REPRODUCTIVE
RIGHTS AND WRONGS

REPRODUCTIVE RIGHTS
AND WRONGS

THE GLOBAL POLITICS
OF POPULATION CONTROL
AND CONTRACEPTIVE CHOICE

BETSY HARTMANN

PERENNIAL LIBRARY

Harper & Row, Publishers, New York
Grand Rapids, Philadelphia, St. Louis, San Francisco
London, Singapore, Sydney, Tokyo, Toronto

To Jim, who gave support

To Jamie, who gave inspiration

*To my grandfather, Henry Bothfeld,
who helped teach me the value of giving*

FIRST EDITION

Designer: Ruth Bornschlegel

Copyeditor: Ann Finlayson

Indexer: Maro Riofrancos

Library of Congress Cataloging-in-Publication Data
Hartmann, Betsy.
    Reproductive rights and wrongs.

    Bibliography: p.
    Includes index.
    1. Birth control. 2. Population policy.
3. Contraceptives. I. Title.
HQ766.7.H37   1987   304.6'6   86-46070
ISBN 0-06-055065-1   87 88 89 90 91 MPC 10 9 8 7 6 5 4 3 2 1
ISBN 0-06-096171-6 (pbk.)   90 91 MPC 10 9 8 7 6 5 4 3 2

Contents

Acknowledgments

This book was not written in isolation. Throughout I have benefited enormously from the encouragement, support, and advice of many people. They have helped deepen my analysis and broaden the scope of the book, as well as renew my faith in the possibility of cooperative effort. My greatest pleasure in writing this book has been the valuable friendships and contacts I have made in the process.

Thanks must first go to Gretta Goldenman. The book was her idea originally, and her commitment, insight, and endless patience helped carry it through to completion. Marge Berer of the Women's Global Network on Reproductive Rights gave freely of her time to comment extensively on the first two drafts of the manuscript. Her contacts and experience in reproductive rights work were formative in the development of my own thinking. Norma Swenson of the Boston Women's Health Book Collective played a vital role as book midwife. She not only gave detailed comments on the manuscript, but provided much needed moral support and continually shared her valuable insights on the subject. Judy Norsigian of the Boston Women's Health Book Collective cast a critical eye on the contraceptive chapters, guided me through the collective's extensive resource collection, and helped keep me up to date. At the Population Council Judith Bruce gave me excellent comments on two drafts of the manuscript, and I benefited greatly from her expertise in international family planning and women's issues.

Other people who gave generously of their time to comment on the manuscript are Jim Boyce, Gena Corea, Lynn Duggan, Joan Dunlop, Deborah Eade, Adrienne Germain, Andrew Graham, Keith Griffin, Polly Griffith, Judith Helzner, Jocelyn Knowles, Frances Moore Lappé, Amanda Milligan, and Edward Passerini.

Others who contributed are Jenneke Arens, Kai Bird, Audrey Bronstein, Therese Budoumit, Rebecca Chalker, Elizabeth Coit, Joseph Collins, Judith Condor, Sonia Corrêa, Belita Cowan, Ireen Dubel, Posey Gault, Forrest Greenslade, Teresa Hayter, James Hobbs, Barbara Holland, Tony Jackson, Bernard Kervyn, Loes Keysers, Rodger King, Barbara Klugman, Brian Landers, Stephen Minkin, Ivan Nutbrown, Vivian Orlowski, Richard Palmer-Jones, Paula Park, Cheryl Payer, Sunanda Ray, Paul Rice, Andrew Rutherford, Rashid Shaikh, Weena Silapa-archa, Peter Stalker, Hilary Standing, and Jomo Kwame Sundaram.

Judith Hoffman gave many months to the project as a research assistant. Christopher Glazek also helped do research. At the IPPF Library in London, Graham Peck provided valuable assistance. Hilary Sloin painstakingly word-processed the manuscript in its final stages. Jesse Markham's advice and support gave peace of mind at a difficult time.

My editor at Harper & Row, Janet Goldstein, shepherded the book along with enthusiasm and insight. I am very grateful for her belief in it and for her excellent editorial skills.

I must also thank Ingrid Palmer, Clare Green, Daria Nielson, Donna Dowal, Mary Ellis, and the staff of the Dinky Do Nursery for their loving care of my daughter, which allowed me to work on this book.

Last but not least, I must express my gratitude to my husband, Jim Boyce, who saw me through all the ups and downs and never lost faith in the project. Other members of my extended family also gave much encouragement and hospitality, particularly my parents, Thomas and Martha Hartmann. My friends helped me keep a sense of humor and perspective.

While all these individuals helped me complete the book, I alone bear responsibility for the opinions and errors contained herein.

Introduction:
A Question of Choice

I arrived at the population issue from two different directions.

Coming of age in the late 1960s, I was a member of the "pill generation." While the media extolled the contraceptive revolution as the key to sexual liberation, the college health clinic prescribed the pill with great enthusiasm. Like so many other young women, I soon discovered that the pill made me feel heavy and depressed, and that "sexual liberation" was often a euphemism for being readily available to men. As feminism began to reshape my view of sexual politics, and politics in general, I abandoned the pill and returned to the safer barrier birth control methods of my mother's generation. I wondered why the clinic never encouraged their use. Elsewhere some of my friends had far worse experiences, ending up in the hospital with IUD complications and worrying that they would never be able to bear children.

Then in the mid-1970s my long-standing interest in South Asia and international development took me to a village in Bangladesh, one of the poorest and most densely populated countries in the world. Here in the West, Bangladesh is typically thought of as an international basket case, a country whose population growth has already outstripped its resources. In the village, however, I encountered a very different reality. I found fertile land, plentiful water, and a climate warm enough for crops to be grown throughout the year. I met families with six or seven children who ate well and families with only two children who were starving.

The vital difference between them was land *ownership*. Almost a quarter of the village people owned no land at all and had to work for rich peasants and landlords for pitiful wages. They not only lacked the land on which to grow food, but did not have enough cash to buy adequate supplies in the market. The real problem was not food scarcity, but land and income distribution.

Up to a point, villagers viewed children as an irreplaceable asset. From an early age, children worked in the home and the fields; instead of draining the family rice bin, they helped fill it. They also provided their parents' only source of security and support in old age. Because of inadequate nutrition and health care, one out of every four Bangladeshi children dies before the age of five. Thus families had to produce many children in order to ensure that a few would survive. My neighbor's first five children had all died in infancy—she bore six more, and the youngest daughter died too.

Yet once villagers had enough children to meet their needs, they often wanted to limit family size. They complained about lack of living space and the fact that through inheritance, land was being subdivided into smaller and smaller plots. Suffering the burden of repeated pregnancies, women especially were desperate for birth control and repeatedly asked me to help them get it.

This widespread desire for birth control came to me as a surprise. Up to that point, it had been my understanding that the main obstacles to the use of birth control in Bangladesh and elsewhere in the Third World were ignorance and tradition, not the availability of contraception. Now I discovered that many women wanted birth control, but could not get it, even though the United States government and other nations were financing multimillion dollar population control programs in Bangladesh.

Later I learned that in other areas of Bangladesh, population control programs were in full force, indiscriminately putting women on the pill, injecting Depo-Provera, or inserting IUDs, without offering adequate medical screening, supervision, or follow-up. As a result many women experienced negative side effects and became disillusioned with contraception. The government's response was not to reform the programs to meet the women's needs, but instead to further intensify its population control efforts by pushing sterilization, even though its irreversibility and risks make it an unsuitable method for many women.

In both instances, whether they lacked access to contraception or had it forced upon them, Bangladeshi women were being denied control over their own reproduction.

As a woman, I could not help but feel angered and intrigued by the connection between their experience and the experience of me and my former classmates in the United States. The two directions had converged, and I found myself increasingly absorbed by the population issue. On my return to the United States in 1976, I learned that many people were making the same connection. The women's health movement was gaining strength, and the campaigns against Depo-Provera, the Dalkon Shield IUD, and sterilization abuse were bringing to public attention the misuses of contraceptive technology occurring both at home and abroad.

I began work on this book in the summer of 1983. I naively envisioned a six-month project; instead it has taken me over three years. Not only was there a vast amount of research to be done, but I found at every stage I had to do a lot of hard thinking, formulating and reformulating ideas. Although the book is now completed, I view my own thinking on population as an ongoing process.

My research followed several different lines. At first, I concentrated on reading a wide spectrum of the available population literature. My previous research and writing on international development proved a useful background. Then as I developed a framework for the book, I focused more closely on specific countries and contraceptives. I corresponded with people actively involved in family planning, health, and women's issues, particularly in the Third World. In England, where I wrote most of the book, and in the United States I made contact both with people in the population field and with health and reproductive rights activists, who not only guided me to resources, but gave me crucial feedback and support.

Beginning in the spring of 1984, I became involved in exposing United States involvement in sterilization abuse in Bangladesh. Much to my surprise, I was contacted by antiabortion activists in the United States, who were interested in taking up the issue in Washington. While their basic objections to sterilization abuse were no doubt sincere, it was clear that they also had another agenda. They wanted more ammunition for the battle they were waging against public support of family planning. Today in the United States the more extreme members of the antiabortion movement are seeking to eliminate all government funding of abortion and "artificial" contraception both at home and abroad. They believe women's place is in the home, bearing children.

There are some who argue that in the present political climate, any criticism of population control only plays into the hands of these conservative forces. Better to remain silent, they say, than to provide ammunition to these dangerous adversaries of reproductive freedom. I reject this logic.

The population control and antiabortion philosophies, although diametrically opposed, share one thing in common: They are both antichoice. Population control advocates impose contraception and sterilization on women; the so-called Right to Life movement denies women the basic right of access to abortion and birth control. Neither takes the interests and rights of the individual woman as their starting point. Both approaches attempt to control women, instead of letting women control their bodies themselves.

The time is ripe for the emergence of a separate, genuinely prochoice alternative, which challenges both the population control and antiabortion positions and which guides family planning and contraceptive development policy. If instead prochoice supporters turn a blind eye to coercive population control practices, they allow the antiabortion movement to capture the issue and to posture as champions of individual reproductive freedom. Such an abdication of responsibility is not only ethically bankrupt, but politically disastrous.

In the course of writing this book, I have come to believe more firmly in the inviolability of individual reproductive rights. The state and local community can play an important role in expanding and protecting those rights, through education and the provision of health and family planning services. However, no matter how perilous the population problem is deemed to be, the use of force or coercive incentives/disincentives to promote population control is an unjustifiable intrusion of government power into the lives of its citizenry, amounting in many cases to physical violence against women's bodies. Similarly, the use of government power to deny women access to abortion and birth control is also a violation of individual rights.

I do not believe this stand is culturally specific, simply the product of Western civil libertarian philosophy, as many in the population establishment argue. The United Nations World Population Plan of Action clearly endorses the principle that population policies should be consistent with "internationally and nationally recognized human rights" of individual freedom and justice. While writing this book, I have met many people from different cultures who share this point of view. They are working throughout the world to ensure that women have access to safe, effective birth control methods. At the same time, they are not prepared to see human rights sacrificed on the altar of population control.

The philosophy of population control rests upon three basic assumptions:

1. Rapid population growth is a primary cause of the Third World's development problems, notably hunger, environmental destruction, economic stagnation, and political instability.

2. People must be persuaded—or forced, if necessary—to have fewer children without fundamentally improving the impoverished conditions in which they live.

3. Given the right combination of finance, personnel, technology, and Western management techniques, birth control services can be "delivered" to Third World women in a top-down fashion and in the absence of basic health care systems. In both the development and promotion of contraceptives, efficacy in preventing pregnancy should take precedence over health and safety concerns.

In the last two decades this philosophy has shaped the activities of most population organizations and international aid agencies in Asia, Africa, and Latin America, as well as among ethnic minorities and poor communities in many parts of the industrialized world.

The organizations and agencies constituting the population establishment have undoubtedly helped in many instances to make birth control more accessible. However, as I will demonstrate in this book, when the overriding goal of family planning programs is to reduce population growth, rather than to expand the freedom of individuals to decide whether and when to have children, the results are often detrimental to women's health and well-being, and ineffective even in terms of the stated goal of lowering birth rates.

In contrast to the assumptions of the population control philosophy, this book will explain the following:

1. Rapid population growth is not the root cause of development problems in the Third World; rather it is a *symptom* of those problems.

2. Improvements in living standards and the position of women, via more equitable social and economic development, motivate people to want fewer children. In the absence of such improvements, the scope for voluntary reduction of population growth is limited.

3. Safe, effective birth control services cannot be "delivered" in a top-down, technocratic fashion, but instead require the development of a popularly based health care system. Health and safety should be the primary concerns in the development and promotion of contraceptive technology.

The book is organized into four parts. Part One begins by analyzing the causes and consequences of rapid population growth in order to put the population problem into perspective. It then describes the reasons why many women lack control over their own reproduction and investigates how population control has distorted Third World family planning programs. It concludes with case studies of Indonesia and Kenya.

Part Two traces the history of the population control movement and its evolution into a powerful political lobby. It considers how the population control philosophy has changed over time and the limitations and positive aspects of current family planning reforms. It ends with a case study of China, which currently has the most drastic population control policy in the world.

Part Three examines the forces behind the development of today's major contraceptive technologies. It details how population control programs have sacrificed women's health and safety in the indiscriminate promotion of hormonal contraception, the IUD, and sterilization, at the same time as they have neglected barrier methods and natural family planning. It argues for the redirection of contraceptive research and for the consideration of legal abortion as fundamental to reproductive choice. The case of Bangladesh highlights the serious ethical problems with sterilization incentives.

Finally, Part Four presents an alternative view of the solution to the population problem. It explores the forces behind the "demographic transition" from high to low birth rates and presents examples of societies that have reduced population growth through more equitable paths of social and economic development. It describes how health and family planning programs can better meet people's needs and charts the growing impact of the reproductive rights movement.

While working on this book, I have become convinced that population control not only restricts reproductive choice, but dangerously obscures the real causes of the earth's afflictions, helping to perpetuate poverty and heighten tensions. When the affluent few regard the impoverished majority as simply a faceless crowd overpopulating the earth, they deny poor people their humanity and diminish their own. In this nuclear age we cannot afford to erect such an unnecessary barrier between human beings. My hope is that this book, in some small way, will contribute to removing that barrier.

I have understood the population explosion intellectually for a long time. I came to understand it emotionally one stinking hot night in Delhi, a few years ago. . . . The streets seemed alive with people. People eating, people washing, people sleeping. People visiting, arguing, and screaming. People thrusting their hands through the taxi window, begging. People defecating and urinating. People clinging to buses. People herding animals. People, people, people, people . . . since that night I've known the feel of overpopulation.

PAUL EHRLICH
The Population Bomb

Once men begin to feel cramped in their geographical, social and mental habitat, they are in danger of being tempted by the simple solution of denying one section of the species the right to exist.

CLAUDE LÉVI-STRAUSS
Tristes Tropiques

PART ONE

THE REAL POPULATION PROBLEM

1

Rethinking the Population Problem

An art historian turns to me at a party: "You're writing a book on population control? My field is aesthetics, and I feel that overpopulation is destroying the beauty of great cities like Paris. Ugly immigrants' housing is springing up all over the place."

The babysitter turns off the TV. "I've been thinking about it," he says. "If they don't force people to be sterilized in India, how are they going to cope with the population explosion?"

An accounting professor explains how pharmaceutical companies could develop cures for many of the basic diseases that afflict poor people, but don't because the people who need them are too poor to pay. "Maybe it's not such a bad thing," he adds. "After all, if more poor people survive, it will only exacerbate the population problem."

An economist, known for his radical views on the United States economy, surprises me by saying that many Third World countries have no choice but to initiate harsh population control measures. "Their economic survival is at stake," he asserts.

I grow to expect such responses from people, no matter how well-meaning or well educated they are. They are repeating a message they have read in the newspaper, heard in the classroom, and seen on television so many times that it has become conventional wisdom. It first captured the popular imagination in 1968, when Stanford University biologist Paul Ehrlich published his famous book *The Population Bomb*. He warned that mankind was breeding itself into oblivion and endorsed stringent population control measures, including compulsion if necessary. Probably most readers of *Reproductive Rights and Wrongs* have the same impression: that the population bomb is exploding out of control. It is the starting point of most discussions about population—and, unfortunately, the end point as well.

The myth of overpopulation is one of the most pervasive myths in Western society, so deeply ingrained in the culture that it profoundly shapes the culture's world view. The myth is compelling because of its simplicity. More people equal fewer resources and more hunger, poverty, and political instability. This equation helps explain away the troubling human suffering in that "other" world beyond the neat borders of affluence. By procreating, the poor create their own poverty. We are absolved of responsibility and freed from complexity.

But the population issue is complex. To put it into proper perspective requires exploring many realms of human experience and addressing difficult philosophical and ethical questions. It entails making connections between fields of thought that have become disconnected as the result of narrow academic specialization. It demands the sharpening of critical facilities and clearing the mind of received orthodoxies. And above all, it involves transcending the alienation embodied in the very terms "population bomb" and "population explosion." Such metaphors suggest destructive technological processes outside human control. The population issue is about people, about individuals. More than we may realize, it concerns ourselves.

The belief that overpopulation is the cause of the Third World's problems has a boomerang effect in the West. Harnessed to the goal of reducing birth rates as fast and effectively as possible, the contraceptive industry has neglected health and safety concerns. The Western women who developed blood clots from the pill, who became infertile from the IUD, who were sterilized without their consent, or who, more commonly, are not fully informed of contraceptive risks and side effects, are just as much the victims of population control as their counterparts in the Third World. This is the link that closes the chain, that brings the population issue closer to home.

It is not surprising that many of the more powerful—and positive—challenges to population control have emerged from the feminist movement. It is in every woman's interest to have access to safe contraception and to the kind of health and family planning services that can provide it. But this is not the goal of population control—far from it.

The myth of overpopulation is destructive because it prevents constructive thinking and action on reproductive issues. Instead of clarifying our understanding of these issues, it obfuscates our vision and limits our ability to see the real problems and find workable solutions.

FAMILY MATTERS

On the surface, fears of a population explosion are borne out by basic demographic statistics. In the twentieth century the world has experienced an unprecedented increase in population. In 1900 global population was 1.7 billion, in 1950 it reached 2.5 billion, and today nearly 5 billion people inhabit the earth. Three quarters of them live in the Third World. The United Nations predicts that world population will reach 6 billion by the end of the century and will eventually stabilize at about 10.5 billion by the year 2110, though such long-term demographic projections are notoriously imprecise.

Initially, this rapid increase in population was due to some very positive factors: Advances in medicine, public health measures, and better nutrition meant that more people lived longer. In most industrialized countries, the decline in mortality rates was eventually offset by declines in birth rates, so that population growth began to stabilize in what is called the "demographic transition." Many countries have now reached the "replacement level" of fertility and in some the population is actually declining.

Today birth rates are also falling in most areas of the Third World, with the exception of sub-Saharan Africa. In fact, the *rate* of world population growth has been slowing since the mid-1960s, and this decline is likely to accelerate in the years ahead.[1*] While world population is still growing in absolute terms, the "explosion" is gradually fizzling out.

Nevertheless, there is still considerable discrepancy between birth rates in the industrialized world and birth rates in the Third World. Conventional wisdom has it that Third World people continue to have so many children because they are ignorant and irrational—they exercise no control over their sexuality, "breeding like rabbits." This "superiority complex" of many Westerners is one of the main obstacles in the way of meaningful discussion of the population problem. It assumes that everyone lives in the same basic social environment and faces the same set of reproductive choices. Nothing is further from the truth.

In many Third World societies, having a large family is an eminently rational strategy of survival. Children's labor is a vital part of the family economy in many peasant communities of Asia, Africa, and Latin America. Children help in the fields, tend animals, fetch water and wood, and care for their younger brothers and sisters, freeing their parents for other tasks. Quite early in life, children's labor makes them an asset rather than a drain on family income. In Bangladesh, for example, boys produce more than they consume by the age of ten to thirteen, and by the age of fifteen their total production has exceeded their cumulative lifetime consumption. Girls likewise perform a number of valuable economic tasks, which include helping their mothers with cooking and the postharvest processing of crops.[2]

In urban settings, children often earn income as servants, messenger boys, etc., or else stay home to care for younger

---

* *(Crude) birth rate* is the number of births per thousand people in a given year.

(Crude) mortality rate is the number of deaths per thousand people in a given year.

Replacement-level fertility is the level of fertility at which women on the average are having only enough daughters to "replace" themselves in a given population.

Population growth rate is the rate at which a population is growing or declining in a given year from natural increase and net migration, computed as a percentage of the base population.

children while their parents work. Among the Yoruba community in Nigeria, demographer John Caldwell found that even urban professional families benefit from many children through "sibling assistance chains." As one child completes education and takes a job, he helps younger brothers and sisters move up the educational and employment ladder, and the connections and the influence of the family spread.[3]

Recently some analysts have claimed that the value of children's labor is declining in many Third World countries, especially among the rural poor. As the landholdings of the poorest get even smaller, they no longer need as many children to work the land. At the same time, falling wages mean that the landless cannot afford to raise many children to the age at which they would become productive. For these reasons, the desired family size may fall.[4]

However, this argument ignores the other crucial reason for having children: security. In most Third World societies, the vast majority of the population has no access to insurance schemes, pension plans, or government social security. It is children who care for their parents in their old age—without them one's future is endangered. The help of grown children can also be crucial in surviving the periodic crises—illness, drought, floods, food shortages, land disputes, political upheavals—which, unfortunately, punctuate village life in most parts of the world.[5]

By contrast, parents in industrialized countries and their affluent counterparts among Third World urban elites have much less need to rely on children either for labor or old age security. The economics of family size changes as income goes up, until children become a financial burden instead of an asset. When children are in school, for example, they no longer serve as a source of labor. Instead parents must pay for their education, as well as for their other needs, which cost more in a high consumption society than in a Third World village. Today in the United States the cost of raising one child to the age of eighteen ranges close to $100,000, not including the cost of a college education.[6]

At the same time, in industrialized societies personal savings, pension plans, and government programs replace children as the basic forms of social security. These social changes, arising from higher incomes, fundamentally alter the value of children, making it far more rational from an economic standpoint to limit family size.

Son preference is another important motive for having large families. The subordination of women means that economically and socially daughters are not valued as highly as sons in many cultures. Not only does daughters' domestic work have less prestige, but daughters typically provide fewer years of productive labor to their parents, because in many Third World countries, they marry and leave home to live with their in-laws shortly after puberty.

Son preference, combined with high infant and child mortality rates, means that parents must have many children just to ensure that one or two sons survive.* A computer simulation found that in the 1960s an Indian couple had to bear an average of 6.3 children to be confident of having one son who would survive to adulthood. In the African Sahel, the delicate ecological zone on the southern edge of the Sahara desert, the figure is even higher—the birth of ten children is needed to provide a 95 percent chance of one son surviving to the age of thirty-eight.[7]

High infant and child mortality rates are in fact one of the most important causes of high birth rates. Each year in the Third World more than 10 million children die before reaching their first birthday. The average infant mortality rate is more than 90 deaths per 1,000 live births, compared to 20 in the industrialized countries. The situation is especially severe in Africa, where sixteen countries have infant mortality rates in excess of 150 per 1,000.[8]

High infant mortality means that parents cannot be sure their children will survive to contribute to the family economy and to take care of them in their old age. The poor are thus

---

* *Infant mortality rate* is the number of deaths of infants under one year of age per thousand live births in a given year.

Child mortality rate is the number of deaths of children aged 1 to 4 per thousand children in this age group in a given year.

caught in a death trap: They have to keep producing children in order that some will survive.

For many parents, the death of a child is a profound reminder of the basic insecurity of life, leading to the desire for more surviving children than they might have wanted otherwise. A study in an Egyptian village found that a mother who has lost at least one child will have more births and desire more surviving children than women in the same community who have lost no children. In the Philippines, too, total fertility is lower among couples who have not experienced the death of a child.[9]

At first glance, it might appear that reductions in infant mortality would actually *increase* the rate of population growth, since there would be more surviving children to grow up into fertile adults. The Third World population surge of the 1950s and 1960s came about through such a reduction in mortality rates without a corresponding reduction in birth rates. Experience has shown, however, that once mortality rates fall to around 15 per 1,000 people per year, the average for the Third World today, each further decline in the mortality rate is generally accompanied by an even greater decline in the birth rate, as people adjust their fertility to improved survival possibilities. This has led UNICEF director James Grant to conclude:

> Paradoxically, therefore, a "survival revolution" which halved the infant and child mortality rate of the developing world and prevented the deaths of six or seven million infants each year by the end of the century would also be likely to prevent between 12 and 20 million births each year.[10]

To date no country has achieved a low birth rate as long as it has had a high infant mortality rate.

High infant mortality is primarily caused by poor nutrition, both of the mother and of the child. In situations of chronic scarcity, women often eat last and least, with a profound impact on infant health. Inadequately nourished mothers typically give birth to underweight babies, and low birth weight has been identified as the "greatest single hazard for infants," increasing their vulnerability to developmental problems and their risk of death from common childhood illnesses.[11] Severely undernourished women also give lower quality breast milk; for a woman to breast-feed successfully without damaging her health, she must increase her calorie and nutrient intake by up to 20 to 25 percent, an impossibility for many poor women.[12] Significant reductions in infant mortality cannot occur without significant improvements in women's nutrition (see Box: The Breast-Feeding Connection).

THE BREAST-FEEDING CONNECTION

Breast-feeding has relevance to the population issue on several different but interconnected levels.

In many countries, increases in infant mortality are linked to the switch from breast-feeding to bottle feeding. Infant formula lacks the antibodies in breast milk that help to protect babies from disease. Poor women, moreover, often cannot afford a steady supply of formula and dilute it with too much water. Proper sterilization of bottles, nipples, and drinking water is also problematic in poor households. As a result, Third World infants breast-fed for less than six months are *five* times more likely to die in the second six months of life than those who have been breast-fed longer. Overall the mortality rate for bottle-fed infants in the Third World is roughly double that for breast-fed infants.[1]

According to the 1982 World Fertility Survey of twenty-eight developing countries, the vast majority of women are still breast-feeding, but for decreasing lengths of time.[2] Intensive sales campaigns by multinational corporations, such as the Swiss-based Nestlé Company and American Home Products, bear a large share of the responsibility for this change. Advertisements with pictures of plump, smiling white babies and the penetration of local health establishments by company representatives have helped convince Third World women that they will have healthier children if they switch to formula. An international campaign against these formula "pushers" finally led the World Health Organization (WHO) to establish a voluntary code of conduct, setting standards for the advertising and marketing of formula.

Although the code has brought improvements in terms of mass advertising, the companies still widely promote formula through health establishments. A recent Population Council study of breast-feeding in four Third World cities found that formula marketers had close commercial ties with physicians, pharmacists, and midwives, and that as a result, women who used Western-type health and maternity services tended to introduce formula earlier.[3] The WHO Code is clearly not strong enough.

Another key advantage of breast-feeding is that it happens to be one of the world's most effective natural contraceptives. It causes lactational amenorrhea, the suppression of ovulation and menstruation by the release of the hormone prolactin. Each month of breast-feeding adds up to three weeks to the interval between births, and women who breast-feed often, whenever the baby wants, delay the return to fertility even longer.[4]

A decline in breast feeding, without a corresponding use of effective contraception, hence means that pregnancies are more closely spaced, and the close spacing of births is itself a major cause of infant mortality. The relationship can also go the other way around: A child's death means a woman stops breast-feeding and resumes fertility sooner, with a higher risk of the next child's death. This vicious biological circle may be one of the key reasons high infant mortality and high fertility go hand in hand.[5]

The last (but not least) cause of high birth rates is the subordination of women. Male dominance in the family, patriarchal social mores, the systematic exclusion of women from the development process, and the absence of decent birth control services combine to force many women into having more children than they want (see Chapter 2). The social environment, in effect, leaves them little or no reproductive choice.

Behind the demographic statistics, then, lies a reality unfamiliar to many in the West, who do not have to worry from day to day about who will help in the fields, who will take care of them when they are old and sick, how many children they need to ensure that a few survive until adulthood. High birth rates are often a distress signal that people's survival is endangered. Yet the proponents of population control put the argument the other way around, insisting that people are endangering their own survival—and the survival of future generations—by having so many children. This is the basis of the Malthusian philosophy which for so long has defined the dimensions of the population problem.

THE MALTHUSIAN ORTHODOXY

The impact of population growth is a source of endless debate. There is a vast literature on the subject, by demographers and economists, sociologists and development planners. The subject not only involves the impact of population growth per se, but problems of population distribution between urban and rural areas and imbalances in the age structure of populations. What emerges most strongly from the literature is the difficulty of generalizing on a global level; the impact of population growth differs from country to country and is influenced by a variety of factors.

Even within the population establishment there is no single point of view. Spurred by Third World criticisms of population control in the 1970s, more liberal members have come to see population issues in a broader development perspective, favoring social welfare policies and voluntary family planning services as the way to address high birth rates (see Chapters 5 and 7). Yet the complexities of the argument and the wide variation in opinion have largely been screened from public view. Instead, the Malthusian alarmists, who range from environmentalists like Paul Ehrlich to senior international technocrats like former World Bank president Robert McNamara, command the widest public audience. In the 1980s their ideas have also enjoyed a revival within the population establishment (see Chapter 6).

There are several reasons why the alarmist message enjoys such credibility. It not only makes good shock headlines in the press, but draws on deep undercurrents of parochialism, racism, and elitism in Western society, complementing the Social Darwinist "survival of the fittest" view. The most extreme Malthusians even advocate that famine relief be cut off to poor overpopulated countries: Let the unfit starve until their numbers are brought under control. In 1985 at the height of the African drought, Governor of Colorado Richard D. Lamm wrote in the *New York Times* that the United States should stop giving emergency relief to African countries that failed to reduce their population growth, since such aid would "merely multiply empty stomachs."[13]

The fact that such suggestions are taken seriously is a sad commentary on just how far Malthusianism has penetrated our value system. So pervasive are its assumptions that many of us have internalized them without even realizing it. Only by understanding the basic fallacies of the Malthusian approach can the way be cleared for a fresh look at the population problem.

The alarmists draw their ideological inspiration from Thomas Malthus, the British clergyman-turned-economist who wrote in the late 1700s and early 1800s. Malthus maintained that, unless restrained by "preventive checks," human populations would double every twenty-five years. The result would be geometric growth—1, 2, 4, 8, 16, 32, 64, 128, etc.—outstripping the earth's capacity for food production, which could at best be expected to increase in an arithmetic progression— 1, 2, 3, 4, 5, 6, 7, etc. Humans were, according to Malthus, little different from animals or plants in this respect; their numbers would be held in check by the limited carrying capacity of the planet. "The race of plants and the race of animals shrink under this great restrictive law," he proclaimed, "and man cannot by any efforts of reason escape from it."[14] Only "misery," the poverty, famine, and pestilence brought on by overpopulation, supplemented by the man-made deprivations of war and slaughter, would keep human numbers down.

Malthus was wrong on two basic counts. First, contrary to his predictions, it is possible for population growth to slow and ultimately to stabilize, not because our numbers are held in check by "natural" forces of famine and pestilence, but rather as a result of voluntary choices by individuals who have experienced improved living standards and an attendant expansion in control over their own reproduction. Malthus' native land underwent such a demographic transition.

Malthus' second mistake was to underestimate greatly the capacity of the earth to feed and clothe a growing human population. It is perhaps not surprising that someone writing at the close of the eighteenth century failed to foresee the tremendous advances in human productive powers that would soon unfold in both industry and agriculture, outstripping population growth. In fact, at least one school of economic history maintains that the crucial force behind technological change— the "prime mover" of economic progress—was none other than *population growth.* In their influential study *The Rise of the Western World: A New Economic History,* historians Douglas North and Robert Thomas conclude that population growth "spurred the institutional innovations which account for the rise of the Western world."[15] Far from blocking any long-term improvement in mass living standards, population growth is thus seen by some historians as the basic *explanation* for such improvements.

The modern-day proponents of population control have reinterpreted Malthusian logic, selectively applying it only to the poor majority in the Third World. It is not a giant step from this partitioning of Malthusian laws to a similar partitioning in the realm of human rights: *We* in the industrialized countries have the right to voluntary choice as to whether and when to bear children, but *their* rights are subordinate to the overriding imperative of population control.

In support of this scientific and ethical double standard, the new Malthusians (neo-Malthusians) point to the correlation between high birth rates and low living standards in the Third World today. It is undoubtedly true that Third World countries generally have higher birth rates than industrialized ones, East and West, and that among Third World countries, those with higher population growth tend to have lower per capita incomes. Drawing sustenance from this simple correlation, the Malthusians then move on to blame a host of complex social ills on overpopulation, with varying degrees of intellectual sophistication and according to the fashions of the time.

In the 1960s and 1970s it was fashionable to attribute hunger and food scarcity to overpopulation. "World food production cannot keep pace with the galloping growth of population," warned the Washington-based Environmental Fund, in one of the less sophisticated applications of Malthusian logic.[16]

"The battle to feed all humanity is over," claimed Ehrlich's 1968 *The Population Bomb*. "In the 1970s the world will undergo famines—hundreds of millions of people will starve to death."[17] Computer projections, such as the Club of Rome's famous *Limits to Growth*, gave these dire predictions a pseudo-respectability, which the hard facts could not. For the galloping horse of population had met its match in the steady march of the tractor: We were about to enter the era of food surplus.

Tremendous advances in agricultural productivity mean that today the world produces enough grain alone to provide every man, woman, and child on earth with 3,000 calories a day, well above the 2,200–2,500 calorie average considered a minimally acceptable dietary level.[18] At least on a global scale, there is no shortage of food.

Nor does a correlation exist between hunger and population density. The Netherlands, with 246 people per square kilometer, has almost one and a half times the population density of India, and only one quarter as much cropland per person. But the Dutch enjoy one of the highest standards of living in the world, while India has one of the lowest.[19] Hunger and poverty in the Central American nation of El Salvador are often blamed on its high population density. "El Salvador, a country about the size of Massachusetts, has 4.5 million people today," a book coauthored by Paul and Anne Ehrlich expresses in horror. Yet Massachusetts itself has a population of 5.8 million.[20]

Simple Malthusian arithmetic says that more mouths to feed mean less food per person. This would be true if the supply of food was somehow fixed and unaffected by the size of a country's population. But food supplies are *not* fixed and can be influenced by population growth in positive ways. This is not only because population growth expands the labor force—each additional mouth brings with it an additional pair of hands—but because the pressure of population on resources can induce technological and institutional change so as to raise output per person. Economist Colin Clark, for example, sees population growth as the principal force behind the extensive clearing of land, drainage of swamps, and the introduction of better crops and manures, changes which "historians tend to describe as 'agricultural revolutions.' "[21]

There is, of course, no guarantee that population growth will automatically trigger corresponding increases in food production, but neither is there an iron law that ensures that it will not. Indeed, in the past three decades, world food production has grown *faster* than world population. World food production doubled between 1959 and 1980, and according to a recent United Nations Food and Agriculture Organization (FAO) study, it could double again by the year 2000. The increase has been larger in the Third World than in the industrialized nations. With the exception of sub-Saharan Africa, most Third World countries have experienced rising per capita food output in the past two decades. Today most countries have enough food to meet the needs of their growing populations.[22] Yet even when food is plentiful, millions of people go hungry.

They go hungry because individual families do not have land on which to grow food, or the money with which to buy it. The main problem is not that there are too many people and too few resources, but rather that too few people monopolize too many resources. The problem is not one of absolute scarcity, but one of distribution.

The FAO's world land census, conducted in 1960, found that 2.5 percent of landowners control 75 percent of the arable land in the world, and that the top 0.23 percent control over half.[23] This unequal distribution of land is especially critical in the Third World, where the majority of the population lives in rural areas.

The agricultural laborer in Asia, the small subsistence farmer in Latin America, and the African peasant who must migrate seasonally to work on plantations or in the mines belong to the 97.5 percent who own only one quarter of the land. They live at the margin of survival. When crops fail or jobs are scarce, they do not have the cash to buy food, even when it is plentiful in the market.

Even famines have more to do with poor people's inability to command access to food than to its actual scarcity. During the Sahelian famine of the late 1960s and early 1970s, for example, almost all Sahelian countries had enough food to feed their populations, had that been a government priority. In fact, agricultural exports from the area actually *increased* during the period.[24]

Today sub-Saharan Africa is the only region in the world where the Malthusians can more readily make their case. At the same time that the region is experiencing the world's highest rates of population growth—the average African woman now bears six living children in her lifetime—per capita food production appears to be declining. (There are few reliable statistics.)[25] "I fear that many African countries, if they do not take positive action to encourage a drop in fertility rates, are speeding headlong to disaster," warns FAO Director General Edouard Saouma (see Box: Africa: Overpopulated, Underpopulated, or Both?).[26]

AFRICA: OVERPOPULATED, UNDERPOPULATED, OR BOTH?

Historically, many areas of Africa actually suffered from *depopulation*, as the result of the slave trade, exploitative colonial labor policies, and the introduction of new diseases from Europe. In the eighteenth century, 20 percent of the world's population lived in Africa; by the year 2000 the figure is expected to be less than 13 percent, despite present high rates of growth. Only since the beginning of this century did Africa begin to rebuild its population.[1]

Today, the problem is not so much absolute numbers of people, but their distribution. "In many African countries, people are alternatively crowded into overused lands and elsewhere spread too thin," explains a report on the Ethiopian famine by an international commission.[2] Most of Africa in fact has very low population densities. The average density in sub-Saharan Africa, for example, is only sixteen people per square kilometer. In interior central Africa there is a belt of relatively low population growth, where women suffer from high rates of infertility associated with sexually transmitted diseases. The continent has millions of hectares of potential rainfed crop land in the humid tropics, most of which is uncultivated and underpopulated.[3]

Yet there are also areas of very high population density in
continued

---

continued

the cities, along the coast, and in the highlands, where population pressure has contributed to environmental degradation. In Ethiopia, for example, the highest densities are in the drought-prone, environmentally vulnerable highlands, while there are thousands of acres of uncultivated arable land in the south and the east.[4]

In West Africa, anthropologist Richard Franke identifies the demand for labor as the crucial determinant of population densities and high fertility. West Africa is currently characterized by a very high birth rate, a very low level of economic development, and an undersupply of labor in many parts of the region. Franke traces this pattern back to the colonial era when the forced recruitment of labor, forced growing of cash crops, taxation, and military reprisals by colonial troops compelled African peoples to "produce as many children as possible to increase labor supply and reconstitute as much of their local economy as possible under colonial conditions."[5]

Added to this was the impact of large-scale male migration to plantation zones and coastal cities for employment. With husbands absent, women depended even more on children as a source of agricultural labor and security.

Today this same migration pattern continues, with adverse consequences in many cases on food production and environmental improvements. In Burkina Faso, for example, during certain times of the year when young men migrate to raise cash for taxes and consumer needs, there is not enough labor to clear bush for new farms or maintain wells, and food production suffers accordingly. A number of observers have in fact noted how low population densities serve as a brake on agricultural production in Africa.[6]

Is there any way out of this vicious cycle? Franke calls for development planners in Africa to drop the simplistic notion of overpopulation and instead focus on the specific demographic reality of each location, so that creative and effective solutions can be found to the problems of migration and agricultural labor shortage.

Africa's food crisis has less to do with high population growth, however, than with low productivity. Sixty to 80 percent of the African rural labor force works at extremely low levels of productivity; the most common agricultural implement is a hand-held hoe, little advanced since the Iron Age. Not surprisingly, African cereal yields have stagnated since 1965, while they have risen in other parts of the Third World.

One of the main reasons food production has stagnated is that resources have been concentrated on growing cash crops for export. This export-oriented policy can be traced back to the colonial period when peasants were made, by the use of oppressive taxation, or force if necessary, to grow export crops. Subsequent research and development programs centered on the needs of commercial farmers and plantation managers, ignoring basic food crops and their producers, who were usually women.[27] (See Chapter 2 for discussion of women in African agriculture).

This same trend continues today, with most African governments giving low priority to peasant food production and neglecting women's role in agriculture. Instead the focus is on plantations, state farms, and land settlement schemes which produce export crops, often in cooperation with foreign agribusiness corporations. In Burkina Faso, for example, cotton production has increased more than twenty times since 1961, while the staple food crops of millet and sorghum remain at 1960 production levels.[28]

Since cash crops are typically grown on the best land, their expansion squeezes subsistence food producers into marginal areas, and the result is land degradation and declining yields. In Niger, for example, grain yields fell from 500 kilograms per hectare in 1920 to 350 in 1978, and are expected to fall even further by the year 2000.[29]

Through state marketing boards, "parastatals," which set low prices for agricultural products, and biased taxation policies, African agriculture has also been bled to finance the development of urban areas and the luxurious life-styles of elites. Meanwhile, foreign aid programs have tended to favor expensive, imported technology over indigenous techniques and labor and to push grandiose commercial schemes over the painstaking provision of training, credit, and inputs to the small (female) farmer or herder.[30]

Although bringing down Africa's birth rate would no doubt relieve pressure on land and food supplies, it will never solve the productivity problem at the heart of the continent's agrarian crisis. Contraceptives do not increase yields. Instead, major agricultural reforms are necessary. Zimbabwe, for example, has recently experienced impressive increases in peasant food production through breaking white farmers' monopoly over rural credit and transportation facilities and by fairer pricing policies for agricultural inputs and produce.[31]

The weight of the evidence means that finally now, in the late 1980s, blaming hunger on overpopulation is going out of style. The cover of a 1986 World Bank report on poverty and hunger announces, in what for the Bank is a daring departure from the Malthusian norm:

> The world has ample food. The growth of global food production has been faster than the unprecedented population growth of the last forty years. . . . Yet many poor countries and hundreds of millions of poor people do not share in this abundance. They suffer from a lack of food security, caused mainly by a lack of purchasing power.[32]

The Malthusians, however, have other arguments in reserve. The harmful impact of population growth on the environment is one which is currently very much in vogue.

Ecologists, like any other members of a scientific discipline, are not a homogenous group. On one side are what I call the human racers, people who perceive the battle over the environment as an inevitable race between man and nature and who believe the earth is already nearing the limits of its "carrying capacity." Because they view mankind itself as the enemy, the human racers are Malthusians. "In the simplest terms, we are in a race to see if we can slow, and eventually halt, population growth before local life-support systems collapse," warns Lester Brown of the Worldwatch Institute.[33]

On the other side are the structuralists, who view environmental destruction as the outgrowth of inefficient, and often inequitable, forms of social organization, which can and should be reformed. They recognize that in some instances population pressure can contribute to environmental degradation, but ask what are the underlying social dynamics that cause that pressure to come about.

The human racers of course have a point. No one wants a world of standing room only, where every bit of land, drop of water, and unit of energy are pressed into producing sustenance for an endlessly expanding human mass. Other species have a right to inhabit the earth, and our own quality of life is enhanced by respect for the natural environment. However, while limiting human numbers makes sense in the long run, it does not follow that in the short run overpopulation is the main cause of environmental depletion.

On the contrary, it is the consumption explosion in the industrialized world rather than the population explosion in the Third World which is putting the most pressure on natural resources. For example, the U.S., with only 5 percent of the world's people, uses one-third of the world's flow of nonrenewable resources and one quarter of the gross planetary production of goods and services. The average U.S. citizen uses almost 300 times as much energy as the average citizen of Bangladesh. A small rate of population increase in the industrialized countries thus puts much more pressure on resources than a rapid population increase in the Third World. Within Third World countries too, elites are shifting to the same high consumption patterns, using up far more resources per capita than their poor compatriots whom they accuse of overbreeding.[34]

Moreover, as the structuralists would point out, many of the main ecological crimes being perpetrated on the earth today—chemical and nuclear wastes dumped in the sea, radioactive clouds from faulty reactors and weapon tests, acid rain from dirty smokestacks—have considerably more to do with unregulated and inappropriate patterns of technological development than with the procreative powers of peasants.

What about the serious environmental deterioration which is occurring in many Third World countries, through deforestation and desertification in particular? Although here the Malthusian case would seem more compelling, there is much more to the story than just population pressure.

When the Center for Science and Environment in New

Delhi investigated deforestation in India, where millions of hectares of forest land are disappearing each year, it found a very different state of affairs from the official government view that the "population explosion is mainly responsible for depletion of our valuable forests."[35] The Center cites a number of studies which reveal how private contractors, through payoffs to corrupt forest officials, have illegally felled huge sections of India's forests, at the same time as they were declared off limits to the local communities who have long depended on them for a livelihood. Meanwhile, "official" forestry projects, aided by international agencies such as the World Bank, are encouraging the export of India's hardwoods and the destruction of mixed, ecologically sound forests in favor of monoculture plantations of pine, eucalyptus, and teak.[36]

Even the poor's desperate need for firewood may have fewer ecological consequences than is commonly imagined. The wood they collect for cooking fuel is largely composed of branches, twigs, and roots—only the rich can afford logs. A village study by the Indian Institute of Science found that gathered firewood did not contribute in any significant way to deforestation, casting "serious doubts on the widespread belief held by many environmentalists that the firewood demand of the poor is leading to extensive deforestation."[37]

Similar processes are occurring in many other Third World countries. The destruction of the Amazon rain forest in Brazil, one of the world's last great tropical forests, is a sad tale of corporate greed. National and multinational corporations, including Goodyear, Volkswagen, Nestlé, and Mitsubushi, have stripped millions of acres for lumber and cattle ranching.[38] In the Philippines, before he was deposed, dictator Ferdinand Marcos gave illegal logging concessions worth over a billion dollars to relatives and political cronies, depleting the country's forest reserves from 34.6 million acres in 1965, when Marcos took power, to only 5.4 million acres today.[39]

Like deforestation, desertification, which threatens almost 20 percent of the earth's surface, is frequently attributed to overpopulation. "Excessive population pressure on limited land resources means desertification," claims a United Nations news feature. "That is the bottom line."[40]

But for many peasants there is another bottom line: the monopolization of land resources by the rich. El Salvador is a case in point. Just as the war ravaging this small Central American nation is often blamed on rapid population growth, so is its deteriorating environment. Today El Salvador faces accelerated erosion of an estimated 77 percent of its land. The country is generally steep and mountainous, with fertile lands located in the middle of volcanic slopes, river basins, and coastal plains. These few productive areas belong to large estates growing cotton, sugar, coffee, and cattle for export.

El Salvador's land ownership pattern is highly skewed: Fewer than one in a hundred farms is more than 250 acres, yet these large farms occupy half the total cultivable land in the country. Meanwhile, the peasants have been pushed onto the higher slopes, where in order to survive, they cut down vegetation and grow subsistence crops on land unsuitable for cultivation. Erosion is the inevitable result.[41]

In such a situation, more people do mean more ecological destruction, since they are crowded onto a limited land space. In this sense, rapid population growth is a factor in desertification, but to call it the primary cause is to simplify a much more complex process. El Salvador's peasants are putting pressure on marginal lands not because of their numbers alone but because they themselves have been made marginal by an agricultural system controlled by the rich.

According to demographer John Caldwell, who has studied the delicate ecological zone of the African Sahel, it is impossible to establish a direct relationship between population pressures and desertification. Over the last decade, he reports, there has been very little scientific investigation of the impact of rising population densities on the environment of poor, arid countries, and many demographers are reluctant even to use the term "carrying capacity."[42]

It will be interesting to see if the environmental argument against population growth, like the hunger argument, also passes out of fashion. Certainly, today more sophisticated Malthusian thinkers are moving away from it, concentrating instead on the deleterious consequences of rapid population growth on the economy at large. For example, in its *World Develop-*

ment Report 1984, the theme of which was population and development, the World Bank argued that rapid population growth is a "serious brake on development," resulting in "lost opportunities for raising living standards, particularly among the large numbers of the world's poor."[43] The World Bank has slightly altered the previous Malthusian line of causality. While it now admits that poverty, not the sheer weight of human numbers, is responsible for hunger and environmental depletion, it blames poverty on the economic consequences of population growth, thus continuing to hold the poor responsible for their own misery.

The economic case against rapid population growth rests on several key assumptions. The first, and crudest, is that rapid population growth slows down the rate of increase of per capita incomes in a number of Third World countries. According to the Population Crisis Committee, this is a matter of "simple arithmetic."[44] Per capita income is measured by dividing gross national product (GNP) by the number of people in a country. Thus the basic argument goes that the more people there are, the smaller each individual's share of GNP will be. But people not only consume wealth and resources, they also create them: the numerator, GNP, seldom stays fixed as the denominator, population, grows. If economic conditions are favorable, population growth may itself contribute to more rapid growth of GNP, so that per capita incomes rise significantly.

In fact, the impressive economic performance of middle-income countries—where per capita incomes have grown by an average of 3 percent per year during the last few decades—has occurred *alongside* rapid population growth.[45] This does not mean, of course, that rapid population growth was the main factor behind their success, but it certainly did not prevent it. Africa's ten richest countries in per capita terms have similar population growth rates as the continent's ten poorest, again suggesting that population is not the crucial explanatory variable.[46]

The next assumption concerns the impact of population growth on government investment. The World Bank argues that rapid population growth makes it necessary to spread a fixed amount of educational and health resources over more and more people, a process it terms "capital widening." Slower population growth, according to the Bank, would allow more investment per person, or "capital deepening."[47] This argument again assumes that the numerator—in this case, the amount of resources available for investment—is fixed, ignoring the fact that people produce those resources in the first place.

It also fails to take into account the basic political fact of life that the amount of resources a country devotes to education and other social services has less to do with population than with government priorities. It is instructive to note, for example, that in the thirty-four lowest-income countries, the percentage of government expenditures on defense rose from 11 percent in 1972 to 18 percent in 1982, while the percentage spent on education declined from 16 percent to 6 percent over the same period.[48] It is also revealing that the densely populated countries of Sri Lanka and Vietnam have achieved nearly universal primary education, while many less populated countries with similar or higher per capita incomes have yet to come close to this goal.[49]

While there is little doubt that slower population growth could help to reduce pressure on Third World school systems, there is no guarantee whatsoever that the resources saved would be used to improve educational quality or to make other socially productive investments, as the World Bank naively assumes. They could just as well be spent on armaments or luxury apartment buildings.

Perhaps the most common economic woe laid at the door of rapid population growth is unemployment. Open unemployment is rare in the Third World for the simple reason that most people cannot afford to be idle; in the absence of unemployment benefits or social insurance, they must somehow try to earn enough to survive. The real problem is *underemployment* in low-paying, low-productivity occupations such as street vending, domestic service, and handicraft production, which constitute the bottom end of the so-called informal sector in Third World economies.[50]

It is undeniably true that millions of people today lack the opportunity to earn a decent living through their own labor.

But is this because there are too many potential workers—or too few jobs?

The problem of surplus labor in Third World countries dates from the colonial period, when European powers appropriated land and other productive resources in Asia, Africa, and Latin America, while destroying any local industries that might compete with their own manufactured goods. Thrown off the land and thrown out of enterprises, thousands joined the ranks of underemployed labor. Political independence did not automatically break this pattern, as industrial development largely continued to be dominated by multinational corporations and international financial institutions, who promoted capital-intensive rather than labor-intensive industries.

Despite the popular Western image of the Third World as a bottomless begging bowl, it today gives more to the industrialized world than it takes. Inflows of official "aid" and private loans and investment are exceeded by outflows in the form of repatriated profits, interest payments, and private capital sent abroad by Third World elites.[51]

Not everyone suffers in the Third World, of course. These neocolonial patterns have continued precisely because of the collaboration of ruling groups in Third World countries, many of whom prefer investing in foreign bank accounts to investing in local job-creating industries. Between 1978 and 1983, for example, the Bank of International Settlements estimates that more than $55 billion was "spirited away overseas" by rich Latin Americans, almost a third of the region's increase in borrowing from foreign banks during the period.[52] Such capital flight provides a rather dramatic counterpoint to the specter of chronic underemployment.

Ironically, at the same time that rapid population growth is seen as a brake on development in the Third World, many economists worry that near zero or declining rates of population growth in industrial countries will have serious negative consequences. The main concern is that there will be too few young people in the labor force to support the social security costs of a large aging population. Japanese economist Naohira Ogawa believes this phenomenon could put an end to his country's spectacular economic growth. The French and West German governments are already offering financial incentives to people to have larger families.[53]

This is not to say that rapid population growth poses no problem at all in the Third World. When agriculture and industry fail to provide employment to the underemployed, then population growth can have negative effects. Indeed, if the number of jobs stays fixed and more and more people vie for them, wages and living standards will tend to fall even for those with jobs. If the numerator remains the same and the denominator swells, then the trend will be for each individual share of the economic pie to get smaller—though the rich could well cut themselves an even bigger slice.

This "matter of simple arithmetic," however, is not an immutable mathematical law. The question is: *Why* do all things remain equal? Why are the majority condemned to a life of chronic poverty and low productivity—and consequently, to high fertility?

The Malthusians do not have the answer to this question because they do not bother to ask it. They do not ask who owns the land, who fells the forests, who draws up the government budget, who steals the international bank loans, who were the colonialists and who were the colonized. By a wave of some magic wand, they deny the role of the rich and powerful in creating and perpetuating the poverty of the powerless. Their ideological fervor masks a profound fatalism: The poor are born to their lot, and the only way out for them is to stop being born.

And what happens when the poor start demanding their rights? The Malthusians call that "political instability," and blame it too on overpopulation. Thus recent writers on U.S. foreign policy, such as General Maxwell Taylor and Robert McNamara, believe the civil war in El Salvador results in part, if not in full, from population pressure, ignoring the extreme disparities of wealth in that country and the violent suppression of any peaceful attempts at social reform.[54] Central America's problem in general is portrayed as too many underemployed young males, who, according to Leon Bouvier of the Population Reference Bureau, increase "the availability of people for revolutionary activity."[55] In this way Malthusianism directly serves to legitimize the status quo: If poor people are rising up, it is only because their numbers are rising too fast.

The Reverend Mr. Malthus himself put it succinctly two centuries ago:

> That the principal and most permanent cause of poverty has little or no *direct* relation to forms of government, or the unequal division of property; and that, as the rich do not in reality possess the *power* of finding employment and mainte-nance for the poor, the poor cannot, in the nature of things, possess the *right* to demand them; are important truths flow-ing from the principle of population. . . .[56]

The essence of Malthusianism boils down to this simple political imperative.

THE CORNUCOPIANS

In recent years, Malthusian fatalism has met its match in the unrepentant optimism of certain influential New Right econ-omists. In their book *The Resourceful Earth,* Julian Simon and Herman Kahn challenge the "limits to growth" philosophy and claim that "if present trends continue, the world in 2000 will be less crowded (though more populated), less polluted, more stable ecologically, and less vulnerable to resource-supply dis-ruption than the world we live in now."[57]

These conservative Cornucopians believe that free enter-prise and nuclear energy can do the trick, just as long as there isn't too much government interference through environmental regulation. According to Simon, temporary shortages of re-sources simply spur the development of new techniques to find them, so that in the end we are better off than if the shortage had never occurred. Meanwhile, population growth produces the "ultimate resource," "skilled, spirited and hopeful people," who, provided they live in an unfettered market economy, can come up with the new ideas to make the system work.[58]

The Cornucopians, who found a sympathetic ear in the Reagan White House, heavily influenced the drafting of the official U.S. Policy Statement for the 1984 U.N. International Conference on Population. In a major reversal of policy, the document described population growth as a "neutral phenomenon," which has become a problem only because of too much "governmental control of economies" and an "outbreak of anti-intellectualism, which attacked science, technology and the very concept of material progress" in the West.[59]

There are a number of obvious flaws with the Cornucopian approach. The unbridled faith in science, technology, and human inventiveness translates into a lack of concern for the very real constraints on the environment we face at the end of the twentieth century and begs the question of appropriate versus inappropriate technologies. Arguably, what is needed is more government environmental regulation, not less. Nor will higher rates of population growth necessarily yield more geniuses if the majority of the world's people remain trapped in poverty. Even the best of brains need food for sustenance and education for development. And before debating the pros and cons of the free market, it is important to point out that the free market simply does not exist, except perhaps in Disney World. Even the Third World countries Simon et al. herald as the great free market successes—South Korea, Taiwan, Singapore—have substantial government involvement in the economy. In the end, the Cornucopians dodge the real issues of power and inequality just as the Malthusians do.

They have performed a great service, however, by opening up the population debate. After more than two decades of hegemony, the Malthusian orthodoxy is on the defensive and has had to cede some ground in order to save the church.

The relaxation of the Malthusian position is reflected in a 1986 U.S. National Academy of Science report, which retreats substantially from past alarmist assessments of population growth, including one issued by the academy fifteen years ago. While concluding that population growth is more likely to impede progress than promote it, the report finds it is not the unmitigated environmental and economic evil it has been portrayed to be. According to the report, there is no "necessary relation" between population growth and resource exhaustion, and the effect of population growth on the economy is mixed. Even when population growth has a negative impact, slower growth alone will not guarantee progress.[60] The report has helped to establish a "middle ground" in the population debate, a middle ground, one might note, already occupied by many demographers and economists who have consistently held a more reasoned view of the issue.

Within the population establishment, the likely effect of the academy's report will be to push the Malthusians into an even more selective application of their logic, as they search out areas of the globe where it is easier to make their case. In a 1986 issue of *The New York Review of Books*, for example, Jonathon Lieberson of the Population Council concedes there is "no universal problem of overpopulation," but then describes the "genuine" and "grave" problem in sub-Saharan Africa.[61] The World Bank recently announced that population assistance is its "highest priority" in sub-Saharan Africa and called for a massive increase in foreign population aid to the region, from $50 million today to $320 million in the year 2000.[62] "Into Africa" has become the place to be.

Along with the ever more selective application of Malthusian logic may also come the ever more selective application of ethics, so that the kind of population programs foisted on Africa and other countries still deemed overpopulated, such as Bangladesh, could easily be disrespectful of basic human rights (see Chapters 4 and 11). For example, Lieberson argues that stringent population policies, notably China's one-child limit, which Americans would find unethical in their own society, might be less objectionable in different circumstances. The most dangerous aspect of Malthusianism is that wherever it makes population growth the devil, it crosses ethical boundaries where angels fear to tread.

WRONGS AND RIGHTS

Because it makes the wrong diagnosis of the population problem, Malthusianism does not prescribe the right cure, and often makes the problem worse. This occurs on several different levels.

In terms of social policy, Malthusianism diverts attention and resources away from addressing the real causes of poverty, and hence of high birth rates. It provides a smoke screen behind which Third World governments and Western aid agencies can hide their failure to challenge the unequal distribution of wealth and power, which prevents broad-based economic development. Population control is substituted for social justice, and much needed reforms—such as land redistribution, employment creation, the provision of mass education and health care, and the emancipation of women—are conveniently ignored. The unfavorable survival conditions that cause high birth rates remain in place.

On the level of culture, Malthusianism reinforces Western ethnocentrism. "Our" nuclear family is supposed to be right for "them" too, even though the circumstances of a U.S. suburb and a Third World village are very different indeed. Modern Western culture also tends to isolate children from adult activities, viewing them as a social as well as an economic burden. By contrast, many Third World cultures are more appreciative of children, a fact that Malthusians find hard to grasp. Today, many Third World elites are embracing Malthusianism with as much, or even more, zeal than their Western counterparts. This not only reflects the penetration of Western values, but the great social barriers of class and caste in many countries, which are often stronger than bonds of nationality. In the most extreme cases, Malthusianism is wielded as a weapon of cultural genocide, through, for example, the forced sterilization of Native American women in the United States and ethnic minorities in South Asia (see Chapters 11 and 12).

On the individual level, Malthusianism has intimately and negatively affected the experience of millions of women with birth control. Married to population control, family planning has been divorced from the concern for women's health and well-being that inspired the first feminist crusaders for birth control. The goal of many Third World health and family planning programs is simply to achieve or exceed specified "contraceptive acceptance" targets; counseling, follow-up, the provision of a range of contraceptive options, and information on risks and benefits are secondary concerns, if they are concerns at all. This is not the fault of individual health and family planning workers—they are themselves caught in a system where sensitivity in meeting women's needs goes unrewarded, and merit is judged by how well they achieve population control targets. The approach typically backfires: Suffering from unexplained and untreated contraceptive side effects and disillusioned with the quality of service, a high percentage of women drop out of family planning programs. This is another way Malthusianism contributes to the persistence of high birth rates.

In the field of contraceptive technology, Malthusianism has put a madness into the methods. The goal of pregnancy prevention has taken precedence over safety in contraceptive research, leading to a lopsided emphasis on the "more effective," or high tech methods, such as the pill, the injectable Depo-Provera, the IUD, and now the hormonal implant. Whatever their virtues in preventing pregnancy, these methods entail substantial health risks, risks which are compounded by the lack of screening and follow-up in many clinical trials and population programs.

Meanwhile, safer methods such as the condom and diaphragm have been grossly neglected, both in terms of the allocation of research funds for their improvement and their promotion and distribution in population programs. In a number of ways, these barrier technologies are highly appropriate to Third World conditions—they help prevent the spread of sexually transmitted diseases, have no adverse impact on breastfeeding, and are very suitable for birth spacing, even if they are not 100 percent effective in preventing pregnancy. Yet population agencies do not consider them effective enough, because they are under the user's control. The thrust of contraceptive research in fact has been to remove control of contraception from women, in the same way that women are being increasingly alienated from the birth process itself (see Part Three).

On the ethical plain, Malthusianism diminishes human rights. In order to ensure the rights of future generations to environmental and economic resources, the Malthusians believe it is acceptable to abrogate the reproductive rights of the present one. Where they differ is over means. The more liberal favor friendly persuasion in family planning programs, the more conservative openly support coercion.

The Malthusians are fundamentally wrong. The solution to the population problem lies not in the diminution of rights, but in their *expansion*. This is because the population problem is not really about a surplus of human numbers, but a lack of basic rights. Too many people have too little access to resources. Too many women have too little control over their own reproduction. Rapid population growth is not the cause of underdevelopment; it is a symptom of the slow pace of social reform.

Two basic sets of rights are at issue. First is the right of everyone on the earth today, not just in the future, to enjoy a decent standard of living through access to food, shelter, health care, education, employment, and social security. Despite present high rates of population growth, most—if not all—societies have the means to guarantee this right to all their people, if wealth and power were shared more equitably. A fairer distribution of resources between the industrialized world and the Third World is just as necessary.

Once people's physical survival is ensured and children are no longer their only source of security, history shows that population growth rates fall voluntarily. Higher living standards across the board were the motor force behind the demographic transition in the industrialized world. Similarly, those Third World countries, whether capitalist, socialist, or mixed economy, which have made broad-based development a priority have also experienced significant reductions in population growth, often at relatively low levels of per capita income. These include Cuba, Sri Lanka, Korea, Taiwan, and China (see Chapter 14). Meanwhile, a country like India, where the benefits of substantial economic growth have flowed disproportionately to a small elite, still has high rates of population growth despite the massive amount of resources the government has devoted to population control.

The right to a decent standard of living is necessary but not sufficient. The other critical right is the fundamental right of women to control their own reproduction. The expansion of reproductive choice, not population control, should be the goal of family planning programs and contraceptive research.

What exactly is reproductive choice? Narrowly conceived,

it means offering women a broad range of birth control methods, including legal abortion, from which they can freely choose. But the choice is really less in the specific product than in the ongoing relationship between the provider and recipient of family planning services. Good screening, counseling, follow-up, and genuine informed consent depend on respect for the needs and the experience of the individual woman (or man). She must be the ultimate arbiter in the decision of whether or not to use contraception and which method to choose. Her womb belongs to her.

The question of reproductive choice ultimately goes far beyond the bounds of family planning programs, involving women's role in the family and in society at large. Control over reproduction is predicated on women having greater control over their economic and social lives and sharing power equally with men.

While reducing poverty reduces birth rates, so does reducing patriarchy. The sheer physical burden of many pregnancies in close succession means that women who are free to control their reproduction seldom opt for having all the children it is biologically possible for them to have. And when women have access to education and meaningful employment, they tend to want fewer children for the obvious reason that they have other options.

To say that guaranteeing these two basic sets of rights will help to reduce population growth is not to say that these rights should be pursued for this purpose. On the contrary, once social reforms, women's projects, and family planning programs are organized for the explicit goal of reducing population growth, they are subverted and ultimately fail. The individual no longer matters in the grand Malthusian scheme of things, which is by its very nature hostile to social change (see Chapter 7). Instead, these basic rights are worthy of pursuit in and of themselves; they have far more relevance to the general improvement of human welfare than reducing population growth alone ever will.

There are of course no simple prescriptions for ensuring these rights. Social change is a complex process, involving subtle cultural transformations as well as not-so-subtle political shifts and power struggles between countries, classes, and sexes. One thing is clear, however: Malthusianism stands in the way of progress. For how one poses the population problem profoundly affects how one supports—or chooses not to support—the concrete attempts of Third World people to improve their lives and the efforts of women around the world to exercise meaningful reproductive choice.

2

A Womb of One's Own

There isn't much understanding in some marriages. My sister has six, and another one has eight. And I said to one of them that she shouldn't have any more. And she said, "What can I do? When my husband comes home drunk, he forces me to sleep with him." And that is what happens to a lot of women. And if the women don't do it, the men hit them, or treat them badly. Or the men get jealous and think their wives must be with other men. And the women have to do whatever they say. I think it is changing a little, because the young women are more aware.

—RENÉ, *a twenty-nine-year-old Peruvian woman,*
unmarried mother of one son

It took place in the room of a gentleman whose name I did not know . . . it was fairly dark and the only light for the operation was an electric torch. Only the desire to get rid of the child I was carrying gave me the courage to stay. It was unthinkable that I should be expelled from college, and I couldn't bear my parents to find out that I was pregnant.

He began the operation. I felt a sharp and intense pain, worse than I had ever felt before. I wanted to cry out and scream. I felt as though part of my flesh was being ripped out by his metal instruments. . . . Gradually the pain lessened. I lay stretched out on the wooden table, almost unconscious, but only for a few moments. Then the man wrote a prescription and gave it to me, and showed me out. . . .

This operation traumatized me and made me think that I might not be able to have children. . . . So when I did become pregnant, I felt so happy and liberated, as though I was being reborn. . . .

Several years after we were married, my husband and I discussed my abortions. It turned out that my husband had known of the existence of contraceptives, but hadn't wanted to talk to me about it because he thought I was too young, and because he thought it could have gone to my head and led me to go off with someone else.

—ALIMA, *a thirty-year-old Senegalese woman who works as a secretary with a private firm in Dakar*

I am Indrani from Sri Lanka. I was living and working in the tea estate area. . . . The only birth control method we know is sterilization. . . .

All medical and social welfare staff, including foreign aid people, are forcing us to be sterilized. . . . The tea plantation community is given 500 rupees for a female sterilization, and in the rest of the country half of this amount is given. When there is a serious illness, the factory management are supposed to provide transport to the hospital. But even if someone is unconscious, they are not given transport. But when a woman decides to say yes for a sterilization, immediately the lorry is ready to go to the hospital.

During or soon after childbirth, women are asked if they want sterilization. When a woman does not agree, she can be refused work in the fields and she may be refused Thriposha [a protein-enriched flour, provided free by CARE]. During the work in the fields, the supervisors are also encouraging women to be sterilized. If you do not agree to a sterilization after your second child, you are not admitted to hospital for your next delivery.

After sterilization, women feel very weak, and after years many still have complaints. Some women did not know that the operation is permanent and stops fertility forever.

—INDRANI, *a member of the Tamil minority in Sri Lanka, who is now living as a refugee in India*

On 1st March 1982, Mrs. K. gave birth by caesarian section to a second daughter. In the days following delivery, a young woman doctor put a great deal of pressure on Mrs. K. and her husband to sign forms of consent for what it appears were injections for rubella vaccination and Depo-Provera contraceptive cover. It seems no attempt was made to explain why the injections might be beneficial or the future effects or side effects of Depo-Provera. They were repeatedly told that the injections were a "good thing" and, as Mr. K. put it, "push, push, pushed" to have them. Mrs. K. was in fact readmitted to the Accident and Emergency ward twice and once for a longer stay to the hospital with massive bleeding in the two months that followed the birth. The Ks seemed to think that this had something to do with these injections.

Although the Ks are native Bengali speakers, Mr. K. speaks reasonable English and understands more. I certainly found it perfectly possible to explain to him that Depo-Provera is a contraceptive—a fact which came as an obvious surprise to him.

—letter dated July 1982, from Bloomsbury Community Health Council, Great Britain[1]

Although René, Alima, Indrani, and "Mrs. K." come from different societies and different walks of life, their experiences reflect a common plight: women's lack of control over their own reproduction. Today what should be a woman's birthright—the right to decide when to have a child and to practice safe birth control—is denied millions of women around the world. Pitted against them are a number of obstacles: economic discrimination, subordination within the family, religious and cultural restrictions, the nature of health care systems, and the distortion of family planning programs to serve the end of population control. Women's biology need not be her destiny, but today her reproductive fate is largely shaped by forces beyond her control.

WOMEN IN UNDERDEVELOPMENT

In many Third World countries the economic subordination of women is directly linked to high birth rates, since it both increases their need for children and impedes their access to birth control. It is the result of a long history of exploitation, which in many cases was intensified by colonialism.

In much of Africa, for example, although women played an important role in food production, male-dominated colonial bureaucracies geared credit and extension services for cash crops exclusively to men, and overturned communal land tenure systems, vesting private ownership in the male "head of household." While men entered the cash economy not only as farmers, but as migrant laborers in the mines, plantation fields, and industries of the colonialists, women remained in subsistence agriculture. When the men migrated, the women had to take over the men's share of domestic tasks, leading to overwork and the subsequent decline in food crop production. This pattern repeated itself in trade. Although in a number of countries women dominated or actively participated in traditional marketing, under colonialism trade became the province of men.[2]

At the same time the processes of migration and urbanization encouraged by colonialism disrupted traditional patterns of life, including social mechanisms to space births. In many areas of sub-Saharan Africa, for example, an interval of up to four years between births was achieved through a taboo on intercourse during lactation, reinforced by the practice of polygamy. "Long before the influx of Western ideas, the understanding of the importance of child spacing to maternal and infant health was widespread in these cultures," concludes a study of traditional birth control methods in Zaire.[3] Meanwhile, the "Western ideas" of the colonialists were strongly pronatalist, encouraging many births and discouraging birth control. Contraception and abortion were generally proscribed by law, and missionaries actively campaigned against abstinence and polygamy[4]

Although women played a key role in many nationalist movements, political independence all too often brought little in the way of concrete improvements in their position. The new native male elites continued to follow many of the same policies as their colonial predecessors.

Today women's work is still consistently undervalued, not only in terms of financial reward, but social recognition as well. In most countries, the nonmonetary yet productive activities of women are not included in labor force statistics or measurements of the GNP. In North Africa, only 4 percent of women are supposedly members of the labor force; in Latin America the figure is 11 percent.[5] Women's work remains largely invisible, uncounted, unrewarded.

Yet researchers now estimate that women produce almost

half the food crops grown in the world. In Africa women contribute two thirds of all hours spent in traditional agriculture and three fifths of the time spent in marketing. In Asia, they constitute over half the agricultural labor force; in Latin America at least 40 percent.[6] In many Third World agricultural societies, women not only labor in the field, but are responsible for the arduous postharvest processing of crops, the provision of water and cooking fuel, the care of small livestock, cooking, looking after the children, to name a few of their responsibilities. Many women are in fact desperately overworked and need many children just to relieve their workload. This is especially true in sub-Saharan Africa, where women and children perform nearly all the agricultural labor.[7]

Rather than relieve a woman's workload or reward her adequately for her labors, modernization of agriculture along Western lines has usually worsened her predicament. Commercial farming still remains a male enclave in most parts of the Third World (though women are an important source of cheap labor for plantations), and it is men who receive access to credit, technology, and extension services. The few outside resources that trickle into subsistence food production generally end up in the hands of men, even if it is women's hands that are doing most of the work. With the exception of a few countries such as Thailand and the Philippines, agricultural training and extension work are limited to men.[8]

The increasing mechanization of agriculture has also worked to the detriment of women. Although technology has the potential of eliminating the importance of differences in physical strength between men and women, it has seldom been used to female advantage. Instead, because of their greater command over resources, men (and usually rich men) inevitably take control of new technologies. When women's traditional tasks of palm oil pressing in Nigeria and rice husking in Indonesia and Bangladesh have been mechanized, for example, it is men who own and work the machines, cutting women out from yet another economic process.[9]

In many Third World countries, the position of women is not much better in the urban economy, where most women are employed in the "informal sector," working for low wages as servants or street vendors, with virtually no job security. In industry women are channeled into unskilled, labor-intensive jobs, in the professions into the traditionally female ghettos of nursing, clerical work, retail sales, and teaching, which are low-pay, low-status occupations.

In the formal labor force, women are generally paid less for equal work, often on the basis that they are simply supplementing their husbands' income. In reality, however, a large percentage of families are headed by single women, and many young women work before they marry.

A job in either the formal or informal labor force seldom relieves a woman of her domestic duties so that she effectively has to manage two jobs at once.[10] Of course, there are middle and upper class women, with high-paying professional jobs and low-paid servants, whose life-styles approach or surpass those of their counterparts in the West. These privileged few are the exception, however, not the rule.

Today as multinational corporations expand their control over the world economy, Third World women, especially in Southeast Asia and Latin America, are joining the "global assembly line" in growing numbers. Over 2 million Third World women work in industry, many employed by multinational electronic, textile, and food-processing industries in labor-intensive, low-skilled jobs. In fact, 80 to 90 percent of low-skilled assembly jobs in the Third World are held by women.

Employment on the global assembly line offers little in the way of seniority benefits or job security. On the contrary, the expectation is that most women will "retire" when they are in their midtwenties. This constant turnover allows the companies to dispose of women suffering from occupationally related infirmities and to avoid payment of maternity and other benefits. Of the discarded women, the "lucky" ones settle into marriage, the less fortunate may be forced by economic necessity into even worse jobs or prostitution.[11]

The marginalization of the peasant woman, the exploitation of the female urban worker—these are two sides of the same coin of modernization. Women's economic powerlessness meanwhile is reinforced by deeply ingrained patriarchal cultural and religious attitudes. The world's great religions all have the unfortunate practice of placing the ideal woman on a pedestal, while knocking the real woman down. Together these forces limit women's power within the household, as well as in the fields and on the job.

SURVIVING PATRIARCHY

Today a new generation of feminist research has articulated what many women have known for centuries: The harmonious household is largely a myth. While men command resources and make decisions, many women battle to survive, emotionally, physically, or both.[12]

Women whose lives are bound by the subsistence household, for example, generally depend on men—who derive authority from working away from home, bringing in cash, and developing broader social and political connections—to mediate with the world outside. This dependence not only undermines a woman's ability to make independent decisions, but in poor families can have a direct bearing on her physical condition. Unable to exert much control over limited family resources, women are often the last to eat and the last to receive medical attention when they are sick.[13]

Despite the many deprivations they face, poor women often have more power within the family than more prosperous women because their labor power is recognized as vital to family survival. According to Indian political scientist Dr. Vina Mazumdar:

> Upward economic mobility, instead of solving the problem of the oppression of poverty, begins the oppression of prosperity, and the entry of some form of social seclusion, withdrawal from public economic activity, and relative loss of individual freedom and status within the family.[14]

Physical violence often serves to reinforce women's subordinate position within the family. Wife beating is unfortunately common all over the world, among all classes. In Mexico, where the phenomenon of *machismo* is particularly strong, an estimated 80 percent of women who live with men suffer from direct physical violence. In Peru, a common male saying is:

"The more I love you, the more I beat you."[15] Wife beating can be symptomatic of the powerlessness men feel themselves, of their need to be lords of the home, because they are vassals in the outside world.

Deprivation, seclusion, violence, all these serve to keep women "in their place." And part of being in that place is having children. For with no other option but the home or at best a low-paying job, women turn to children as their primary source of power. The birth of a first child, especially a son, brings a woman an automatic status that other domestic roles such as cooking and cleaning do not. A child pleases a woman's husband and her in-laws, the people who control her life. *Children are a woman's constituency within the narrow political world of the family;* the more she has, the stronger her clout. If she is infertile, her status plummets, and she often falls victim to polygamy, desertion, or divorce.

Children are often the main sources of a woman's pride and self-respect. "Social systems whose positive images of women are all linked to the reproductive role leave women with only one way to achieve a sense of purpose and accomplishment," concludes Kathleen Newland in her comprehensive study of women.[16] Children may also be a woman's only hedge against an uncertain future. Faced with the very real possibility of widowhood, divorce, or abandonment, women need children, especially sons, both for old-age support and to protect their rights to land and other property. In Kenya, for example, where roughly a quarter of rural households are headed by women, women do not generally inherit land but instead are given the right to use land owned by male family members, including sons.[17] Children are a husbandless woman's lifeline; without children, her prospect is often utter destitution.

When a team of demographers studied a Bangladesh village, they found that under the pressure of deepening poverty, male bonds of obligation to women were weakening, increasing women's vulnerability. At the same time, outside employment opportunities for women were severely limited, so that there was little chance of earning an independent livelihood. Widows were particularly at risk. The study cites the case of a once prosperous village woman reduced to beggary upon her husband's death. The study concludes:

> The risk and insecurity that patriarchy imposes on women represent a powerful systemic incentive for high fertility. . . . The best risk insurance for women . . . is to produce sons, as many and as soon as possible.[18]

Today in many areas of the Third World, the traditional family is breaking down, and there are a growing number of female-headed households. According to one study of seventy-four Third World countries, one in five households is headed by a woman. Although many of these women work outside the home, it is usually in low-paying occupations. Their short-term independence then counts for precious little in the way of long-term security. They too must rely on children as their basic form of risk insurance.[19]

In some cases, in fact, women want children, but not husbands. In Kenya's Central Province journalist Paula Park found that many young mothers preferred being single, since men drank too much liquor and spent too much money, undermining a woman's ability to care for her family.[20]

If women's powerlessness increases their need for children, then steps toward their empowerment could presumably have the opposite effect. This appears to be true in the case of literacy. The educational level of women is the single most consistent predictor of fertility and contraceptive use, even more important than income level.[21]

Not only do educated women generally marry later and have access to better jobs, which compete with motherhood, they also tend to have a broader world view. As a study of fertility in India explains:

> An educated woman is usually less closely confined, physically and psychologically, with her husband's family and its narrow familial concerns than is the woman who is brought into their home as an uneducated girl. . . . She is more likely to feel that she can do something about the conditions of her life, including the conditions of pregnancies in close succession or conceiving during her later reproductive years.[22]

Unfortunately, the female literacy rate for the Third World as a whole is only 32 percent, compared to 52 percent for men. However, female primary school enrollments are rising and catching up with males', though the male-female gap continues in further education, where there were only three girls for every five boys in 1985. The quality of education girls receive also tends to be inferior to boys', with girls typically channeled away from math and sciences toward subjects such as home economics and literature.[23]

Women's employment in the skilled labor force is also linked to fertility decline, not only because of competition with motherhood, but because the availability of such jobs serves as an incentive to families to educate girls.[24]

Although poverty and patriarchy serve as inducements to high fertility, it does not necessarily follow that women want to bear as many children as is biologically possible—eight, ten, even more. Many women would like to practice birth control, to space their pregnancies or to end them altogether once their need for children is met. What then is standing in their way?

BARRIERS TO REPRODUCTIVE CONTROL

A number of surveys have tried to provide a precise measurement of how many women would like either to limit or to space births. The recent World Fertility Survey, conducted in twenty-seven Third World countries, found that almost half the married women questioned wanted no more children, and that younger women especially tended to desire a smaller family size. In general, the number of women who wanted no more children exceeded the number of those using contraception, and this was interpreted as indicating a large "unmet need" for birth control.[25]

More compelling—though perhaps less "scientific"—evidence of women's unmet need for birth control comes from women talking to women. For when women, even of different class and cultures, sit down and speak seriously to each other, one thing that they share in common is both the blessing and curse of fertility.

In 1978, author Perdita Huston broke ground with her

classic *Message from the Village,* based on in-depth interviews with village women from Kenya, Egypt, Sri Lanka, Tunisia, and Mexico. In almost every society she visited she found women eager to learn about birth control, although there were many obstacles in their way.[26]

Similarly, Audrey Bronstein, in her study of Latin American peasant women, reports:

> Every woman I spoke to, with one exception, wanted reliable information about how to control her own fertility. The fact that most women had been forced to have more children than they wanted was the most damning evidence of the suffering and loss of human rights experienced by peasant women under the rule of both their husbands and the political factors controlling their lives.[27]

Similar findings have emerged from studies in Bangladesh, from a recent Oxfam survey of rural women in Kenya, from the reports of Third World women's organizations.[28]

Why women want to space or limit births is not difficult to fathom. The physical hardship of repeated pregnancies can exact a terrible toll on a woman's health. Between the ages of fifteen and forty-five, a woman in rural Bangladesh can now expect to have an average of eight pregnancies and to spend nearly seventeen years either pregnant or breast-feeding. This would be hard for any woman, but for already undernourished women the difficulty is greatly magnified. An estimated two thirds of all pregnant women in the Third World are anemic.[29]

Childbirth literally kills hundreds of thousands of poor women every year. Maternal mortality rates in excess of 500 per 100,000 live births are not uncommon in many Third World countries, compared to 5 to 30 in the industrialized world.

Put another way, the complications of pregnancy account for between 10 and 30 percent of *all* deaths of women of reproductive age in areas of Asia, Africa, and Latin America, but less than 2 percent in the United States and Europe.[30] The risk is greater for women under twenty or over thirty-four, and for women who have borne three or more children and suffer from the nutritional maternal depletion syndrome.[31] Many women do not have access even to rudimentary medical care during childbirth, much less sophisticated emergency equipment, so that even minor problems can lead to death.

For desperately poor women, having many children can be a heavy economic and emotional burden. A Mexican woman told Perdita Huston: "If I am going to have more children, who is going to feed them? When my children are crying, is it God who comes to comfort them?"[32]

The large number of induced abortions that occur worldwide every year—an estimated 30 to 50 million—also reflects the desire of women to limit births. Half of these are illegal. The medical complications of improperly performed illegal abortions are now reaching epidemic proportions in many parts of the Third World, and represent a leading cause of death among women of childbearing age.[33]

In Latin America, where abortion is outlawed in most countries because of opposition from the Catholic Church, one fifth to one half of all maternal deaths are due to illegal abortion, and scarce hospital beds are filled with victims. In Bolivia, complications from illegal abortions account for over 60 percent of the country's obstetrical and gynecological expenses.[34]

Seeking to limit their pregnancies, women, then, are also risking their lives.

Even in countries with liberal abortion laws, poor women often resort to illegal abortions because they lack access to legal abortion facilities or cannot afford to pay for the legal operation. In 1978, six years after the enactment of India's relatively liberal abortion law, for example, there were only 1 million legal abortions in the country compared to an estimated 5 million illegal ones.[35]

Recourse to dangerous illegal abortion not only underlines the need for widespread, cheap, legal abortion facilities, but the need for access to safe contraceptive alternatives. The problem is not simply supply—in many Third World countries the per capita availability of contraceptives is quite high—but more fundamental social barriers blocking women from contraceptives.

Male dominance is one of the strongest obstacles. In most cultures wives must have their husband's consent before they can decide to limit their fertility. And many men are reluctant to agree: They fear the possibility of their wife's infidelity or the loss of their control over her. As a doctor in a rural Mexican clinic explained to Perdita Huston,

> When a wife wants to do something on her own, such as trying to limit the number of mouths to feed in the family, the husband will become angry and even beat her. He thinks it is unacceptable that she is making a decision on her own. She is challenging his authority, his power over her—and thus the very nature of his virility.[36]

Not surprisingly, in households where men and women share power more equally, acceptance of family planning is much higher.[37] Including men in discussions with family planning workers also seems to make a difference. But more often than not, family planning programs are geared exclusively toward women, ignoring the basic reality of male dominance.

Male control of the medical profession also discourages many women from visiting family planning clinics. As a Mexican anthropologist explains:

> A woman is supposed to be the property of one man: her husband. If she goes to a clinic another man, the doctor, is going to see and touch her. Her husband won't let her go . . . and she, too, is reluctant. This is a great barrier to the acceptance of family planning in Mexico.[38]

In many Muslim cultures the problem is intensified by the practice of female seclusion. If no men other than a woman's husband and close male relations are allowed to see her, much less touch her, how likely is it that she will be able to consult a male doctor about family planning?

More female doctors and health workers are only part of the answer, however, for the problem lies more fundamentally in the very nature of health services. In most Third World countries, the scant resources devoted to health are usually spent in urban areas, on modern hospitals which serve a small elite. In rural areas, where people lack access to even rudimentary health care, they also usually lack access to decent family planning services. In Kenya, 58 percent of married women between the ages of fifteen and forty-nine who are exposed to the risk of pregnancy do not even know where they can obtain modern methods of contraception; in Mexico, the figure is 47 percent.[39]

Even when people do know where to get contraceptives, the time it takes to travel to a clinic, wait there, and return serves to discourage them—in Kenya, such a journey typically takes six hours. And once at the clinic, Kenyan women are sometimes refused birth control, especially if they are young and unmarried.[40] For people who can hardly afford basic medicines, the cost of contraceptives can also be prohibitive.

Many Third World health systems prefer modern Western-style medicine, undervaluing traditional forms. For family planning, this means that birth control methods in use for generations, whether they be herbal pessaries, withdrawal, abstinence, or prolonged breast-feeding, are passed over in favor of modern contraceptives, which are often less culturally acceptable and more disruptive of traditional practices. A Nigerian doctor warns of the implications for Africa: "The impact of a carelessly designed family planning program that may interfere with local beliefs and constraints can only serve to increase fertility levels."[41]

In order for women to feel confident about contraception and to use it effectively, they need to understand how the reproductive system works. Basic health education, however, is seldom emphasized in most health care systems or family planning programs. Even in an industrialized country like the United States, sex education is a source of endless controversy, for keeping women in the dark about their bodies is another powerful way of keeping them "in their place."

In many countries organized religion also presents a barrier to women's use of contraception. This is most obvious in the case of the Catholic Church's condemnation of all "artificial" forms of birth control. In the Church's view using contraceptives or having an abortion is a sin.

In the case of Islam, according to Egyptian feminist Nawal El Saadawi, nothing in the *Koran* either explicitly supports or opposes contraception. Thus among Islamic religious authorities, some "maintain that Islam approves of family planning and even abortion; yet others hold firmly to the position that

Islam not only opposes abortion, but even the utilization of contraception." In the Arab world, she maintains, it is not religion per se that is the issue, but the way religion is used "by those who rule to keep down those who are ruled."[42]

Many governments also follow pronatalist policies in the belief that an expanding population is vital to national development, prestige, and security. In sub-Saharan Africa, for example, five countries—Chad, Ivory Coast, Gabon, Guinea-Bissau, and Mauritania—do not support family planning, and until recently the number was much higher.[43] To facilitate economic growth (and some speculate to increase the proportion of the Malay ethnic group in the population), the Malaysian government wants to achieve a fivefold increase in the population over the next 115 years. The Prime Minister is telling families to "go for five" children.[44]

In Latin America the Catholic Church has prevented many governments from establishing national family planning programs. In Peru, for example, the Church helped to block the implementation of the government's 1977 Population Policy, which called for voluntary family planning services, and recently succeeded in pressuring the government to eliminate voluntary surgical sterilization as a birth control method. As a result, only the most privileged Peruvian women have access to modern forms of contraception, and thousands of women are forced each year to resort to dangerous illegal abortions.[45] Left-wing movements in Latin America have also tended to oppose family planning, failing to distinguish between population control interventions from abroad and women's real need for birth control. However, this opposition is beginning to fade under the influence of feminism.

Unfortunately, many governments that have implemented national family planning programs have done so not for reasons of women's health or reproductive freedom, but because of pressure from international donors to control population growth. Ironically, population control itself often blocks women's access to safe birth control, as we shall see in the next chapter.

It would be mistaken to view this lack of reproductive control as simply a Third World women's problem. In the Western world too, economic powerlessness and low status combine to place restrictions on women's reproductive choice. In fact, the basic pattern of sex discrimination shares much in common with the Third World. Women in Western countries are paid only one half to three quarters of what men earn at the same jobs; in the formal labor force their traditional occupations— clerical work, teaching, nursing, and unskilled factory jobs— are scandalously low-paid, and their domestic work is under-valued and unrewarded, even though it is estimated to con-tribute as much as one fifth to one third of the GNP.[46]

Many women in the West also face difficulties gaining ac-cess to legal abortion and safe birth control. In several European countries, including Belgium and Ireland, abortions are still illegal, and even in countries with more liberal laws, such as Great Britain and the United States, many women cannot afford them or obtain them easily. In Ireland, until recently even sell-ing condoms on a nonprescription basis was illegal![47]

In the United States, the absence of a national health sys-tem, which serves everyone, regardless of ability to pay, means that family planning services which provide a wide range of contraceptive choices are something that only the well-off can afford. As political scientist and reproductive rights activist Rosalind Petchesky explains:

> The careful and sensitive counseling that would be necessary for poor and uneducated women to use nonpermanent birth control successfully is reserved for private offices and clinics that cater mainly to middle-class women; in truth, there is little such care in the hurried, overcrowded conditions of large hospital outpatient clinics, on which poor women rely.[48]

In the United States, teenagers' lack of access to contraception is reflected in record pregnancy rates. Out of every 1,000 teenagers aged fifteen to nineteen, 96 become pregnant, more than double the rate in Canada, England, and France.[49] Yet conservatives continue to fight sex education in the schools and the provision of contraceptives to minors without parental consent.

The practice of population control is also not limited to the Third World. In the United States poor black, Native

American, and Hispanic women have been forcibly sterilized in federal programs; in England recent immigrants have been given Depo-Provera without their consent (see Part Three).

The situation is not much better in a number of Eastern European countries and the Soviet Union. Although female labor force participation is high in these countries, women are still locked, like their Western sisters, into low-pay, low-prestige occupations, are responsible for almost all domestic work without as many modern conveniences, and are restricted in terms of contraceptive choice. In the Soviet Union, for example, abortion is the primary means of birth control, not by choice but because other forms of contraception are virtually unavailable. According to one Soviet feminist:

> The scarcity of contraceptives is due to the Soviet Union's not considering women's needs an industrial priority; furthermore, the government wants (white [that is, the dominant Russian ethnic group]) Russians to have more children, because of its racist concern about the greater growth of the ethnic populations in the other Soviet republics.[50]

In Romania, pronatalism has had particularly seriously consequences for women. Concerned about a drop in the birth rate, the Romanian government overturned liberal abortion legislation in 1966 and prohibited the use of modern contraceptives except for medical reasons. The birth rate did rise as planned, but at the cost of women's lives. In 1977 the maternal mortality rate from illegal abortion was three times the 1966 rate, and it is still rising.[51]

In 1984 the Romanian government launched a new campaign to increase births, calling for every woman to have at least three to four children as part of her "patriotic duty." The legal marriage age for girls has been lowered to fifteen, men and women still single at twenty-five pay an additional 5 percent income tax, and all women in their twenties have to undergo compulsory medical checkups, with pregnant women closely observed to make sure they do not have abortions. One of the motives behind the present campaign may be racist concern over the high growth rate of the gypsy population.[52]

These are just some of the barriers to women's reproductive control in the industrialized world. Just as in the Third World, then, the issue goes far beyond the simple question of contraception to involve power relationships at almost every social level, from the family on up to the national government. Recognizing this basic reality, many feminists today are defining reproductive rights much more broadly. Their demands include the following:

- The right to economic security through the opportunity to work for equal pay for equal work, so that women can adequately care for themselves and their families.
- The right to a safe workplace and environment for all, so that women are not exposed to hazards that threaten their ability to bear healthy children, or forced to choose between sterilization and jobs.
- The right of quality child care, so that women can enter the work force secure in the knowledge that their children will be looked after.
- The right to abortion and contraceptive choice.
- The right to reproductive education, so that women and men of all ages are better able to understand and control their own bodies.
- The right to decent medical care, necessary not only to ensure contraceptive safety, but a basic human right.
- The right to choose how to give birth, and to have control over the development and use of new reproductive technologies.
- The right of lesbian women and women with disabilities to be mothers.
- The need for men to participate as equal partners in childbearing, housework, and birth control, so women no longer have to shoulder the "double burden."
- An end to discrimination so that all people—regardless of race, sex, or class—can lead productive lives, and exercise real control over their own reproduction.[53]

Clearly, reproductive rights are predicated on achieving basic rights in almost every sphere of life. For while reproduction may be an intensely personal experience, it is also a fundamentally social one, at the center of a web of human relations. It is important never to lose sight of the whole while focusing on the center. Indeed, it is the failure to see the whole that lies behind the narrow conception and single-minded pursuit of population control.

3

The Plan Behind Family Planning

Women the world over want family planning.

This statement is probably not much of an exaggeration. The difficulty comes when trying to define precisely what family planning means. In the Third World context many people believe family planning and population control programs are one and the same. So if you oppose population control, they automatically assume you are against any form of family planning.

Family planning, however, is a generic term, encompassing all types of birth control programs, in the same way that "health care" can refer to many kinds of medical treatment. Family planning programs can thus vary widely from each other, depending on whose interests they serve. A family planning program designed to improve health and to expand women's control over reproduction looks very different indeed from one whose main concern is to reduce birth rates as fast as possible.

Family planning programs of the first type aim to offer the following:

- A wide choice of contraceptive methods, with full information on benefits and risks, and supportive counseling on how to use them.
- Good screening and medical follow-up.
- A full range of reproductive health services, including treatment for infertility, antenatal and postnatal care, prevention of sexually transmitted diseases, and support for breast-feeding.

- Counseling on male as well as female responsibility for contraception.
- Respect for the local culture and local health providers, and the incorporation of traditional fertility control methods practiced by the community, if they are safe.
- Freedom from pressure and coercion.

In trying to meet ambitious, and often unrealistic demographic objectives, population control programs on the other hand impose birth control on women from above. They typically limit choice of contraceptive method, fail to give adequate information and counseling, neglect screening, follow-up, and the overall health of the woman, ignore the sexual politics of reproduction, and are insensitive to local culture. The result is a tragic waste of resources, which in different hands could serve to expand reproductive choice.

Women the world over want family planning. This is the story of what population agencies have done to them in its name.

RHETORIC AND REALITY

Most of the major international agencies that shape Third World population policy are perched high atop Western metropolitan centers. In offices with the latest in communications equipment, a host of administrators, researchers, and consultants consider the business of "delivering" birth control to the Third World. A few peasant women's faces peek from glossy covers of promotional brochures or an occasional photograph in the lobby, but otherwise Third World women are mainly numbers in computer printouts, unidentified "targets," "clients," or "acceptors" in the technical journals adorning the office shelves. Their fate figures only in demographic calculations of "births averted" and "couple-years of protection."

A plane trip away, in the capital cities of the Third World, the offices of government family planning ministries are seldom so well appointed. There are ceiling fans and open windows rather than automated thermostats, an army of clerks instead of word processors, dusty files rather than crisp reports. But the peasants are missing there as well. The villages where family planning will or will not succeed lie just beyond the bounds of the city, but to the urban civil servant they are often an alien world. Distances are not only measured in miles.

Between the peasant "target groups" and the population experts yawns a wide social gulf, which is rarely crossed. The family planners plan, the contraceptive deliverers deliver, the acceptors accept. What could be simpler? The people on top decide what is best for the people on the bottom. Thus family planning becomes a profoundly technocratic exercise. This is no accident, but rather the direct outcome of three decades in which the philosophy of population control has won intellectual and political ascendancy.

From the 1960s Western policymakers, especially in the United States, embraced "overpopulation" as a primary cause of poverty and instability in the Third World. It was this concern—not concern for women's well-being—that shaped the initial pattern of family planning interventions overseas. Although these interventions have varied from country to country, they have usually involved a combination of these steps:

- Support for fledgling local family planning organizations, often staffed by Western-trained nationals with population control values, by private population agencies such as the International Planned Parenthood Federation (IPPF).
- The larger involvement of institutions such as the Ford Foundation, the Rockefeller Foundation, and the Population Council in the establishment of population research institutions, the training of top Third World personnel in the United States, and the sending of advisory missions to encourage governments to embark on population control programs.
- A flow of funds and personnel from the United States government's Agency for International Development (AID) as an integral part of foreign aid.
- The entry of multilateral institutions, such as the United Nations Fund for Population Activities (UNFPA) or the World Bank.[1]

Out of these interventions has grown a whole imported science of family planning in the Third World, based on several key assumptions.

The first assumption is that there is already a large demand for modern family planning services among recipient populations and that people are prepared to use them right away, regardless of social, economic, and cultural conditions. In the early days, many foreign agencies designed and promoted programs on this basis. They developed the KAP (Knowledge, Attitude, and Practice) Survey, in which outside interviewers asked women sensitive questions about reproduction and fertility. When a woman answered yes to the questions of whether she was interested in contraception or already had enough children, she was assumed to be an immediate candidate for a family planning program.

Harvard researcher Donald Warwick provides an important critique of the KAP approach in his book *Bitter Pills,* an evaluation of family planning programs, which was commissioned and then disavowed by the United Nations Fund for Population Activities (UNFPA) for being too critical. He points out how the surveys ignored the cultural context of fertility decisions in which women often have no authority, have never viewed themselves or their husbands as able to determine family size, or may change their minds over time.[2]

Moreover, many of the questions were slanted toward positive answers. As Mahmud Mamdani found in his classic 1972 study of a Harvard-sponsored family planning project in an Indian village, the peasants were often willing to comply with the interviewer's biases. "It is sometimes better to lie," one villager told him. "It stops you from hurting people, does you no harm, and might even help them."[3]

The continued use of KAP surveys, despite mounting criticism of their methodology, may have something to do with the fact that they were not only intended to measure demand for family planning, but to serve a political purpose. As Bernard Berelson, former head of the Population Council, stated candidly:

A survey should probably be done at the outset of any national program—partly for its evaluational . . . use but also for its political use, in demonstrating to the elite that the people themselves strongly support the program and in demonstrating to the society at large that family planning is generally approved.[4]

Today KAP surveys have been improved, but there is still too little emphasis on in-depth discussions and personal contact, which are often much more effective in finding out what people really want and need.[5]

A second key assumption of family planning theory is that people can be motivated to practice family planning through information, education, and communication (IEC) campaigns— e.g., through billboards showing an affluent two-child family, messages over the radio and cinema, lectures in schools and public meetings. Although there certainly is a role for public education on family planning matters, IEC programs are typically beset with a number of problems.

First is the failure to recognize that the family planning message is bound to fall on deaf ears as long as people need children for their economic survival or the subordination of women means they cannot use family planning even if they want to. Moreover, those spreading the message often hold elitist attitudes and have no idea of how to communicate effectively with people who are beneath them on the social ladder. For example, an Indian official responsible for holding public meetings on family planning complained:

> It is very difficult to have public meetings here because the villagers will disturb them. For example . . . one fellow got up and started to discuss the price of rice prevailing here. "Why can't you give one measure of rice for one rupee, as you are doing in Madras? If you do that, we may start to think about family planning." Now how can we conduct meetings when conditions are like this? These Harijans [previously called Untouchables] are lazy![6]

Such elitism is also reflected in the inappropriate nature of the message itself. In Indonesia, the main motto of the family planning program is that with two children, "We are a happy and prosperous family,"[7] a common refrain in many other countries as well. But for a peasant without land or employment opportunities, limiting fertility hardly brings prosperity or happiness; the cozy image of the Westernized nuclear family belongs to an alien and unobtainable world. Moreover, although many women want to limit births, they usually want more than two children.

As Mamdani points out, the fundamental premise of the IEC approach is questionable:

> The underlying assumption is that the behavior of the population, given the environment and its constraints, is not rational: it is thus susceptible to "education." If education fails, it is a question of not having used the right techniques.[8]

Hence, today, ever more sophisticated techniques are being employed. In Mexico, for example, television soap operas promote family planning. "I don't want my child to grow up in a place like this," shouts a poor Mexican woman, pregnant for the third time in three years, from the television screen.[9]

In Bangladesh, Population Services International, with U.S. Agency for International Development (AID) funding, advertises condoms and the pill, helping, according to the International Planned Parenthood Federation's (IPPF) *People* magazine, "to associate family planning with widespread aspirations such as better health, prosperity and a Westernized lifestyle."[10] The project even attempted the novel approach of air-dropping advertising leaflets, though this was abandoned after the leaflets landed on a girls' secondary school in the capital city of Dhaka!

The last assumption shared by both foreign agencies and many Third World governments is that there is a neat congruence between the goals of population control and the improvement of individual health and welfare. In practice, however, emphasis on population control profoundly affects how family planning programs are organized and implemented in the field, and means, in a number of cases, that they function *in actual contradiction* to the goal of individual welfare.

In the drive to lower birth rates, the population establishment has developed what Donald Warwick calls the "machine theory of implementation," in which family planning programs consist of mechanical delivery systems on the one hand and program clients, who are "receptacles for the services delivered," on the other.[11] Standard models have been developed and applied irrespective of different cultural contexts, with authority centralized within the national government and passed down through a rigidly defined hierarchy of officials. Success has typically been evaluated solely in terms of numbers of acceptors and of targets met, not in terms of people's satisfaction with the services delivered.

Although the goal of this machine model is above all "efficiency," in practice its top-down organization and target orientation can cause a high degree of bureaucratic bungling. In the Philippines, for example, Warwick describes how the pressure on family planning workers to meet numerical quotas of acceptors has led to unproductive competition between local agencies vying for funds.

A national administrator of the Family Planning Organization of the Philippines complains that the agencies engage in "acceptor grabbing" to support their claims to be the better agency to implement family planning: "This boils down to their motivation of getting more funds. . . . They feel that family planning is where the money is, and this is the root of all evil."[12]

Thus mobile clinics from one Filipino religious group who distributed the pill and IUD in slum areas claimed "credit" for all their acceptors, but when some of the women subsequently suffered from adverse effects, the mobile units were nowhere to be seen. Staff members from permanent clinics in the area, run by another organization, were meanwhile reluctant to admit these patients for treatment because they could not count them as acceptors.[13]

While local agencies fight for numerical victories in the field, the centralization of authority in the capital has led, in the words of one AID-sponsored evaluation, to "the development of big buildings in Manila, with large, underutilized staff, and with little trickle down of resources to the field where they can be used."[14]

By its very nature, the donor-imposed model of family planning neglects, and sometimes outright disrespects, local culture. This has meant that many family planning programs have lost the opportunity to build on existing fertility control practices such as birth spacing, breast-feeding, and herbal contraceptives, and have failed to address people's other reproductive needs, especially problems of infertility.

Many family planning programs, instead of winning over and involving trusted local healers and midwives, have alienated them. In Egypt, for example, where the traditional midwife is an important figure in rural communities, the Ministry of Health decided that midwives did not have the proper training to operate in the health system as family planning workers. As might be expected, many midwives perceived the government's family planning program as a threat to their positions and authority and worked against it.[15]

Today, some donor agencies are trying to involve local midwives, called Traditional Birth Attendants or TBAs in official jargon, more closely in the provision of family planning services, though it is unclear whether this will be a lasting practice or just another fad.[16]

The most serious drawback of the machine model of family planning is limitation of choice, whether through subtle pressure or outright coercion. The emphasis on meeting targets means that people are often pushed into accepting contraception or sterilization against their will, so that family planning workers can fulfill the quotas on which their jobs depend. "No program with targets can be completely free of coercion," write demographers John and Pat Caldwell.[17]

Target orientation can also distort the kind of education family planning workers receive, so that they have imperfect information on the relative risks and merits of different contraceptive methods and are thus ill-equipped to meet people's needs. In South Asia, the World Bank notes, "Where it exists, supervision takes the form of enforcing accountability and targets rather than supportive training and advice."[18]

While in theory most programs follow the "cafeteria" approach to family planning, in which the widest choice of contraceptive methods is made available, in practice the drive to bring down birth rates means that only the so-called more ef-

fective methods—IUDs, hormonal contraception, and sterilization—are promoted. In the Philippines, for example, AID
pressure led an agency to circulate this warning to its clinics:
"Discourage condom acceptors and encourage more IUDs and
pills. The clinic is evaluated on the method accepted by the
clients. There will be no more supply of condoms: so convince
your condom acceptors to shift to pills and IUDs."[19] Such biases
are reinforced by incentive systems, where both providers and
acceptors are "rewarded" for particular methods.

In order to meet quotas for "effective" methods, family
planning workers often consciously decide not to disclose potential adverse effects to acceptors. As one Kenyan field worker
explained, "We don't tell them of the major side effects for
fear of losing them."[20] In the short run, this may win higher
acceptance rates, but in the long run, it can lead to disillusionment with specific contraceptives and family planning in general. Indeed, it is now commonly accepted that the greatest
single obstacle to continued use of family planning services is
adverse experience with methods adopted.[21]

For these reasons, the machine model of family planning
has not only failed to expand reproductive choice, but in many
places—notably India, Pakistan, Egypt, and Kenya—has
proved inefficient even in terms of its own goal: to lower the
birth rate. Nevertheless, critical evaluations have been remarkably rare. In the early days, donors such as the World
Bank performed cost-benefit analyses of population projects
by measuring the benefits from "averted births" compared to
the costs of family planning services, and translated actual rates
of contraceptive acceptance into estimates of demographic
change. It was assumed that once people accepted family planning, they would continue to use it effectively. The result was
an unrealistically rosy picture.

Today cost-effectiveness analysis, which seeks to estimate
the cost per acceptor, has become more popular. Both methods,
however, view *quantity* of acceptors as more important than
quality of services delivered.[22] Indeed, as Donald Warwick
points out, because family planning programs have been designed in quarters far removed from the people who actually

use them, evaluations typically ignore "the sensitivities of local clients and communities," favoring instead "statistical results."[23]

When, on occasion, consultants do go to the field for on-site inspections of family planning programs, they still tend to avoid the crucial question of whether or not people are satisfied with the services they are getting. As one former IPPF official said of his organization:

> There is no such thing as a really hard evaluation. It's the old fly-in, fly-out routine. For a day or two the evaluators are feted by the project staff and the village leaders and take a few glossy pictures. No discussions are arranged with the actual recipients of the services. In the rare case a critical evaluation is made, it is usually buried by the bureaucracy. . . . Not only is there very little proper research, but there is a positive dislike of field trips that don't stick to the cocktail circuit.[24]

More often than not, any problems are simply attributed to "management" difficulties. The basic assumption is that if officials could only organize things a little better, making use of new management information systems, then programs would function more effectively. Computerizing program data thus assumes a higher priority than instituting fundamental changes.

Even in the absence of many critical evaluations, high dropout rates from family planning programs and the persistence of high birth rates in many countries have indicated clearly enough that the family planning machine is in need of repairs. The response of the population establishment has been mixed. More liberal elements have tried to reform family planning programs through integrating them with health, community, and women's development projects (see Chapter 7). More hard-line population control advocates, however, have stepped up the pressure on target groups through the use of incentive and disincentive schemes to induce sterilization or contraceptive use. These not only limit choice, but in many cases lead directly to coercion.

THE INCENTIVE DEBATE

Within the population community incentives are a source of much controversy. For example, while the International Conference on Family Planning in the 1980s, co-sponsored by the United Nations Fund for Population Activities (UNFPA), the Population Council, and IPPF in 1981, reached a happy consensus on almost every other issue, there was "fundamental disagreement" over incentives.[25]

This disagreement is reflected in differences in official policy among population agencies. In principle, the UNFPA and a number of private agencies such as the Pathfinder Fund and the IPPF are against incentives, although in practice they often cooperate with governments who use them. The World Bank, on the other hand, openly supports and finances incentive schemes. Its senior population adviser, Dr. K. Kanagaratnam, maintains that "Incentives and disincentives are the stock in trade of the business—they help to create a national norm, a milieu."[26] The U.S. Agency for International Development (AID) also joins the incentive supporters' camp, although it disguises incentives as "compensation payments" (see Chapter 11).

Supporters of incentives argue that they are a neutral tool of social engineering, designed as "inducements to change behavior." According to this view, the use of incentives in family planning programs helps to spread information about contraceptive techniques, acts as a trigger-mechanism to start people using contraception who are already interested in limiting births, and encourages those not yet interested to accept family planning through financial benefits that alter their "taste" for children. Ostensibly, incentives are voluntary, since people can either choose to accept them or refuse them if they want.[27]

Such views display a fundamental ignorance of the social context in which incentives are introduced. "What is remarkable is that none of them makes room for a more down-to-earth explanation of the effectiveness of incentives in a culture of poverty," writes Marika Vicziany in her study of the Indian family planning program, "namely, that the main reason a ma-

COUNTRIES OFFERING SMALL, ONE-TIME PAYMENTS

TO INDIVIDUALS		TO DOCTORS OR FAMILY PLANNING WORKERS	
Sterilization	*Contraceptives*	*Sterilization*	*Contraceptives*
Bangladesh	Bangladesh	Bangladesh	Bolivia
India	Egypt	Bolivia	Dominican
Indonesia	India	Dominican	Republic
Malaysia	Mauritius	Republic	Egypt
(industries only)	Nepal	Ghana	Ghana
Nepal	South Korea	Hong Kong	Hong Kong
South Korea	Thailand	India	India
Sri Lanka	Tunisia	Indonesia	Indonesia
Thailand	Vietnam	Malaysia	Malaysia
Tunisia		Mauritius	Mauritius
Vietnam		Philippines	Philippines
		Singapore	Singapore
		South	South Korea
		Korea	Sri Lanka
		Sri Lanka	Taiwan
		Taiwan	Thailand
		Thailand	Tunisia
		Tunisia	

Sources: Population Crisis Committee, Population Council, International Planned Parenthood Federation, and United Nations. From Judith Jacobsen, *Promoting Population Stabilization: Incentives for Small Families,* Worldwatch Paper 54 (Washington, D.C., Worldwatch Institute, June 1983), p. 8.

terial incentive works is that it provides an immediate economic gain."[28] For people who are desperately poor, there is no such thing as free choice. A starving person is unlikely to turn down a loaf of bread, even if it means being sterilized. Thus, in practice incentives often have more to do with coercion than with choice.

The most common form of incentives is one-time payments to acceptors and/or providers of sterilization, and occasionally of other contraceptives, especially the IUD (see Table). These not only bias contraceptive choices toward specific techniques but all too often trade on the desperation of the poor and lead to profiteering on the part of family planning personnel.

When motivators—people from the community who recruit acceptors—are also paid a fee, this can lead to additional abuses, as local bosses use the opportunity to exert pressure and turn a fast profit. A study of mass vasectomy camps in India's Gujarat State found, for example, that the "most influential" motivators were members of the local revenue department and the police.[29] In Pakistan, when incentives for doctors, motivators, and acceptors were introduced for IUD insertion, an "IUD factory" ensued in which all three groups cooperated to have IUDs repeatedly inserted, then removed, then inserted. . . .[30]

Dr. Zafrullah Chowdhury of the People's Health Center in Bangladesh has likened such systems to prostitution, where the "recipients 'sell' their human pride and dignity":

> The prostitute sells the body to survive, knowing that the person who has used them has no concern for the physical/ emotional implications this may have for the prostitute. Similarly, the sterilization acceptor under an incentive scheme is merely a further number of the profiteer. Once the procedure is finished, so is the patient—no one cares about them post-operatively, if they have complications, if further problems arise later. They have served their usefulness.[31]

Such incentive systems also do little to change people's basic attitudes toward family planning, and in fact may make it a very negative experience, leading to a backlash.

In some parts of Thailand, family planning acceptors receive rewards, not in cash but in kind. In one program run by the private Community Based Family Planning Services (CBFPS), women are urged to "space your next pregnancy with a pig." The woman receives a piglet, which she fattens for eight to nine months, during which time she agrees not to get pregnant. She then shares the profits of the grown pig with the CBFPS program. If she fails to keep her word, the pig is not taken from her, but she may lose the opportunity to get another.

Says IPPF's *People* magazine: "There is no need for coercion in [this] program. Thai villagers do not need much 'persuasion' to observe that a neighbor with only two children and two pigs is better off economically than a neighbor with six children and no pigs."[32] But is this necessarily so? Equating prosperity with the number of children one has in relation to the number of pigs is a dubious—and demeaning—way of looking at the more complex realities of Thai rural life.

Community incentives are often deemed less controversial than individual incentives. Although the International Conference on Family Planning in the 1980s recommended, for example, that cash incentives to individuals be restricted, it left room for incentives "which benefit the community and society rather than particular individuals."[33] But are these really any more respectful of basic human rights?

In community incentive schemes, whole villages or groups of family planning acceptors are rewarded if they achieve a high contraceptive acceptance rate. In Indonesia, under a World Bank-financed $3 million community incentive scheme, sixty villages will be eligible for government grants for public works projects if 35 percent of their couples practice contraception. AID also supports community incentives in Indonesia to "promote intercommunity competition," and Thailand has instituted programs where access to environmental improvements, income-generation funds, and health care is contingent on community family planning performance.[34]

The potential for abuses in these cases is obvious. Powerful local leaders, eager to secure the government grants, could easily pressure poorer families into "accepting" family planning, and then proceed to use the outside resources exclusively for their own benefit. Such schemes also raise the question of why villages do not have access to public works and economic improvements *in the first place.*

Some proponents of community incentives admit the possibility of misuse:

> Relying as they do on peer pressure, community incentives involve persuasion, if not coercion, of the most direct kind—from one's neighbors and community leaders. If local power structures favor an elite, the incentive program may also, possibly to the detriment of the community as a whole.[35]

But local power structures that "favor an elite" are the rule, not the exception.

Even where wealth and power are more equally shared among villagers, community incentive schemes would raise difficult ethical questions. By their very nature, they subject individuals to peer pressure in one of the most private areas of their lives, not necessarily because it is in their own best interest, but because a population control agency has decided to offer the community a substantial bribe. Proponents of such schemes might well ask themselves if they would like to be pressed by their neighbors not to have children because then their block could get a road repaved by the World Bank.

Some countries have gone even further and have instituted comprehensive economic incentive and disincentive schemes run by the government (see Chapter 8 on China). In South Korea, for example, two-child couples who are sterilized receive priority for business and housing loans, and their children get free medical care until the age of five. In Singapore, families with more than two children face reduced access to public housing and education, loss of paid maternity leave, higher fees in maternity hospitals, and higher income taxes,[36] although now such measures depend on whether or not you are from the "right" genetic stock (see Box: Lee's Designer Genes).

LEE'S DESIGNER GENES

Singapore's Prime Minister Lee Kuan Yew has long held the eugenicist belief that the poor remain poor and uneducated because they are genetically inferior. In 1969, he described the need for disincentives:

Free education and subsidized housing lead to a situation where the less economically productive people in the community are reproducing themselves at rates higher than the rest. This will increase the total population of less productive people.

Our problem is how to devise a system of disincen-

continued

continued

> *tives, so that the irresponsible, the social delinquents, do not believe that all they have to do is to produce their children and the government then owes them and their children sufficient food, medicine, housing, education and jobs.*[1]

Fertility statistics led Lee to take further action in 1983. Much to his chagrin, he discovered that in Singapore educated women now only have an average of 1.7 children, compared to 3.5 born to the uneducated. If this trend were to continue, he warned: "Levels of competence will decline, our economy will falter, the administration will suffer, and society will decline."[2]

Hence the Singapore government announced a selective incentive scheme, in which uneducated women are discouraged from having more than two children, while educated women are given incentives to have *more* children, including priority access to the best schools and greater tax relief. Unmarried educated women, especially those working in public service, are being pressured to marry under threats of withholding job promotion, and a Social Development Unit has been set up in the Prime Minister's office, whose main task is to match up unmarried male and female graduates, through a computer if necessary. The government even sponsors free "love-boat cruises" for eligible singles in the civil service.

Meanwhile women under thirty, who have no school-leaving certificate and a monthly income of less than US $710, are being offered the incredible sum of $4,750—more than a year's wages for many—if they agree to be sterilized after their first or second child. Their children's access to good schooling is also linked to sterilization.[3]

Opposition has come from many educated women, one of whom wrote the local press that "The only fanatics who have done such things were the storm troopers of Nazi Germany."[4]

Indeed, Lee's views do not differ all that much from those of Hitler, who wrote in *Mein Kampf:* "Since the inferior is always numerically superior to the best, the worst would multiply itself so much faster . . . given the same opportunity to survive and procreate . . . that the best would necessarily be pushed to the background. Therefore a correction in favor of the better must be undertaken."[5]

> After a recent electoral setback, Lee has dropped the incentives for graduate mothers, but the incentives for poor, uneducated women to be sterilized remain in place.[6]

Such incentive and disincentive schemes can further widen the gap between rich and poor. When people need children for their immediate economic survival, they are less likely to pay serious attention to long-term disincentives, although these can punish them in the future. Meanwhile the rich, who are often already motivated to have fewer children, take advantage of the scheme, deriving economic benefit.

These schemes also have the impact of punishing children for the decisions of their parents. After all, it is the children who suffer most when they are denied a place in school or medical treatment at a government clinic just because they happen to be the third child instead of the second.

While critics see in such incentives and disincentives the potential for serious infringement of personal liberty, supporters argue that similar incentives already operate in many walks of life. Tax laws, for example, help to determine how people invest their money; parking tickets are a disincentive to leaving one's car in restricted places. Without such measures for social control, society simply could not operate.

Demographer Kingsley Davis sees nothing wrong with using compulsion to bring down birth rates. "Why does the family planning movement . . . which is the predominant approach to population policy have as its slogan 'every woman has the right to have as many children as she wants'?" he asks. "We would not justify traffic control by saying that 'every driver has the right to drive as he pleases.' "[37]

Such an argument avoids the central question of why people need to be persuaded or forced to have fewer children in the first place. Isn't it because of the very absence of the most powerful incentive of all: the economic and social security of having fair access to the fruits of development? This is not something that can be handed out in local currency when a person is sterilized; instead it involves major social restructuring. When incentive schemes are substituted for social change, the result invariably discriminates against poor people, especially women, if it does not outright coerce them.

Even if one accepts that, broadly speaking, incentives and disincentives are justified—that there must be limitations to personal liberty for the good of the community—another question arises: Just *who* defines what is in the public interest? Who designs the tax system? Who decides that population control must be a priority, instead of women's rights, land reform, health care, and education? Those who hold the reins of power, of course.

In many, if not most, countries, poor people are cut out of the political process, even if they constitute the majority. They are not the ones designing family planning incentive schemes in the capital cities of the Third World, or in AID or the World Bank's offices in Washington. Their definition of the public interest differs fundamentally from that of the politicians, technocrats, and generals who rule *over* them, not *for* them.

This basic political fact of life is largely ignored by even the most liberal family planners, who despite all the evidence to the contrary, persist in believing (or at least maintaining publicly) that governments always operate in their citizens' best interests and mediate between the individual right to choose and greater social goals, between the rights of those living today and those yet unborn. Thus, says the background document to the International Conference on Family Planning in the 1980s:

> When provision of contraceptive information and services does not bring down the fertility level quickly enough to help speed up development, governments may decide to limit the freedom of choice of the present generation so that future generations may have a better chance to enjoy their basic rights.[38]

But sacrificing one generation for the next is a dangerous, and dubious, road to progress. Once basic rights are abrogated, they may be lost for a long time. And forcing people to have fewer children will not "speed up" development. It will only give family planning a bad name, hurt women, and reinforce the authoritarian power structures that prevent development from occurring in the first place. There are far more effective and humane ways to bring about development and a corresponding reduction in population growth (see Part Four).

The next chapter takes a closer look at the experience of two countries, Indonesia and Kenya, where reproductive choice has been subordinated to population control objectives. There are lessons to be learned from both.

4

The Indonesian Success and the Kenyan Failure

INDONESIA: PROS AND CONS

In the last fifteen years Indonesia, whose population of 160 million makes it the fifth most populous country in the world, has experienced a significant, though not spectacular, fertility decline. Although the figures are disputed, the crude birth rate, which was between 40 and 45 in the early 1960s, is probably now in the range of 30 to 35.[1] According to the government's National Family Planning Coordinating Board (BKBBN), contraceptive use has also increased from 2 percent of married women of reproductive age in 1972 to 58 percent in 1984. These latter figures are widely believed to be inflated, however.[2]

Population agencies often give credit to Indonesia's family planning program for this fertility decline. Indonesia, asserts a U.S. Agency for International Development (AID) document, is a " 'success story' unrivaled in family planning history."[3] Demographers are more cautious, however, pointing to a number of broad social and economic changes, such as rising male and female educational levels, reductions in childhood mortality, rural to urban migration, and changing employment patterns in the countryside, as being conducive to smaller families.[4]

Whatever the precise causes of Indonesia's fertility decline, it is true that the country has a strong national family planning program, particularly on the densely populated islands of Java and Bali. The history of family planning in Indonesia dates back to the 1950s, when the Indonesian Planned Parenthood Association first introduced contraceptive services. At that time, however, Indonesia's first president, the nationalist Sukarno, was strongly pronatalist, and family planning received no government support.

Sukarno's independent foreign policy greatly antagonized Western powers, and during his regime international agencies such as the Ford Foundation focused on sending the country's intellectual elite abroad for training, in the hope that one day they would inherit power.[5] Their investment paid off in 1966, when a bloody military coup, which left a million dead, brought the country's current ruler, Suharto, to power. Under the influence of Western-trained technocrats, Suharto embraced the philosophy of population control. Today he has become one of its most prominent spokesmen in the Third World.[6]

In 1970 Suharto set up the National Family Planning Coordinating Board (BKBBN) to oversee, financially and organizationally, the country's population control effort. During the first years of the family planning program, contraceptive services were delivered mainly through the Ministry of Health's network of rural clinics. Later the BKBBN, with foreign assistance, set up its own network of family planning field workers, who visited individual households and referred acceptors to family planning clinics. In the mid-1970s the BKBBN adopted the Village Contraceptive Distribution Center approach, which, according to United Nations Fund for Population Activities (UNFPA) official Jay Parsons, was "based on the assumption that the monthly trek by acceptors to the family planning clinic represented an unacceptable burden on women whose motivation to use contraception was tenuous at best."[7]

Under the new approach women contraceptive users were joined together in Acceptor Clubs. The leader of the club, typically the wife of the village headman or another prominent official, acted as the intermediary between the village women and the family planning clinic, helping to ensure a steady supply of contraceptives at the local level. Today the concept of the Acceptor Clubs has been expanded, so that through them women receive access to credit, training, and some basic mother and child health services.

What are the pros and cons of the Indonesian approach?

On the positive side, Indonesia has been successful in making certain kinds of contraception widely available. It has emphasized birth spacing rather than sterilization, and has created a contraceptive delivery system that reaches right down to the village level and depends on the participation of local communities to keep it going. Through widespread educational and publicity efforts, Indonesia has also demystified the subject of birth control, so that the vast majority of the population have heard about it and are not afraid to talk about it or use it.

There is another side to these achievements, however, which has to do with the way the Indonesian family planning program has been implemented as a tool of population control. The negative aspects of the program include limitations on contraceptive choice, the use of authority, and the quality of acceptance.

Limitations on Contraceptive Choice   Target orientation, one of the central features of the machine model of family planning, is a key component of the Indonesian family planning program. BKBBN officials, for example, are encouraged to outperform each other in meeting targets, as they compete for performance incentives, such as AID-financed trips and training programs. Their style of work ranges, according to AID, from "calculated, strategic planning characteristic of the military to missionary zeal and a messianic conviction that the program is predestined to succeed."[8] Today the government's target is a reduction in the crude birth rate from about 30 to 35 at present to 22 by the beginning of 1991.[9] This kind of ambitious target easily leads to distortions in the provision of contraceptive services.

The Indonesian program pushes the so-called more effective contraceptives. "Though contraceptive services adopt the 'cafeteria system,' " writes the BKBBN, "potential acceptors are encouraged to take effective methods such as the IUD and the pill."[10] The profile of contraceptive use follows accordingly. In 1984, for example, of the new family planning acceptors on the islands of Java and Bali, 52 percent chose the pill, 30 percent the IUD, 10 percent the injectable, 4 percent the condom, and 3 percent sterilization.[11]

In parts of Java, traditional fertility control methods, such as withdrawal and abstinence during breast-feeding, are believed to have been practiced effectively for many generations.[12] Now they are actively discriminated against. An article in *Tempo*, Indonesia's leading weekly news magazine, revealed in 1984 how in one district in East Java, villagers complained that they were being penalized for using traditional methods rather than modern contraceptives distributed by the government. One civil servant was threatened with the denial of his salary if his wife refused the IUD, even though they had practiced traditional methods successfully for four years.[13]

At the same time that the official family planning program pushes the pill and IUD, adequate health infrastructure does not exist for the treatment of side effects, routine checks of women with IUDs, or long-term monitoring of hormonal contraceptive users through cervical smear tests for cancer, etc.[14] In fact, primary health care in general has suffered from the emphasis on population control, although there is now an attempt to "piggyback" health services onto the family planning program (see Chapter 7). A long legacy of elitism in the country's medical education system also means, according to Indonesian specialists Terence and Valerie Hull, that "Many doctors treat patients with disinterest bordering on disdain. . . . This is nowhere more dramatic than in the case of women's reproductive health care . . . where there is no assurance that health professionals will do internal examinations, take a case history, or schedule a series of follow-up visits to monitor contraceptive use or medical anomalies."[15]

In the early 1980s, as part of an intensification of population control efforts, the BKBBN launched a mass IUD insertion campaign. (The pill is in disfavor because of high drop-out rates, which offset its efficacy in preventing pregnancy, and hence population growth.) There apparently is little concern for the fact that the IUD is an inappropriate form of contraception for many women, because of side effects such as heavy bleeding and the risk of infertility.

The campaign includes mass IUD "safaris," where thousands of women are brought together, often under pressure from local officials to have IUDs inserted in a "picniclike" atmosphere. There are now signs, however, that the safaris will be scaled down for the program is experiencing high IUD failure and discontinuation rates.[16]

A key element of safari entertainment is the presence of high-level government officials, including occasional appearances of President Suharto himself (see Box: On Safari). The use of authority, in fact, is a finely developed art in the Indonesian program.

ON SAFARI IN INDONESIA

In 1985 British writer Jill Tweedie traveled to Indonesia to observe firsthand the position of women in that country. She was able to attend an IUD Smiling Safari. Her description of the event is excerpted from *Women: A World Report*, a New Internationalist Book (London: Methuen; New York: Oxford University Press, 1985). Tweedie has also written a novel on population control, *Internal Affairs* (London: Heinemann, 1986).

One morning, people gather at the entrance to Hendra's village, staring across at a bungalow flapping with banners. Two helmeted policemen, their hips slung with guns, truncheons and handcuffs, stand with their legs apart cheerfully grinning as groups of young women are shepherded inside by stripling youths in flared trousers and high wedge heels. At the top of the room, focus of the women's most absorbed attention, numbers of substantial males lounge at flower-decorated tables, their pastel safari suits immaculate. More chairs are set up and more women squeezed in. The safari suits surge to the microphone, gold rings and watches gleaming, and talk on and on. . . . At a gesture from the floor, three older women leave their seats to be given large brass plaques. Time passes, flies dance, corn and peanuts and glasses of jasmine tea are brought to the head tables and the compere announces a fashion show.

These occasions, into which the peasant women are ushered, are repeated in villages and towns all over Java and Bali and, to a lesser extent, across most of the 13,500 islands that make up the long archipelago of Indonesia. Called 'Smiling Family Safaris', they are the cornerstones of the country's family planning drive and every ingredient occurs again and again. Local bigwigs, along with functionaries of the BKBBN, proclaim the inestimable benefits of contraception, promise health, wealth and happiness to those who limit their fertility (*Dua Anak Cupuk,* Two Children are Enough), describe in dramatic detail the squalor in store for those who do not and chart the progress of the particular village towards that promised land where smiling nuclear families will live happily ever after.

Afterwards, health workers swarm round the women, busily weighing the babies to monitor their growth, immunizing them, while behind screens and partitions their mothers lie on tables, patiently waiting to be transformed into angels. *Apsari* is the Indonesian word for angel, and that is what you become when you accept contraception. New angels are given some immediate reward, perhaps four kilos of rice prettily tied with blue ribbon. In devoutly Muslim villages, long-term angels sometimes receive a more spiritual bonus—a trip to Mecca, all expenses paid. *Per IUD ad astra.*

Not so much a program, more a religious crusade, population control in Indonesia. Under their navy baseball caps and neat blue suits its officials crackle with fervor, their eyes burn with an evangelical flame. This hearts-minds-bodies operation has the personal backing of President Suharto. His faded fleshy face looks down upon his flock from a million plaster walls and rattan huts, gravid with his revelation that the future greatness of his country has less to do with land reform or job creation or education (first, contraception, *then* a new school) than with the closure of wombs as fast as possible and in almost any way bar physical force. "The Indians were too brutal," says one of his officials. "We have learnt from them."

Today Indonesian women are dragooned towards contraception as, once, they were doomed to uncontrolled fertility. This is, without doubt, a kind of beginning but it falls a long way short of choice and also seems, particularly to the Western observer, unnecessary. In every society in the world, women have been, are and always will be diligent in their search for ways to avoid constant childbearing and reckless in the risks

continued

continued
they are prepared to take with their own health to achieve that
end. In Indonesia, contraception is freely available and em-
phatically approved. Why, then, is it not possible simply to
clear the way for them by removing one of the obvious obstacles
in their path—the objections of men—so that they may avail
themselves, without coercion, of what they have always wanted?

The Use of Authority   The structure of political authority
in Indonesia has profoundly influenced the organization of
family planning services. When Suharto first seized the reins
of power, he streamlined the bureaucracy by purging suspected
leftists and dissenters, placed military officers in key civil service positions to ensure loyalty, and filled the prisons with political detainees.

Such "administrative reforms," as they are euphemistically
termed in AID's case history of the Indonesian family planning
program, did little for civil liberties, but did facilitate population control. According to AID: "The most ready explanation
given for the success of the Indonesian family planning program
is the strong hierarchical power structure, by which central
commands produce compliant behavior all down the administrative line to the individual peasant."[17]

Today Suharto still brooks no political dissent. Yet many
people in the population field applaud Indonesia's "political
stability" and "strong political commitment" to population
control, without acknowledging that such stability and commitment have been achieved at the price of a repressive military
dictatorship.[18]

The extent of direct coercion in the Indonesian family
planning program is a matter of some debate, though most
observers agree there have been cases. In the late 1970s in
East Java, for example, the military became directly involved
in promoting IUD insertion during a special drive to meet high
targets. A subsequent study of four villages involved in the
drive reported that almost half the acceptors said they were
coerced, and most admitted that they feared the government.[19]

In 1984, *Tempo* reported that in Jepara District primary schoolteachers were told that their salaries would not be paid if they could not produce certificates of participation in the official family planning program, and in Pati District village women were threatened with heavy fines for becoming pregnant.[20]

Responding to reports of coercion, Dr. Haryono Suyono, head of BKBBN, told *Tempo*, "We have to deal with 20,000 people a day so some people are bound to get trodden on in the process.[21]

In general, the Indonesian government relies far less on direct coercion in its family planning program than on more subtle forms of paternalism and social pressure. National, provincial, local, and even foreign authority figures visit IUD safaris and attend village pageants in order to drive home the message that population control is a patriotic duty, and that women who accept family planning are appreciated by those on high. The flip side of this paternalism, of course, is that women who do *not* accept are *not* appreciated.

It is not high-level authority figures who make the crucial difference in the Indonesian program, however, but the ones in closest everyday contact with the villagers. They help create the peer pressure necessary to sustain contraceptive acceptance.

The Quality of Acceptance   In his article sympathetic to the Indonesian program, Jay Parsons concludes that despite its great success in recruiting acceptors, it essentially relies on "externally imposed motivation." According to him, program managers at the subprovincial level report that although the majority of couples in their areas are practicing contraception,

> few know or understand why they are doing so except that they have been encouraged to by their village elders or that not to accept family planning is considered in some way treachery against the national good. . . . Should there be a break in the now externally imposed pressure exerted on couples, it is questionable whether current contraceptive use levels would continue as high as they are at present.[22]

This is because, he maintains, the socioeconomic setting in Indonesia is not yet conducive to individuals wanting to limit their fertility in their own right.

The great *quantity* of acceptors recruited by the program has thus been achieved at the expense of the *quality* of acceptance.

The mechanisms by which people are pressured to accept family planning are intimately tied to the social structures of community life. On Bali, for example, the main form of social organization is the *banjar,* a small community of kin-related families. Every thirty-five days the *male* heads of these families meet to discuss issues of common concern. Working with the heads of the *banjars,* the BKBBN introduced discussions of overpopulation and family planning into these meetings. Soon each household head had to report publicly the household's family planning status, and detailed maps of the *banjar* were prominently displayed, where each house was color-coded according to contraceptive use.[23]

In Central and East Java the BKBBN builds on what Parsons calls the "mystical reverence" of the Javanese "common folk" toward authority figures.[24] The BKBBN has displayed great ingenuity in harnessing the support of local village headmen, teachers, religious officials, policemen, etc., in the population control cause. Is it reverence, or is it fear, that motivates poorer and less powerful villagers to accept the message and join the Acceptor Clubs? While the Indonesian program is commonly praised for the extent of community participation, the Hulls point out that few commentators have really analyzed to what extent club membership is voluntary or borders on "community exploitation" by virtue of bureaucratic pressure from above.[25]

Once women join Acceptor Clubs, however, there is a steady supply of carrots to help make up for the stick. The provision of credit, training, resources, and awards through the clubs acts as a material incentive for contraceptive acceptance.

Defenders of the Indonesian program like to point out that even though community pressure is instrumental in getting individuals to practice contraception in Indonesia, in the long run those individuals benefit, through the improvements family planning brings to their health and lives. And after seeing these improvements, individuals will eventually develop their own personal motivation to use contraception.[26]

In the process, however, damage is done. The emphasis on population control means contraceptive choice is limited, with the consequence that women's health is adversely affected by the indiscriminate promotion of the pill and IUD. Through their involvement in the family planning program, powerful local leaders gain another source of leverage over the less fortunate, which reaches into the most private corners of people's lives. Focusing on family planning with such zeal also diverts community energies from other pressing development problems, such as nutrition, basic health care, land use and distribution. The top-down approach toward birth control means it is not popularly perceived as a tool of reproductive choice, but as a means of social control. Rather than increase personal motivation to use birth control, this approach could provoke a backlash against family planning.

Today Indonesia has become *the* family planning showcase in the Third World. Courtesy of AID and other international agencies, officials from other countries are flown there to observe the program, in the hope that they will carry the model back home. They visit villages, where they are treated to sumptuous meals and elaborate entertainment, where officials tell them about the remarkable progress they have made in reducing birth rates.[27] The visitors learn all about the pros, but the cons remain unseen.

KENYA: WHOSE FAMILY PLANNING FAILURE?

Today Kenya enjoys the dubious distinction of having one of the highest birth rates in the world. A Kenyan woman on average bears more than eight children in her lifetime, and if this pattern persists, demographers expect the country's population to triple from about 20 million today to almost 60 million by the year 2010. Yet in 1967 Kenya became the first African nation south of the Sahara to launch an official population control program. What explains this apparent contradiction?

There are two key elements to understanding the Kenyan experience. First, social and economic conditions are not yet conducive to a significant fertility decline. Infant mortality is still high, children are needed as a source of labor and security in rural society, and the status of women is generally low. Women not only lack opportunities in the modern sector of the economy, but in agriculture they bear most of the workload, since men migrate for jobs.

There are also strong social pressures on women to have children. As an editorial in *Viva*, a Kenyan women's magazine, explains:

> Socially and culturally, we women have been made to believe that our primary role in life is to be a producer of children. We have been told again and again that only through marriage, pregnancy and motherhood can we find dignity and respect. Men in our society are probably the biggest obstacle to a successful family planning campaign. The hard facts are that men do not want women to have the ability to control their reproductive functions. Women freed from continual pregnancies are free to develop themselves as productive members of the larger society. Undeniably men see this a threat.[28]

Men also have very little economic incentive to want fewer children, since women bear most of the responsibility for child support.[29]

Nevertheless, in Kenya, as in most countries, there is an "unmet need" for contraception among women, a need the official family planning program has largely failed to fulfill.[30] The way the program has been conceived and organized is the second element of the Kenyan failure.

In the early 1960s, expatriate advisers in the Kenyan Ministry of Economic Planning and Development pressed the government to promote population control. In accordance with conventional development theory at that time, they blamed rapid population growth for the country's economic problems, avoiding the sensitive issues of uneven distribution of land and a capital intensive industrial strategy leading to high unemployment.

Hoping that accepting the expatriate advice might improve Kenya's credit rating in international banking circles, the government invited the Population Council to study the population problem in 1965. A team of four U.S. consultants spent three weeks in the country and produced the report which formed the basis of Kenya's first population policy. The advice was simple: Declare the urgent need for population control, promote the IUD, and hire more foreign advisers.

The report not only ignored the cultural context of fertility decisions in Kenya but, coming from outsiders, it laid the government open to charges of a white plot of "genocide." Without popular support, the family planning program floundered. As one Kenyan official admitted, the people were reluctant at the outset because "family planning was introduced wrongly, i.e. as population control, and people did not like the idea. The wrong introduction to family planning could have been avoided by only mentioning the improvement of the health of the mother and child."[31]

Despite this experience, population control is still the dominant motif of the Kenyan family planning program. Today the World Bank is the coordinator of a consortium of donors, which includes the UNFPA, the U.S., Sweden, West Germany, Denmark, and Britain, who have helped fund and organize the Kenyan population program. Since its inception, the main thrust has been the delivery of MCH (Mother-Child Health) and family planning services through the expansion of rural health facilities and the training of staff in contraceptive techniques. On paper it sounds fine, but in practice it is a different matter.

A 1980 World Bank evaluation provides some valuable insights as to why the first stage of the program, from 1974 to 1978, produced such dismal results. The project's goal was "to reduce the high annual rate of natural increase . . . by recruiting 640,000 new Family Planning acceptors and thereby helping to avert some 150,000 births."[32]

While setting such targets can easily distort the nature of any family planning program, in the Kenyan case the targets were not even based on the country's own data (which didn't exist), but on models derived from as far afield as Taiwan. In addition, the target was based on the use of only one method, the pill, which accounted for 80 percent of contraceptives dispensed. Confusion resulted in the field when the various donors gave different brands of pills.

The donors also failed to face up to the weaknesses of the government health services, which, given their poor record on delivering even basic health care to rural people, could hardly be expected to provide adequate family planning assistance. This was not only a problem of lack of infrastructure and staff—there is currently only one doctor for every 10,000 people and one nurse for every 2,500 in Kenya—but lack of government commitment to providing services to those who need them.[33]

As a result, the Kenyan family planning program, in the words of the World Bank, did not succeed "as well in retaining acceptors as it did in recruiting them."[34] The average client came back to the clinic fewer than four times and then dropped out of the system altogether.

A study cited by the Bank found that one of main reasons for high dropout rates was contraceptive side effects, which is also supported by anecdotal evidence. Writer Paula Park reports, for example, that many rural women she spoke to were frightened of modern birth control methods because of negative experiences with them. In particular, they disliked the injectable Depo-Provera.[35]

No effective program evaluation was possible, however, due to lack of data. Furthermore, what little data there was concentrated on the family planning side, neglecting MCH services. According to the World Bank:

> One of the basic premises of the Kenyan program is the link between maternal/child health and family planning; however, no information is available as to whether this link has proved a helpful factor in the program.[36]

Another persistent problem faced by the Kenyan program, both past and present, is the inability of family planning field educators to communicate effectively with village women. Drawn from the middle classes, they tend to have an attitude of superiority toward the poor. As the editors of *Viva* explain:

> There's no communication between the family planning people and the villagers. The women who go there to talk, like

Mrs. ——, she is so painted, everyone just stares at her. She's got eight children. What does she know? In any case they are too elitist. How can you say fewer are better? People see a family of 10 well off, while the one without any child is suffering. How can they think that the second situation is supposed to be better?[37]

In addition, family planning field workers have been paid more than the community nurses to whom they are supposed to report, causing friction where there should be cooperative effort.[38]

Even those health personnel who have a genuine commitment to family planning face real practical difficulties in meeting women's needs. A public health nurse from Nyanza Province writes that because of the shortage of health personnel, "the explanation of the side effects of conventional contraceptives is not done properly, and in the end the users become discouraged when they find themselves experiencing some side effects."[39]

Meanwhile, fears of the genocidal intention of family planning programs still persist. Recently, as the Kenyan government was concluding negotiations with AID for a contraceptive marketing drive, rumors spread that free milk provided at schools in the central highlands was treated with contraceptive chemicals. The children stopped drinking it. Fueling the rumor was the belief that the government wanted to reduce the population increase of the region's ethnic groups.[40] Ironically, the population control push is also helping to strengthen Right to Life forces in Kenya, who can criticize family planning as a foreign plot.

Today the Kenyan government is launching another family planning initiative, with the assistance of the World Bank and other international donors. The focus is much the same, with the expansion of rural health facilities and staff training in family planning techniques.[41] Whether this project helps meet women's needs for safe contraception remains to be seen, since it seems to break little with the past, and for some donors at least population control still comes first.

A 1983 World Bank report identified Kenya's rapid population growth as "the single most important obstacle to sustaining rising living standards in Kenya over the long term."[42] If by the Bank's calculations, population growth rates don't come down fast enough, it may be necessary for the government to use incentives and disincentives to encourage family limitation, such as eliminating tax relief for large families, limiting maternity leave and benefits, and loss of access to public housing. While the Bank points to the "serious administrative difficulties" in making such programs effective in rural areas, it scarcely addresses the much more serious ethical issues involved.

The Kenyan government appears to have taken the Bank's message to heart. In the autumn of 1985 President Moi warned the nation that *women* who bore more than four children risked losing a number of social benefits, including maternity leave.[43]

Such a strategy once again ignores the reasons why Kenyan women continue to have many children. They not only lack access to contraception but to economic resources and to the social and political power that would enable them to control their reproductive lives. Ultimately, a fertility decline depends on giving them that access, not on turning them into demographic targets and punishing them for the failure of both the Kenyan government and international donors to meet women's legitimate needs.

PART TWO

POPULATION CONTROL COMES OF AGE

5

Birth of an Ideology

Population control, as a major international development strategy, is a relatively recent phenomenon, dating back to the aftermath of World War II. Yet its origins reach back to the intellectual currents and social movements of the nineteenth and early twentieth centuries, which culminated in an organized birth control movement in Europe and the United States. The conflicts and contradictions in that movement's history presage many of today's debates.

STRANGE BEDFELLOWS

The human race has long sought to control births. Abstinence, withdrawal, and abortion are age-old techniques, sanctioned by many ancient societies. Barrier methods such as vaginal sponges and cervical caps were also used in the Middle East several thousand years before Christ. In seventeenth- and eighteenth-century Europe, condoms (made of linen or dried sheep gut), vaginal sponges, and pessaries were available in some countries. In 1843 the vulcanization process allowed the production of more reliable rubber contraceptive devices, and the diaphragm, or "Dutch cap," gained great popularity in the Netherlands in the late nineteenth century. IUDs and spermicides were also used in Europe at the time.[1]

The availability of contraceptive devices in Europe did not mean that birth control was always socially acceptable in the West, however. In the modern era, the struggle for the legitimization of birth control is a drama spanning two centuries and involving many actors with radically different scripts. The early neo-Malthusians supported birth control as a means of improving the condition of the poor by limiting population growth; feminists and socialists believed it was a fundamental woman's right; eugenicists embraced it as a way of influencing genetic quality. These strange bedfellows combined to give the birth control movement its unique character: It carried within it the seeds of birth control as a liberating force, as well as a means of coercive population control. The following analysis of the birth control movement draws largely on the historical interpretation advanced by Linda Gordon in her book *Woman's Body, Woman's Right,* as well as on research done by Bonnie Mass for her book *Population Target,* one of the first major critiques of population control as an international phenomenon.[2]

The first major public advocates of birth control were the English radical neo-Malthusians. Although Malthus had warned of the dire consequences of rapid population growth, he had *opposed* contraception in principle and had deployed his arguments mainly to justify the wide gap between rich and poor in late eighteenth century Britain. According to him, welfare measures such as England's Poor Laws only led to further impoverishment, since they enabled the poor to breed more. The radical neo-Malthusians, by contrast, viewed overpopulation as a cause of poverty and believed that contraception, by enabling the poor to have fewer children, could help to alleviate poverty and improve the condition of the working class. In 1823, in his "diabolical handbills" addressed to the English working class, neo-Malthusian Francis Place advised the use of the vaginal sponge and withdrawal.[3]

These first attempts to publicize the possibility of birth control took place against a backdrop of deep cultural conservatism about sexuality. By the beginning of the nineteenth century, the prevailing view, as filtered through the churches, was that the main purpose of sexuality was procreation within marriage.

Robert Dale Owen, the son of the famous British reformer Robert Owen, brought radical neo-Malthusianism to the United States in the early part of the nineteenth century. In the United States Owen broke with his English mentors, supporting birth control primarily on the grounds of women's right to self-determination. For him the cause of poverty was unequal distribution of wealth, not overpopulation.

Owen's ideas fell on fertile ground. The United States was a new country, with plenty of land and growing employment opportunities; overpopulation was clearly not a threat. Social reformers at the time were largely utopians, believing in the possibility of a "perfect" society based on a preindustrial vision of economic independence. Individual reform was the key to social reform, and women's rights, including the right to control reproduction, were a cornerstone of individual freedom.

This emphasis on women's rights helped lay the basis for the growth of a feminist movement in the United States in the middle of the nineteenth century, composed of suffragists, moral reformers (such as temperance advocates), and those who challenged the convention of legal marriage. Although many feminist groups disapproved of contraceptive devices per se as "unnatural," they believed in voluntary motherhood, the right of women to choose when to become pregnant, with abstinence the preferred means.

Motherhood was seen as a skill and a talent, rather than an instinctive practice. Unwanted children, the feminists argued, were more likely to be physically and morally defective. Although voluntary motherhood was an important step forward, feminist thinking of the day failed to address the concerns of the growing proportion of immigrant and working class women in the United States, since the values it preached were largely white, Protestant, and middle-class.

THE WOMEN REBELS

In the United States two trends combined to make birth control a more broad-based issue in the second decade of the twentieth century. Among the intelligentsia and social reformers, a new philosophy of sex radicalism spread from Europe and increasingly undercut traditional Victorian views. Among these circles, sexuality was now valued independently of reproduction.

At the same time working class militancy was on the rise, as the International Workers of the World (IWW) and the Socialist Party supported drives for unionization. Women were key actors in these struggles, proving to be militant and persevering strikers in many major industrial disputes.

The combination of sexual rebellion with social rebellion produced the spark that ignited the U.S. birth control movement. The famous anarchist Emma Goldman, one of its most outspoken advocates, was arrested for distributing a pamphlet, *Why and How the Poor Should Not Have Many Children,* which described condoms, cervical caps, and diaphragms. But it was a young Socialist activist, Margaret Sanger, who became the main organizer of the movement. Her early writings in the New York socialist paper *The Call,* under the title "What Every Girl Should Know," were not directly concerned with birth control, but reflected a general concern about women's health.

Sanger's interest in birth control was deepened by visits to France, where it was widely practiced, and to several other European countries, where birth control had become a demand of political activists. As early as 1882 in Holland, a trade union-sponsored birth control clinic had been opened, and in Germany female members forced the Social Democratic Party to give up its opposition to birth control.

Returning to the United States in 1914, Sanger started her own paper, the *Woman Rebel,* supported by the IWW, the Socialist Party, and the anarchists. In its pages she combined her now compelling interest in birth control (a term she coined) with continued support of the working class movement. Sanger's political militancy started to fade, however, into a romantic philosophy of individual expression. She claimed that birth control could free the "absolute, elemental, inner urge of womanhood."[4] Sanger fled to Europe when the *Woman Rebel* was closed down by the Post Office, and she was indicted on two counts of obscenity.

Spurred by the news of her indictment, the birth control movement continued to grow in her absence. When Sanger returned from Europe, she campaigned for public support for her trial, and in 1916 the charges against her were dropped. Turning to direct action, Sanger and her sister were arrested for opening their first birth control clinic in the Brownsville area of Brooklyn, and Emma Goldman was arrested again for handing out contraceptive information.

After 1916, the alliance between Sanger and the radicals began to weaken. This was to have a decisive influence on the future course of the U.S. birth control movement. Many radicals believed that a focus on women's problems detracted from the more important issue of class conflict, and that revolution, by ushering in a new era of socialist prosperity, would take care of women's problems automatically. Why worry about birth control when under socialism women would be able to support any number of children? Others feared that a focus on birth control and sexual matters could alienate people who might otherwise support a radical economic program. In addition, World War I led to a wave of antiradical hysteria. Facing severe government repression, socialists were forced on the defensive, and their interest in birth control waned.

Social changes in the 1920s also contributed to the decline of a radical, feminist birth control movement in the United States. As in the 1950s, the postwar economic recovery led to the view of women as consumers, housewives, and beauty objects. Sexual mores loosened among the middle class, making birth control more privately acceptable if not publicly so. The feminist movement faded after achieving the major victory of the women's suffrage amendment to the Constitution in 1918.

Sanger herself, though remaining an ardent birth control advocate, drifted toward political conservatism. Already in 1917 she was considering a new tactical approach. She wrote her sister from jail: "It is true that the fashionable seem far removed from the cause, and its necessity—but we cannot doubt that they and they alone dominate when they get an interest in a thing. So little can be done without them."[5]

By 1917, Sanger had split formally with the radicals over control of her *Birth Control Review*. As the radicals left the cause, professionals and eugenicists came to fill their shoes.

"MORE CHILDREN FROM THE FIT, AND LESS FROM THE UNFIT"

In 1921 Sanger and her associates set up the American Birth Control League (ABCL). Although she continued direct action tactics, such as setting up clinics, Sanger's quest for respectability led her to court professionals, especially doctors. In the 1920s a few liberal doctors moved toward public support of birth control—as long as they were guaranteed a monopoly over its dissemination. Sanger supported their demands for legislation that would limit the right to prescribe contraceptives to doctors.

Other birth control groups opposed such bills on the grounds that they would limit birth control to that small number of women who had access to clinics and regular medical care. As historian Linda Gordon remarks, "The impact of professionals—particularly doctors—on birth control as a social movement was to depress it, to take it out of the mass consciousness as a social issue. . . ."[6]

A more ominous development was the influence of eugenics, the science of improving human heredity. One branch of eugenics maintained that the rich and powerful were *genetically* superior to the poor, and that whites were in general superior to other races. To the United States elite, such a philosophy provided a convenient justification for their privileged position.

In 1904 steel magnate Andrew Carnegie established a center for the study of "hybridized peoples" or racial mixtures. Bonnie Mass quotes a Carnegie researcher who wrote about racial integration in Jamaica:

> The moral disharmony in hybrids may often be due to the even greater contrast between the psychology of the various races, as, for instance, between the ambition, the love of power and the adventurous spirit of the whites, and the idleness, the inconstancy, the lack of self-control and often of adequate intelligence of many colored people.[7]

The wealthy Harriman family funded the Eugenics Records Office and the Kellogg family the Race Betterment Foundation in 1913.

The eugenicist conclusion that the poor were genetically inferior led to calls for compulsory sterilization. Paul Popenoe, a leading eugenics spokesman, estimated that 10 million Americans should be sterilized on the basis of IQ testing. By 1932 compulsory sterilization laws for the feeble-minded, insane, criminal, and physically defective had been enacted by twenty-seven states.

Eugenicists soon joined the birth control movement in growing numbers, providing it with a new direction to replace the discarded one of women's rights. As early as 1919, Sanger's *Birth Control Review* published eugenicist arguments, including her own famous statement, "More children from the fit and less from the unfit—that is the chief issue of birth control." In her book *The Pivot of Civilization*, she warned that the illiterate "degenerate" masses might destroy "our way of life." By 1932 she was calling for the sterilization or segregation by sex of "the whole dysgenic population" (those who are suspected of being producers of "unfit" offspring).[8]

The American Birth Control League now advocated "racial progress" and sterilization. At one period the organization was led by Guy Irving Burch, director of the American Eugenics Society and founder of the Population Reference Bureau, who supported birth control because he had long worked, in his own words, "to prevent the American people from being replaced by alien or negro stock, whether it be by immigration or by overly high birth rates among others in this country."[9]

By 1940 the eugenicists and birth controllers' interests had so overlapped that Henry Pratt Fairchild, former president of the American Eugenics Society, said at the annual meeting of the Birth Control Federation (formerly the ABCL):

> One of the outstanding features of the present conference is the practically universal acceptance of the fact that these two great movements (eugenics and birth control) have now come to such a thorough understanding and have drawn so close together as to be almost indistinguishable.[10]

It was left to a man named Adolf Hitler, however, to carry the racial purity/superiority school of eugenics to its logical—and lethal—conclusion. The German sterilization laws passed in 1933 (based on the Model Eugenical Sterilization Law developed by the U.S. Eugenics Record Office) eventually led to over 200,000 sterilizations of "inferiors," while millions more were murdered in Nazi gas chambers.

Some eugenicists greeted Hitler's initial efforts with enthusiasm. Bonnie Mass notes how the British *Eugenics Review*, for example, wrote that, "It would be quite wrong and unscientific to decry everything that is going on in that country. . . . In Germany, the most advanced eugenics legislation is carried through without difficulty."[11] In 1939 Guy Burch campaigned against the admittance of "non-Aryan" children, Jewish orphans who were refugees from the Nazis, into the United States.[12]

Although the Nazi atrocities helped to discredit this brand of eugenics in the Unites States, it never completely disappeared. In fact, some of the concepts resurfaced two decades later in the drive for population control.

Meanwhile, racism also infected the birth control movement. In 1939, for example, the American Birth Control Federation designed a Negro Project with the aim of hiring several black ministers with "engaging personalities" to travel through the South enlisting the support of black doctors for birth control. According to Gordon,

> This project was a microcosm of the elitist birth-control programs whose design eliminated the possibility of popular, grass roots involvement in birth control as a cause. "The mass of Negroes," argued the project proposal, "particularly in the South, still breed carelessly and disastrously, with the result that the increase among Negroes, even more than among Whites, is from that portion of the population least intelligent and fit, and least able to rear children properly."[13]

While eugenicists and racists thus turned birth control into an offensive weapon, it was soon to undergo another transformation, into a tool of top-down social planning.

FROM BIRTH CONTROL TO FAMILY PLANNING

The New Deal and World War II ushered in a new era of social planning into the United States, for both required reorganization of the society on a massive scale.

The New Deal involved the government much more directly in the provision of social services to the poor. The impoverishment of many white, middle-class people during the Depression now made it difficult to blame poverty on genetic inferiority. Instead, poverty increasingly came to be viewed as "environmentally" caused, though it could inflict lasting damage on its victims. The solution was social reform through welfare programs, which could improve the position of the individual.

Although birth control was not an explicit part of federal welfare programs, under the New Deal many social workers began to promote it. This had the advantage of spreading birth control information to many poor women. However, it also placed "birth control in the context of social worker-client, subject-object relations, discouraging mass participation in the programs," as Linda Gordon notes.[14] This legacy unfortunately persists in many family planning programs today.

Following the planning trend, the Birth Control Federation of America changed its name to the Planned Parenthood Federation in 1942, and family planning became the new, and more acceptable, euphemism for birth control. Gordon quotes a family planning poster of the time that aptly summed up the new philosophy:

MODERN LIFE IS BASED ON CONTROL AND SCIENCE.

We control the speed of our automobile. We control machines. We endeavor to control disease and death. Let us control the size of our family to ensure health and happiness.[15]

The goal was to stabilize the family, even if that implicitly meant stabilizing women's inferior role. However, Planned Parenthood did take the step forward of recognizing mutual sexual enjoyment as a prerequisite for a happy marriage and acknowledging men's role in reproduction. Sex and the need for contraception *outside* marriage remained taboo. Planned Parenthood clinics, in fact, would not serve unmarried women, and the last barriers against services to them did not fall until the late 1960s.[16]

Despite their limitations, Planned Parenthood and the organizations that preceded it did perform the very valuable role of making contraception more accessible and acceptable. They helped free many women from the burden of unwanted pregnancies. At the same time, however, they shifted the focus away from women's rights, embraced eugenicist and elitist views of the poor, and adopted a limited, top-down approach to the delivery of services. Margaret Sanger's movement thus helped pave the way for the coming of population control.

THE POSTWAR POPULATION CONTROL BOOM

During the immediate postwar period in the United States, perceptions of demographic issues began to change. Emerging from World War II as the major world power, the United States had a growing need for access to Third World raw materials in order to assure a steady supply for the country's industries. At the same time population growth rates were on the rise in the Third World.[17]

United States access to Third World raw materials and markets depended on the existence of "friendly" governments, at a time when nationalism was on the rise, often tinged with a radicalism unpalatable to the United States. The success of the Chinese Revolution, Indian and Indonesian nonalignment, independence movements in Africa, economic nationalism in Latin America—all these contributed to growing U.S. fears of the Third World. Population growth, rather than centuries of colonial domination, was believed to fuel the nationalist fires, especially given the increasing proportion of youth.[18]

Although government reports touched on these perils of overpopulation, private organizations and foundations were the main force behind the postwar population control boom. In the 1940s the publications of the Planned Parenthood Federation began to emphasize the problem of overpopulation. In 1948, largely due to Sanger's efforts, the International Planned Parenthood Federation (IPPF) was formed. It was initially funded by the Brush Foundation of Cleveland—Dorothy Brush, one of IPPF's most influential board members, was also on the board of directors of the American Eugenics Society. The English Eugenics Society gave IPPF its first London offices free of charge.

In 1952 population control gained impeccable establishment credentials when John D. Rockefeller III invited thirty prominent American conservationists, Planned Parenthood leaders, demographers, and development experts to a population conference in Williamsburg, Virginia. At the conference the Population Council was born, embodying Rockefeller's conviction that "the relationship of population to material and cultural resources of the world represents one of the most crucial and urgent problems of the day."[19] By 1955 the Council was advising the government of India on setting up a family planning program, and in 1959 another technical assistance mission went to Pakistan.

Another early enthusiast was Hugh Moore, founder of the Dixie Cup Corporation, who set up the Hugh Moore Fund in 1954 to rally U.S. businessmen to the population cause. The Fund distributed T. O. Greissimer's *Population Bomb* (forerunner to Paul Ehrlich's book of the same title), which warned: "The population bomb threatens to create an explosion as disruptive and dangerous as an explosion of the atom, and with as much influence on prospects for progress or disaster, war or peace."[20] Moore's generous financial support brought him clout within the American Planned Parenthood Federation, where he served as vice-chairman, and the IPPF, where his former employee Greissimer became head of the New York office.

The 1957 report of an Ad Hoc Committee, consisting of representatives from the Population Council, Laurence Rockefeller's Conservation Foundation, and Planned Parenthood, outlined the emerging strategy of population control. Titled *Population: An International Dilemma,* the report depicted population growth as a major threat to political stability both at home and abroad. In the Third World the solution was not outright promotion of birth control by United States interests, but rather the wooing of national elites who, once convinced of the cause, could build support in their own countries.[21]

The private population establishment was to follow this strategy in the years ahead, building links with prominent Third World government officials, medical personnel, academics, and leaders of private organizations through training programs in the United States and the establishment of research institutions here and in the Third World. One of the first steps was to enlist the cooperation of U.S. academics.

Beginning in the 1950s, large amounts of money began to flow into United States universities from the Ford Foundation, the Population Council, and the Rockefellers to finance population studies.[22] Generous funding facilitated the development of what some observers have called "a powerful cult of population control" in U.S. academia.

According to development economist Charles Wilber, "The influence of this 'cult' is such that most Western development economists have not thoroughly investigated the evidence [on population] for themselves," so that "dubious assumptions were not questioned and contradictory evidence was explained away or ignored."[23] Some of these dubious assumptions can be found in the early economic rationales for population control.

In the mid-1960s, for example, General Electric researcher Stephen Enke produced the first cost-benefit analysis of population control, which claimed that resources spent on family planning could contribute up to 100 times more to higher per capita incomes than could resources invested in production.[24] In other words, population control was a very profitable investment indeed, more profitable in fact than most any other development expenditure!

Enke's findings exercised a powerful influence over United States policymakers. In a speech before the United Nations, President Johnson raised the issue of "multiplying populations" and urged his audience to "act on the fact that less than five dollars invested in population control is worth a hundred dollars invested in economic growth."[25]

From private and corporate support to academic respectability to government policy—population control followed this path to the top. For the powerful, population control was "an idea whose time had come," and official United States government assistance would soon be forthcoming.

THE OFFICIAL STAMP OF APPROVAL

Official acceptance in Washington of the need to counter the "population threat" dates from the Draper Committee. Set up by President Eisenhower in 1958 to study the United States Military Assistance Program and other forms of aid, the committee was chaired by General William H. Draper, a New York investment banker and a key figure in the postwar reconstruction of Europe. Like Draper, many of its members combined high level defense experience with positions of corporate power.

The committee's mandate did not specifically mention population, but on the day it was established, General Draper received a cable from Hugh Moore, the Dixie Cup magnate, warning: "If your committee does not look into the impact and implications of the population explosion, you will be derelict in your duty."[26]

In the following months, Draper took Moore's message to heart, embracing the population issue with a passionate zeal that would last the rest of his life. He told the Senate Committee on Foreign Relations in May 1959: "The population problem, I'm afraid, is the greatest bar to our whole economic aid program and to the progress of the world."[27]

In July, at a White House press conference publicizing the final recommendations of the committee, Draper's dramatic presentation—complete with an alarming map of world population growth—made headlines around the world. The committee recommended that the United States government fund population research as part of its Mutual Security Program, and that aid be given to those "developing countries who establish programs to check population growth."[28]

By the mid-1960s the weight of the United States government began to swing behind population control, and new legislation soon embodied growing Congressional enthusiasm. The 1966 Food for Freedom bill, according to the House Committee on Agriculture, recognized "for the first time, as a matter of U.S. policy, the world population explosion relationship to the world food crisis," and allowed food aid revenues to be

used to finance family planning programs in the Third World.[29]
In 1967 alone, Congress directly allocated $35 million to the
U.S. Agency for International Development (AID) for popu-
lation programs.

The population control lobby was impatient, however, with
what they saw as the slow pace of government involvement.
In 1967 Hugh Moore set up yet another organization, the
Campaign to Check the Population Explosion, which financed
alarmist advertisements in major U.S. newspapers. The campaign attracted powerful support—among the advertisements'
signatories were Eugene Black, former president of the World
Bank, and Lewis Strauss, a founding member of the Population
Council. The rhetoric of the ads was clearly designed to create
a wave of overpopulation paranoia, and their racist overtones
were only thinly disguised. "The ever mounting tidal wave of
humanity now challenges us to control it," warned one ad, "or
be submerged along with all our civilized values. . . ." According to another:

> A world with mass starvation in underdeveloped countries
> will be a world of chaos, riots and war. And a perfect breeding
> ground for Communism. . . . We cannot afford a half dozen
> Vietnams or even one more. . . . Our own national interest
> demands that we go all out to help the underdeveloped
> countries control their population.

Not even the United States was safe from the overpopulation
menace. "How many people do you want in your country?"
an ad challenged, then painted a picture of cities "packed with
youngsters—thousands of them idle, victims of discontent and
drug addiction. . . . You go out after dark at your peril: Birth
Control is an answer."[30]

For some people it was the *only* answer.

RAVENHOLT AND THE WAR ON POPULATION

The U.S. Agency for International Development (AID) is today
the largest single funder of population activities in the Third
World, allocating almost $250 million to "population planning"

in fiscal year 1985. Overseeing the agency's entry on the population scene was the colorful and often controversial figure of Dr. R. T. "Ray" Ravenholt, who became head of AID's Population Branch in 1966. Ravenholt's enthusiasms included the production of red, white, and blue condoms to celebrate the American bicentennial, as well as the promotion of much riskier contraceptives.

Ravenholt's single-minded devotion to the cause of population control not only contributed to AID's "leadership" in the field, but to the specific forms which population control took in the Third World. His approach was simple: Reduce fertility by means of the direct provision of family planning services and the development of new and better contraceptive technology, regardless of social context. And the justification for United States involvement? As he explained, "Without our trying to help these countries with their economic and social development, the world would rebel against the strong U.S. commercial presence."[31]

In 1969 President Nixon upgraded Ravenholt's program into a separate Population Office under AID's Technical Assistance Bureau, with a $50 million annual budget, which increased steadily during the next decade. Enjoying unprecedented bureaucratic autonomy, Ravenholt's Office became a personal population control empire.

Ravenholt sought to translate his rising budget into quick results. Progress should be measured, said an AID memo cited by Warwick, "in the only terms which ultimately matter—births averted."[32] A staff member commented, "A core value for the Office of Population is showing that you can spend money faster than other organizations in the field. . . . Look how quickly we act, how outrageous we dare to be."[33]

Not everyone in the agency agreed with Ravenholt's approach. He had to overcome opposition from senior administrators, who resented his independent empire, from economists who disagreed with his single-minded focus on family planning as the key to development, and from overseas mission directors, who disliked the pressure to perform on the population front irrespective of cultural conditions.

AID increased its leverage in the population field by funding other organizations; by the early 1970s, it contributed over half the budget of the IPPF and the United Nations Fund for Population Activities (UNFPA), 90 percent of the budget of the Pathfinder Fund, a Boston-based "private" family planning organization, and substantial amounts to the Population Council, universities, and other private agencies.

This strategy not only helped AID to win friends, but to get around some of the political sensitivities involved in the promotion of population control in the Third World. As a top State Department population official explained:

> In all of our assistance, we would do well to maintain a low profile. It is probable that we will have to work more and more through international organizations and private voluntary groups since these non-U.S. government entities are rather widely preferred in countries now entering the family planning field.[34]

By the late sixties the United States was putting pressure on the United Nations, where opposition from Catholic and Communist countries had prevented population control from becoming a major concern. In 1969 President Nixon called for the U.N. to take a leading role in population control in his Presidential Message on Population.

That same year the UNFPA was established, under the direction of Rafael M. Salas, a high level Filipino government official and businessman. Over at AID, however, Ravenholt had a very clear idea of who was in charge. "I see AID and the U.N. playing essentially complementary roles," he said. "The Agency is ahead of the U.N., which will follow trails blazed by AID."[35] In 1970 the U.N. General Assembly designated 1974 as World Population Year and began preparations for a World Population Conference to be held in Bucharest.

Confident that it had now built a solid international consensus on the need for population control, the United States government was in for a rude shock.

BUCHAREST: THE PENDULUM SWINGS FORWARD...

Opening the World Population Conference in Bucharest in 1974, U.N. Secretary Kurt Waldheim struck an apocalyptic note, warning that "the problem posed by world population not only constitutes a danger, but the world's population is in danger."[36] His tone was echoed in the draft World Population Plan of Action, written in advance with substantial United States involvement. The draft set out specific targets for world population "stabilization" and concentrated on population growth as the main obstacle to social and economic development. Instead of being readily accepted, however, the draft plan generated disharmony and debate.

Opposition came not only from traditional Roman Catholic quarters, but also from many Third World countries, which saw the focus on population growth as a way to avoid addressing deeper causes of underdevelopment, such as inequalities in international relations. China called on the conference to remember that "of all things in the world, people are most precious." India argued that "development is the best contraceptive," and criticized the high consumption of resources in the West.[37] Feminists, demographers, and representatives of voluntary agencies also added their voices to the critique of population control.

However, the worst shock to the United States population community came with the defection of one of its most senior members. In a speech before a forum of nongovernmental organizations, John D. Rockefeller III, godfather of the population movement, called for "a deep and probing reappraisal of all that has been done in the population field":

> I believe that the place for population planning is within the context of modern economic and social development; I believe that economic growth is truly meaningful to the extent that it enhances the well-being of the people generally; I believe that the developed nations must strive to understand modern development, to be of assistance whenever possible, but to recognize that each nation must solve its development and fertility problems in its own way; I believe that women

increasingly must have greater choice in determining their roles in society.[38]

The United States delegation, led by the then Secretary of Health, Education and Welfare Caspar Weinberger, reacted angrily to these challenges, dismissing calls for a New International Economic Order as rhetoric and denying that Western consumption patterns had anything to do with population issues.

Despite United States opposition, the World Population Plan of Action was substantially revised. Explicit targets were dropped, and population growth was placed within the much broader context of socioeconomic transformation (see Box: Selections from the World Population Plan of Action). A new view emerged dominant from the conference. Population growth was no longer seen as the main barrier to development; instead development itself could help lower birth rates. "Development is the best contraceptive" became a popular slogan.

The World Population Conference's emphasis on the "population-development linkage" did not spring from out of the blue. The seventies were a time of much soul-searching about the meaning and purpose of development. The 1960s unbridled confidence in the "trickle-down" theory—the faith that a narrow focus on economic growth would eventually benefit the poor—gave way to a new focus on "meeting basic human needs" such as food, shelter, education, and health care.

Liberal population experts endorsed the new approach, for not only could meeting basic needs help to lower birth rates by motivating people to have fewer children, but family planning could be an important part of the basic needs package. "Integration" became the new buzzword: Integrate family planning with health, with women's programs, with education (see Chapter 7).

"Integrated development" meant fighting poverty—and population—simultaneously on all fronts. Except, that is, for the front which was politically most sensitive. Few asked the awkward question of why the basic needs of the poor were not being met in the first place.

The glaring inequalities in the distribution of income, land, and power were discreetly avoided, in the belief that Third World governments, with the backing of international donors, could deliver such goods as health and family planning to the poor, without fundamentally altering the social order in which they live. The Bucharest critique was thus interpreted in a way that fell far short of genuine social reform, and as a result many of the ensuing "integrated" programs were doomed to failure. Local elites once again asserted their control over aid-provided resources, and the New International Economic Order never materialized, as Third World nations sank deeper into debt, and the West entered an era of economic recession.

Nevertheless, the acknowledgment of the population-development linkage was a big step forward. But if the 1970s were a decade of soul-searching, the 1980s so far have been a time of retrenchment. Within the most powerful Western development institutions, the basic needs approach has been supplanted by conservative economic strategies, and despite the right-wing attack on family planning, the population pendulum too appears to be swinging backward. Even Malthus himself is back in vogue.

SELECTIONS FROM THE WORLD POPULATION PLAN OF ACTION

The formulation and implementation of population policies is the sovereign right of each nation.

The basis for an effective solution of population problems is, above all, socioeconomic transformation. A population policy may have a certain success if it constitutes an integral part of socioeconomic development; its contribution to the solution of world development problems is hence only partial.

True development cannot take place in the absence of national independence and liberation. Alien and colonial domination, foreign occupation, wars of aggression, racial discrimination, apartheid, and neocolonialism in all its forms, continue

continued

continued

to be among the greatest obstacles to the full emancipation and progress of the developing countries and all the people involved.

Population policies are constituent elements of socioeconomic development policies, never substitutes for them: While serving socioeconomic objectives, they should be consistent with internationally and nationally recognized human rights of individual freedom, justice, and survival of national, regional, and minority groups.

Women have the right to complete integration in the development process . . . by means of an equal access to education and equal participation in social, economic, cultural, and political life. In addition, the necessary measures should be taken to facilitate this integration with family responsibilities, which should be fully shared by both partners. . . .

It is recommended that all countries: Ensure that information about, and education in, family planning and other matters which affect fertility are based on valid and proven scientific knowledge, and include a full account of any risk that may be involved in the use or nonuse of contraceptives.

All couples and individuals have the basic right to decide freely and responsibly the number and spacing of their children and to have the information, education and means to do so; the responsibility of couples and individuals in the exercise of this right takes into account the needs of their living and future children, and their responsibilities towards the community.[1]

The Population Establishment Today

Today about U.S. $1 billion is spent each year on family planning in the Third World. Around $100 million is spent by individuals themselves on contraception, $400 million by Third World governments, with China, India, and Indonesia the biggest spenders, and approximately $500 million by the developed country governments, multilateral institutions, and private agencies that constitute the Western population establishment.[1] Population assistance currently accounts for around 2 percent of total economic aid provided by Western (OECD) governments. Although this is only a small percentage, population aid and the policies it helps to generate influence many other aspects of development planning.[2]

The population establishment is by no means a monolith—it is made up of a wide spectrum of organizations and individuals, pursuing different and sometimes conflicting activities and goals. Yet they are loosely joined together by a common sense of purpose, and often more tightly by a common source of funds. Since the United States government is the largest single donor, contributing roughly half of international population assistance, it is the key actor in the population control drama. However, it generally prefers to play its role behind the scenes.

Following is a list of the major agencies involved in population control:

The Agency for International Development AID population assistance is funneled through two channels—the Office of Population and regional bureaus who work directly with Third World governments. In fiscal year 1984, a little over half of

AID's $212 million population budget was allocated to the Office of Population, the rest to bilateral assistance. Asian countries—particularly Bangladesh, India, Indonesia, the Philippines, and Thailand—were by far the largest recipients of bilateral funds.

About half of the Office of Population budget went to family planning services provided by private agencies, and another quarter directly to the United Nations Fund for Population Activities.[3] AID chooses to channel so much of its funds to private agencies and multilateral institutions not only because of the political sensitivities surrounding direct United States government involvement in population control but, according to Dr. Stephen Sinding, former director of the former AID Office of Population, because Congress appropriates so much money to population that AID has to find ways to spend it! AID field missions, he explains, generally do not ask for population money. The powerful population lobby in the U.S. Congress pushes AID from behind.[4]

Although Ray Ravenholt resigned under pressure in 1980, reduction of population growth remains the primary raison d'être of AID's program. Although AID does not condition the rest of its development assistance on a government's population control performance, according to its 1985 Congressional Presentation: "In countries where continued high population growth rates appear to be eroding economic development, AID includes this factor in its policy discussion with the government."[5]

Theoretically, AID supports programs that provide a wide range of contraceptives and "enhance the freedom of individuals in LDC's to voluntarily choose the number and spacing of their children,"[6] but it is prohibited by law from funding abortion.

Other Developed Country Governments   Japan is now the second largest national donor, contributing 9 percent of worldwide population assistance in 1982. Other major donors are Sweden, Norway, West Germany, the United Kingdom, the Netherlands, Canada, Denmark, Australia, Switzerland, and Belgium.[7]

The United Nations Fund for Population Activities   With a budget of roughly $140 million a year, the UNFPA is the largest multilateral member of the population establishment. Although in theory UNFPA is supposed to support a wide spectrum of population-related activities, in practice its main emphasis is on funding family planning programs, which account for almost half of its budget.

This emphasis is no accident. According to one UNFPA official: "AID, which provides about a quarter of our funds, puts pressure on us to focus on family planning." The UNFPA has identified fifty-three high priority countries—"poor countries with high rates of population growth"—for assistance. Many of these are in Africa.

Officially, the UNFPA is committed to the principle of voluntarism and must abide by the U.N. Human Rights Charter. It projects a public image of an organization, in the words of one official, "in business to do what people want, not to tell people what to do." But in effect UNFPA does not do what people want but what governments want, and what governments want, if it involves pushing population control, can easily conflict with voluntarism. Through its director-general, Rafael M. Salas, the UNFPA has in fact played an important role in building an international "consensus" around the need for population control.[8]

The World Bank   In the late 1960s, then World Bank president Robert McNamara became a powerful voice for population control within the international community. However, to date the bank has committed roughly $500 million to population programs, less than 1 percent of its vast lending resources. Still, by the end of the 1970s this made the bank the third largest contributor of funds to population assistance. Recent large recipients of bank population aid are Bangladesh, Egypt, India, Indonesia, the Philippines, and Thailand, and in the coming years the bank plans to increase significantly population assistance especially to sub-Saharan Africa.[9]

Bank influence in the population arena extends far beyond financial commitments. According to Dr. K. Kanagaratnam, senior adviser in the Population, Health, and Nutrition Department, "When you talk about the bank, you must realize that everything we do is supportive of fertility decline. Maybe we aren't doling out contraceptives, but governments take free population money first, not bank loans."[10]

By virtue of its leverage over other forms of development finance, the bank is able to pressure Third World governments to develop population policies. This is done by discussing the adverse impact of rapid population growth in its influential economic reports, through "dialogues" with senior government officials and by arranging the cofinancing of large population projects with other donors, which gives the bank greater leverage in its role as coordinator.[11] Although officially the bank promotes "humane and noncoercive" population policies, it openly supports incentive and disincentive schemes to increase contraceptive use and sterilization.

The International Planned Parenthood Federation   With a budget of roughly $50 million a year, the IPPF, headquartered in London, is the largest international private agency funding family planning services. The United States, Japan, and Sweden have been its largest contributors, with AID providing about a quarter of the annual budget.[12] In 1985, however, IPPF lost United States government funding because of its refusal to insist that its 117 member family planning associations stop all abortion activities.

The withdrawal of United States funding has provoked a split within IPPF ranks. In the summer of 1985 the Western Hemisphere Region section of IPPF, with the permission of headquarters in London, capitulated and signed an agreement with AID not to give assistance to any foreign nongovernmental organization unless that organization certifies in writing that it does not perform or promote abortion as a family planning method. The Planned Parenthood Federation of America, the U.S. affiliate of the IPPF, was furious, since it has been working to overturn the prohibition on U.S. funding of organizations that support abortion and to find alternative sources of funds so that IPPF could maintain its prochoice position.[13]

At the same time that IPPF promotes family planning as a basic human right, it uses overpopulation rhetoric to build support for its programs and takes an incautious attitude toward contraceptive safety. As a result, its member associations have often played a double role: On the positive side, they have bravely introduced family planning programs into hostile environments; on the negative side, they have helped pave the way for population control interventions and programs that neglect women's overall health (see Part Three).

The Population Council   Located in New York, the Population Council operates on an annual budget of approximately $20 million. Its main funding source is the U.S. government, which provided $10 million in 1985.[14] Since its inception in 1952, the council has played a key role in the design and introduction of family planning programs, the training of Third World personnel, and the transformation of population studies into a respectable discipline. It is not a funding institution.

Today the council is a proverbial mixed bag, with staff ranging from population control zealots to academic demographers to feminist reformers of family planning. Its Center for Population Studies does interesting research on the role of women, migration, development, and the determinants of fertility; its International Programs department is more directly involved in setting up family planning programs; its Center for Biomedical Research develops new contraceptives, often within an implicit population control perspective.

The Population Council is the preeminent liberal population organization today, especially since the Ford Foundation has reduced its population programs. According to one observer, the council ignores the politics of family planning and population control, leaning toward a "politically neutral, culturally universal technical view."[15] Yet over the years the council's good credentials among the upper echelons of the United States establishment have given population control a legitimacy it might otherwise lack.

The Ford Foundation   From 1952 to 1983 the Ford Foundation committed $260 million to population activities, with major program areas reproductive and contraceptive research, demographic training, core support for the Population Council, and technical assistance to family planning programs. Ford played a major role in the early design of family planning, greatly influencing—and by many accounts distorting—the structure and goals of India's population program.[16] Today Ford has phased out funding of these areas and instead concentrates on several specialized fields. In a positive development, feminists in the organization have succeeded in mobilizing support for women's economic programs and better forms of reproductive health care, including abortion services. Ford also works domestically and internationally in child survival programs.

The population control legacy, however, still persists. According to a 1985 Working Paper, Ford actively works to influence and develop population policies in Third World countries in order to achieve "a broad national consensus on the negative effects of rapid population growth on a nation's welfare."[17] Ford supports the research and training of Third World scholars in the population field in the belief that they will have the maximum influence on government leaders.

The other major United States private foundations in the population field are Rockefeller, Mellon, and Hewlett, who together contribute roughly $15 million a year to population activities.

Private Agencies, Consulting Firms, and Academic Centers   While AID, UNFPA, the World Bank, IPPF, the Population Council and the large private foundations are at the hub of the population establishment, a multitude of smaller groups help make the wheels go 'round. The Association for Voluntary Sterilization, the Pathfinder Fund, Family Health International, Family Planning International Assistance—these are a few of the private agencies that develop and deliver family planning services to the Third World. Most profess to be working for the double goals of making family planning services available and limiting population growth. Individuals within these agencies often tend to lean toward one goal or the other—there is not always one unified point of view.

A recent trend in the development business is the growth and proliferation of consultancy firms, which feed off the United States government budget. The population field is no exception.

Among the main consultancy firms involved in population work are Development Associates, the Futures Group, and Westinghouse Health Systems. AID, for instance, funds a project of the Futures Group called RAPID—acronym for Resources for the Awareness of Population Impact on Development—which dramatizes the perils of overpopulation with simple graphs, highly selective statistics, and the kind of elementary Malthusian reasoning that attributes almost every social ill to high fertility. Research and training centers at Johns Hopkins University, Columbia University, University of Michigan, Georgetown University, University of North Carolina, Northwestern University, and Tulane University provide the academic backup to the United States population program, each receiving more than $2 million annually from AID.[18]

Although strictly speaking, most of these organizations are private, in reality almost all depend heavily on United States government funds. This can limit their independence, as in the case of the Pathfinder Fund, which in 1983 was forced to stop all abortion funding, even through private sources, in order to receive its annual appropriation from Congress. It also means that many are reluctant to challenge the AID emphasis on population control, for population money is their lifeblood.

Pressure Groups and Publicists   Public support for population control is vital in order to lubricate the wheel with regular injections of funds. Thus pressure groups and publicists perform an important role in building a United States population control constituency, lobbying Congress and influencing the media. They tend to take an extreme line—the group Zero Population Growth, for example, believes that overpopulation is the second greatest hazard in the world next to nuclear war—but their zeal is tolerated as long as it yields results.

Of all the pressure groups, the Population Crisis Committee (PCC), founded in 1963 by General Draper and Hugh Moore, is the most influential. It exercises leverage far beyond its modest annual budget of several million dollars by using prominent retired military, government, and business leaders to press its case not only on the United States public and Congress, but on senior Third World officials. The activities of the Population

Crisis Committee help to illustrate how the population control message is spread at home and abroad.

Finding the Pressure Points   Ambassador Edward Martin, diplomatic liaison for the Population Crisis Committee, is a gregarious elderly statesman, whose former posts include United States ambassador to Argentina, assistant secretary of state for economic affairs, and senior consultant to the President's Commission on World Hunger. The names he drops are from the highest echelons of United States society. The Population Crisis Committee, he reveals, "plays all around with the people we know."[19]

What does this "playing around" involve? First, it means putting pressure on Congress and key government officials to step up population appropriations. For example, according to its limited circulation *Highlights of 1983 Activities*, the Population Crisis Committee arranged meetings for its directors, William Westmoreland, the general of Vietnam War fame, and Ambassador Marshall Green with top White House and Office of Management and the Budget officials "to raise consciousness among the President's chief advisors about the national security impact of rapid population growth and to encourage greater support for population assistance programs within the Reagan administration."[20]

PCC also reaches out to a wider range of groups. In 1980 and 1981, for example, groups addressed by PCC leaders included the Air War College, the American Security Bank, the Army War College, Brookings Institute Seminars for senior government officials, and the CIA training school.[21]

Through its contacts with the business community, PCC is currently trying to get multinational corporations to use their blocked accounts (local currency which cannot be repatriated because of foreign exchange restrictions) to finance population activities in Third World countries. In 1984 the Mobil Corporation was considering the proposal in Nigeria and Turkey.

More intriguing is the way PCC exerts influence on prominent Third World leaders. Its special "diplomatic liaison team" monitors the development of population policies in Third World countries and makes overseas trips to meet and put pressure on top Third World officials. "Since we have close informal ties to UNFPA and AID-funded activities, we can play our special part without stepping on official toes," says the *Highlights of 1983 Activities*. One highlight was to meet with President Zia ul-Haq of Pakistan, "a country of special strategic importance to Americans." After seeing a RAPID presentation of the perils of overpopulation in his country, President Zia apparently declared total support for Pakistan's new population plan.[22]

Along with IPPF, UNFPA, and the Pathfinder Fund, the Population Crisis Committee has also been involved in the formation of the international parliamentary movement on population and development, which brings together parliamentarians from a number of countries at periodic conferences. This movement appears to be an important pressure point for the promotion of population control. The rationale behind it, according to the PCC, is that: "Meetings of elected parliamentarians, from donor and recipient countries alike . . . help form a political safety net for heads of state who want to move aggressively on the population front."[23]

In 1985 *The New York Times* ran a full-page advertisement sponsored by the Global Committee of Parliamentarians on Population and Development, which called for "population stabilization" and blamed "degradation of the world's environment, income inequality and the potential for conflict" on overpopulation. The ad carried the signatures and photographs of thirty-five heads of state, all but one them a man.[24]

It would be mistaken, however, to view this process as simply the Western population establishment putting pressure on recalcitrant Third World leaders, for many are more than willing to cooperate. This is because there is often a common interest between the population agencies and Third World elites. After all, there is generally more in common between an AID official in Washington, for example, and a government family planning minister in India, than there is between the minister and an Indian peasant. Perhaps the AID official and the minister attended the same training course at a university in the United States; they undoubtedly read the same journals, attend the same conferences, socialize at the same parties when visiting each other's area of the world. Today some liberal Western members of the population establishment complain that Third World colleagues are often much more concerned with rapid population growth and dismissive of human rights concerns than themselves. Ironically, the indoctrination process has proved a little too successful.

Money helps to lubricate the relationship between the population establishment and Third World elites—it is probably no exaggeration to say that foreign support for population control has largely been bought at Western taxpayers' expense. Warwick notes that in the Philippines, for example, AID forged a local population control lobby through the simple strategy: "Buy in, buy out, and buy around."[25] Third World members of the Old Boy population network (for they continue to be mainly upperclass men) are constantly rewarded with scholarships and travel grants, funding for pet projects, prizes, and renown in the international press.

Although these material rewards help to cement the alliance, the identity of interest between foreign agencies and Third World elites goes far beyond the perks. Both are part of the new class of world managers, which has begun to transcend differences in culture. They define most issues as "management problems" rather than as moral dilemmas, failing to question their own values and assumptions and to confront the frequent incompatibility between population control and respect for human rights. And for them, bringing the birth rate down is an enterprise that befits their managerial talents, whereas attacking poverty and inequality head-on would jeopardize their privileged position in the hierarchy of politics and power.

Today the population establishment is truly international— among a small circle of friends.

FROM PRESSURE TO POLICY

The stage is set. The actors are in place. The next step is to finalize the script. This is the job of the technocrats.

Robert S. McNamara is the global manager par excellence. In the 1950s he managed the Ford Motor Company; as Secretary of Defense in the Kennedy and Johnson administrations, he managed the United States war in Vietnam, and his years as president of the World Bank saw its transformation into the preeminent international institution managing development in the Third World. Now, upon his retirement, he has determined how to manage population growth.

Writing in *Foreign Affairs*, McNamara blames rapid population growth for a whole catalog of miseries: unemployment, pressure on food supplies, degradation of the environment, an increase in poverty, and even the rise of authoritarian governments.

He warns that if the world fails to bring down population growth rates through "humane and voluntary measures," either the old Malthusian checks of starvation and disease will take their toll, or governments will be forced to take coercive measures and desperate parents to resort to frequent abortion and female infanticide.[26]

What is the way out of such a situation? For McNamara, the answer is simple: Develop and implement a population policy. He outlines some of the essentials of such a policy—political will, administrative capacity, the strength of community institutions. "But the most important single step that any nation can take to reduce its rate of population growth," McNamara states, "is to establish a frame or a plan within which all of these measures can be formulated and against which progress can be periodically evaluated. . . . As a foundation for such action, country fertility targets must be set for specific time periods."[27]

His is a neat vision of a world in which the policymakers draw up a plan, which the functionaries then implement, and the poor masses respond by limiting their fertility. The chain of command is as clear as a military hierarchy. The technocratic mind, in fact, seeks to manage civil society as it would an army at war.

McNamara's vision is elaborated in the World Bank's *World Development Report 1984*, which lays out a blueprint for developing population policy: First, collect data to document the deleterious effects of rapid population growth. Second, ensure the political commitment of important national leaders. Third, create the right institutions. Fourth, intensify support for family planning services. Fifth, adopt other more stringent measures if necessary.[28]

The bank draws a clear distinction between population control policy and family planning as an individual right:

> Family planning programs provide information and services to help people achieve their own fertility objectives. By contrast, population policy involves explicit demographic goals. It employs a wide range of policies, direct and indirect, to change the signals that otherwise induce high fertility . . . it requires clear direction and support from the most senior levels of government.[29]

To change those "signals" more quickly, the bank endorses incentive and disincentive schemes, such as payments to sterilization acceptors. Carefully designed and administered, these schemes, the bank claims, "meet the criteria of improving welfare and allowing free choice."[30] Instead, they usually restrict free choice and give the green light to coercion.

Some top population policymakers openly counsel the use of coercion. In a deeply disturbing article, Bernard Berelson, the late president emeritus of the Population Council, and Jonathon Lieberson argue for the "stepladder" approach to population policy: Start off with soft measures, such as voluntary family planning services, and proceed if necessary to harsher measures, such as disincentives, sanctions, and even violence. "The degree of coercive policy brought into play should be proportional to the degree of seriousness of the present problem and should be introduced only after less coercive means have been exhausted," they write. "Thus, overt violence or other potentially injurious coercion is not to be used before noninjurious coercion has been exhausted."[31]

They are able to condone coercion so easily because they believe there is no such thing as a "correct" ethical system or universally "approved" ranking of human rights. In their ethically neutral, morally relative universe one thing is clear, however: They rank themselves above others. And it is their responsibility, they say, to make their "best information and policies" known to the "dominant powers" of other societies.[32] If this is their best policy, what could be worse? On Berelson and Lieberson's stepladder the sky's the limit.

From pressure to policy and ultimately to practice—the population control drama plays on. Sometimes all the actors meet in one location, as occurred in Mexico in 1984.

MEXICO CITY: THE PENDULUM SWINGS BACKWARD

As part of their extensive preparations for the August 1984 Mexico City International Conference on Population, the UNFPA produced a film, *Tomorrow's World*, which depicted the perils of overpopulation and extolled the virtues of modern family planning. Among the more memorable scenes in the film are a Tunisian midwife explaining the wide choice of contraceptive methods to women by opening a folder full of birth control pills, a Thai hairdresser giving discounts to customers who buy pills from her, and a closing shot of a woman flat on her back, giving birth in stirrups, as an example of what wonders modern medicine can bring.

But the most vivid picture is of a poor, landless Mexican woman, who has agreed to sterilization after the birth of her fourth child. "Life without land will never be an easy matter," the narrator tells us, "but at least this mother's problems will stop multiplying."

At UNFPA headquarters in New York, Dr. Joep van Arendonk, director of the Program Division, discussed the upcoming conference. "The value of these conferences is that you can reach a number of opinion makers," he explained. "In Bucharest there was not as much awareness, particularly on the part of Africa and Latin America, that there is a population problem. Now there is an awareness, but what action to take? In Mexico, population targets will be a heated issue again, along with contraceptive approaches, the pros and cons of surgical contraception, and the redistribution of population." What about redistribution of wealth? I ask him. "That," he answers, "is not our concern."[33]

The Mexican woman has no land. That is not our concern. Our concern is that she stop having children. Was this the message the UNFPA was bringing to its guests in Mexico?

Certainly in Mexico City the discussion was carefully circumscribed, kept within the narrow bounds of the new population control "consensus." The message of Bucharest—that equitable economic and social development is the key to reducing poverty, and hence rapid population growth—had been swallowed, digested, and regurgitated in a much milder form. "The arguments seem to have fused and become two sides of the same coin," writes UNFPA's Jyoti Shankar Singh. "Rapid population growth is now accepted as both a cause and an effect of poverty." Development can help bring down birth rates, the argument goes, but population control is equally necessary to bring about development. "Governments all over the world now say they would not hesitate to take action if they were worried about population trends," Singh concludes.[34]

After their bad showing in Bucharest, the leaders of the population establishment had also done their homework well. A barrage of preconference publications and expert consultations heralded the new consensus, paving the way for a smooth ride.

The conference scene itself was hardly conducive to challenging the "consensus." Two U.S. women who attended the conference describe it in the *Boston Globe:*

> Mexico City played host to an elaborate production by and for an international elite. . . . That participants were exposed only to the upper echelons of Mexican society and that the conference discussion centered on the ideas of a single world class of administrators raises questions about the international "consensus" which became the watchword of the meeting. . . . Despite the presence of over 700 journalists, coverage of the international meeting was largely cautious and uncritical. . . . Fed a diet of shrimp, wine and information packets, reporters walked an increasingly fine line between intimate observation and collaboration. For all the discussion that took place during the UN conference, neither the participants or the press tackled the fundamental issues underlying the "population problem."[35]

The only real note of discord at the conference sounded when conservative politician James Buckley delivered the official U.S. policy statement of the Reagan administration. The statement not only challenged traditional Malthusian thinking on the impact of population growth (see Chapter 1), but launched a full-scale attack on abortion rights. Since 1974, Congress has prohibited the use of U.S. government funds for the direct support of abortion services overseas; however, private family planning organizations were still able to receive U.S. government aid if they used a segregated, non-U.S. funded account for their abortion work. The 1984 policy went the critical one step further by denying U.S. funds to any private organization which performs or even just promotes (through counseling, for example) abortion as a family planning method. The statement also stipulated that where abortion is legal, foreign governments can only receive U.S. population aid through segregated accounts, and threatened the UNFPA with a cut-off of funds if it supports abortion or coercive family planning programs in any member nations.[36]

Ironically, the policy statement served to legitimize the position of the population establishment by casting them in the role of the defenders of reproductive rights. The press collaborated in this portrayal, for the extremism of the Reagan position made the population control lobby seem moderate by comparison.

Only outside the conference hall were reproductive rights interpreted more broadly, as hundreds of women, men, and children, many from Mexico City's infamous slums, demonstrated on the street. They linked their demands for basic reproductive rights, including the legalization of abortion and an end to forced sterilization, to basic economic rights. Why were Mexico's poorest citizens being forced to pay for the country's debt crisis through austerity measures imposed by the International Monetary Fund? they asked the delegates entering the conference.[37]

No one answered.

While the message of Bucharest was largely lost in Mexico City, it can still be found in the philosophy of many "new style" family planning programs today. The next chapter considers its impact over the last decade and the extent to which population control has been and can be reformed.

7

The "New Look" in Family Planning

The 1974 U.N. World Population Conference in Bucharest forced a reappraisal of the view that family planning alone could bring down birth rates in the absence of more basic social and economic improvements in people's lives. This gave rise to the "integrated" approach, in which family planning services are combined with other development activities, such as women's projects, the provision of health care, and community participation.

Although in theory there is much to commend this approach, in practice it suffers from several shortcomings. First, in many projects the development activities end up as mere smokescreens for population control. The World Bank bluntly states:

> The earlier enthusiasm and commitment of the donors ... was severely bruised by the accusations and allegations that emerged at the Population Conference in Bucharest; to some extent they never recovered from it. Population issues were thereafter offered in a modified focus whether within health or other packages and within the development context *to provide cover* [my emphasis].[1]

Secondly, even when the projects sincerely attempt to integrate development and family planning, the concept of development they promote is often unrealistic, since it ignores inequalities in the distribution of wealth and power. The "basic needs" strategy of the 1970s, for example, has largely proved a failure in the absence of basic social reforms.

Still, it is within this approach that one sees the greatest possibility of reform and of a split between the liberal family planners and hard-line population control advocates.

THE DISCOVERY OF WOMEN

Ever since its inception, population control has focused on women, because of the obvious fact that they are the bearers of children—it is their fertile wombs which must be rendered infertile in order to reduce population growth. Today that focus continues, though it has broadened to include other aspects of women's lives. In recent years the social and economic plight of Third World women has been "discovered" by the international development and population community. Whether that discovery brings progress or plague, however, depends on the motives and methods of the discoverers.

In the summer of 1985 the United Nations Decade for Women drew to a close with a major international conference in Nairobi. If progress on women's issues can be measured by sheer volume of research papers, conference reports, and speeches on the subject, then the decade has been very productive indeed. On paper at least, women have at last been recognized as vital to the development process. Why now and not before? one is tempted to ask. The answer lies in the confluence of three separate currents in the 1970s.

First was the growth of feminism in the West and among sections of the educated elite in the Third World. As a new generation of young, upwardly mobile women entered the professions, a few trickled into the field of international development. They began to ask what was happening to all those "invisible" Third World women. Their efforts helped to identify the problem, though they did not always provide a clear vision of the solution.

Secondly, as growing numbers of women joined the global assembly line, they became strategically important to the multinational economy. Integrating women into industrialization was proving very profitable indeed.

Then, in the 1970s, demographic research yielded the information that enhancing women's status was an important key to fertility decline. The population community took heed.

What has this discovery of women meant in practice? To understand just how much—or how little—has changed, one first has to look at the past record of international development agencies.

In her book *The Domestication of Women* Barbara Rogers describes the inbuilt biases against women in the development profession. At the upper echelons, the profession has long been dominated by men, and rich men at that. Like their colonial predecessors, they have largely failed to recognize women's productive role, seeing women, when they see them at all, only within the context of the family. This has formed the basis of the "home economics" approach to women's development, in which women receive training in nutrition, child care, sewing, etc., at the same time that they are denied opportunities to upgrade their agricultural and commercial skills.[2] Most home economics projects are of little use to peasant women, who have long efficiently managed the home—and often the fields as well—under the most adverse of circumstances.

The discovery of women in the 1970s brought about a shift in approach. Today one of the most popular types of women's projects is "income generation"—a development term that means helping women to earn money. On the positive side, these projects recognize women's role as workers, not just as housewives, and their need for cash. Their disadvantage, however, is that instead of seeking to transform the local economy in ways that would benefit poor women—for example, by raising wages for the vital labor women already perform—they simply graft on additional activities. Many are, in the words of a UNICEF statement, "Unimaginative, unprofitable and often exploitative handicraft or knitting/sewing schemes."[3] A typical pattern is for women to produce handicrafts within the home, which then pass through the hands of male middlemen to tourist and overseas markets. The woman gets but a fraction of the sales price, and her isolation from other workers helps prevent her from organizing for better pay.

Even when income generation activities involve women in more modern industries, in a central workplace, they do not necessarily guarantee greater economic independence, since wages are low and the profits often accrue only to male owners and managers.[4]

The basic problem with the income generation approach is that women not only need income, they need power, and power is just not on the agenda. Why not? In her article "Rethinking Women and Development," Anita Anand provides a clue: "It is easier to propagate reformist measures such as income generating projects, job skills, nutrition education, welfare and the like than to examine the root causes of overt sexism, agricultural displacement, and the marginalization of women in any society."[5] Most women's projects also fail to recognize that women are not a homogenous group; they belong to different classes and have different social and economic needs.

How have these trends influenced the work of the population establishment? Today, few of its members would dispute, in the words of Rafael Salas, director of the United Nations Fund for Population Activities (UNFPA), "the importance of improving the status of women, both for its own sake and to help achieve population goals."[6]

While the international development community as a whole has embraced "integrating women into development," the population establishment has taken the process one step further, by using development projects as another way to push family planning. Initially, this attempt also passed, and in some cases is still passing, through a home economics phase. Consider, for example, the International Planned Parenthood Federation's (IPPF) Women's Development Project in Guayaquil, Ecuador, which combines "cooking and sewing classes for women and dance classes for their children, along with family planning and health services."[7]

Reflecting the general trend, the emphasis today, however, is on income generation. These projects follow the basic logic that if women are given the opportunity to earn cash income, often in a women's cooperative or club, they will gain greater decision-making power within the family, have less need to depend on children, and be able to meet more easily with other women to receive information about family planning. Such projects would not only contribute to fertility decline then, but would also help to increase women's power within the community.

In practice, the latter goal often takes a back seat. In some cases the economic benefits from income generation projects do not accrue to the women directly but are used instead to pay for family planning supplies. In others, women receive benefits only if they agree to accept contraception.[8] In Indonesia, for example, the UNFPA provides funds to women's groups to set up beekeeping, vegetable-raising, and handicraft businesses when the women have agreed to have only two children.[9]

To get a closer look at some of the pitfalls of this approach, it is worthwhile examining one case in depth.

Bangladesh: Clubs, Co-ops, and Contraceptives   The link between women's low status and high fertility led the World Bank and Bangladesh government to launch a major women's program in Bangladesh in 1975, which included the formation of women's cooperatives, mothers' clubs, and vocational training projects. Its aim was not the emancipation of women per se, but, according to the Bank, "to provide alternatives to childbearing."[10] On paper this distinction may seem insignificant, but in practice it is not.

First, consider the Mothers' Clubs. The philosophy of the clubs has been eloquently expressed: "When a woman touches the first *taka* she has earned with her own labor, she feels liberated, and her fertility behavior changes to a great extent."[11]

What "liberating" economic activities have the clubs trained women to undertake? Sewing, basket weaving, knitting, and mat making—all are products for which the market is notoriously fickle, according to Bangladeshi economist Naila Kabeer. She describes how, in the case of basket weaving, "the social workers provide the women with grass and palm leaves to make the baskets, pay them for their labor, and take the baskets away to market. The women remain passive participants throughout the process."[12] Though the women may gain a few *taka* from the enterprise and some family planning information, they hardly gain any real economic or social power.

The cooperative program, on the other hand, represents a more serious attempt to integrate women into the commercial economy. (Whether this is a positive goal is a matter of dispute.[13]) In addition to training in management, agriculture, and family planning, the cooperatives run credit schemes, whereby women who contribute regularly to a common fund become eligible for loans. They can use the loans to start small enterprises such as livestock and poultry raising or rice processing. These may be traditional women's tasks, but they are of far more significance to the rural economy than handicraft production.

The project has been billed as a great success—the World Bank's *World Development Report 1984* proudly describes how women's economic activities are thriving in the cooperatives and how contraceptive acceptance rates are much higher than among the general population.[14] What it fails to mention, however, is just who are the primary beneficiaries of the cooperatives.

When Danish sociologist Kirsten Westergaard investigated a women's cooperative, she found this sorry state of affairs:

> The female cooperative hardly functioned at the time of the study in 1979/80. One of the basic problems is that it was not formed in collaboration with the women in the village but rather by the manager's husband. . . . Almost all women stated that they found no benefit in membership. While this was the almost universal subjective assessment of the women . . . it should be mentioned that one half (10) of the women in the sample had received loans from the cooperative. . . . However, only three of the women had utilized the loans for purposes which could be considered income generating for the women. . . . The vice-chairman of the women's cooperative had lost interest in the organization. Her complaint was against the poor women members who could not save very much and thus reduced the possibility for the other members of getting more loans.

Many poor women had not even been asked to join the cooperative, since, as they explained, "the cooperative was not meant for them, as they had no money to pay weekly savings."[15] Although Ms. Westergaard did find two cooperatives which functioned more effectively in providing loans to members, she concluded that "the program in its present form has the potential to benefit primarily the better-off women."[16] This was also the conclusion reached by another study, which found that even the cooperatives' agricultural training was inappropriate to poor rural women who asked, "What is the use of learning how to grow vegetables if you have no land?"[17]

Such results are unfortunately quite predictable in the context of rural Bangladesh, with its sharp social divisions: The better-off inevitably monopolize control over outside resources. The failure to recognize these divisions afflicts many aid projects, but in the case of the women's cooperatives, the underlying population control motive intensifies the problem. Viewing women mainly in terms of their reproductive capacity makes it easy to lump them together into broad categories such as "women of childbearing age," "married women at risk of pregnancy," etc., ignoring the very real differences in their circumstances. Helping more prosperous women to earn some independent income, learn a few skills, and receive family planning services, is not a bad thing *in and of itself,* but it does little to improve the overall position of women, for in Bangladesh the majority are desperately poor.

Yet the project is a success, says the World Bank, not least because family planning acceptor rates are growing up. But is this a real yardstick of progress?

When those funding women's projects measure achievements mainly in terms of the numbers of contraceptive acceptors, problems can develop. A 1978 internal working paper of the Women's Section of the Bangladesh Ministry of Agriculture and Forestry notes that the Women's Cooperatives reported: "Contraceptives dispensed by the family planning programs have caused complications and ill-health for untold numbers of users. . . . It is only after years of operation that follow-up care is being introduced as part of the program."[18] During the years 1985–1990, the Bangladesh government plans to double the number of women in the cooperatives and increase the percentage of them using contraception from 31 percent in 1983 to 50 percent at the end of the period.[19] Such an ambitious family planning target could easily distort the program.

One of its better features has been that participation is not contingent on contraceptive use.

Undoubtedly, improvements in women's position are likely to hasten fertility decline, but attempts to "improve" their position *primarily as a means to lower birth rates* can lead to the type of problems encountered by the Bangladesh program. In the end population control is a poor motive for women's development, and what's more, it doesn't work.

Today a few women in the population field are critical of past developments and would like to see different approaches to women's projects. Describing herself as one of the few feminists in the field, UNFPA Senior Researcher Malika Vajrathon believes income generation projects should concentrate on professions that are strategic to a country's economy and where women already have a long history of involvement. Organizing women coffee workers in Latin America, for example, could increase both their economic and social power.

She also believes that changing women's role in family planning involves challenging the myth that women alone are responsible for reproduction. "Up to now the picture of world population growth has been a woman's bloated belly," she says. "But what about the men?" She claims that in recent years progress has been made on sex education, but that programs still ignore "the politics of sex, the role of power and exploitation."[20]

At the Population Council, associate Judith Bruce points to positive developments in research on women's roles. "To date research has either been gender blind or gender negative," she explains. Now there is a new emphasis on distinguishing between men's and women's allocation of resources within the household.[21] She also mentions the SEEDS series sponsored by the Population Council. The SEEDS booklets describe a number of income generation projects that directly aim to increase women's economic power.

These include the Hanover Street project of the Jamaican Women's Bureau, which trains women in welding and carpentry, jobs previously held only by men, and the Working Women's Forum in Madras, India. The forum helps provide credit to working women in the slums so they can expand their businesses and includes support services such as child care and family planning.[22]

Women at the Pathfinder Fund in Boston are also funding innovative women's projects, but face obstacles along the way. Bonnie Shepard, Associate for Women's Issues and Family Planning, regrets that she and her colleagues have to use population rhetoric in order to get their women's projects approved. "AID likes to look at women's projects in terms of cost per family planning acceptor," she explained, "whereas we're trying to concentrate on education, counseling, and consciousness raising. Our projects don't necessarily have a family planning component."[23]

Although these are hopeful signs, the fact remains that these women are still a beleaguered minority within the population world. Working within that context, it is difficult in practice to resolve the basic conflict between the goal of population control and the pursuit of women's rights.

THE HEALTH CONNECTION

There is a logical link between health care and family planning. Improved health can lead to reductions in infant mortality, reducing the need for many children, just as birth spacing through family planning can improve mother and child health. In theory, both health care and family planning can be delivered through the same network, by the same personnel. Thus, it is not surprising that the new school of family planning has called for the closer integration of the two.

Not everyone agrees, however. Those whose main concern is population control fear that mixing family planning with health care will dilute its effectiveness. Warwick quotes an AID official in the Philippines who objects, for example:

> My fundamental worry is that if you integrate family planning into all the other things that need to happen like better health . . . you run the risk of making what we call . . . horserabbit sausage. You use one horse and one rabbit; the rabbit is family planning, and you don't get much family planning out of that kind of sausage factory.

Another senior AID administrator worries that health programs might actually "aggravate" the population problem—by lowering death rates![24]

On the other side are those who are concerned that the integration of the two will result in less emphasis on basic health care, as family planning takes priority. Thus, in India, according to health analyst Dr. Debabar Banerji, family planning has grown "at the cost of the health services, because health workers were pressured to attain family planning targets."[25]

In El Salvador, women are refused treatment in government health clinics unless they agree to use contraception. Facing shortages of vital medicines, a hospital director in the Dominican Republic complains, "Here the only things not lacking are contraceptives. . . . I have sent many letters reporting a shortage of supplies, and the only thing they ever send are pills, condoms, and other contraceptives!"[26] In many systems, this bias can be accentuated by the fact that contraceptives are free or heavily subsidized, while other basic medicines are costly.

In some countries government health ministries have had to fight for the right to keep family planning as a basic health measure within their jurisdiction. A senior Latin American official, for example, complains of the way the Malthusians in Western population organizations have exerted pressure on his government to institute independent population control programs, free of any oversight by the health ministry.[27]

In the end, the real issue is not integration of family planning and health per se, but the larger social context in which specific programs occur. In countries where governments do little to meet the basic needs of the people, population control tends to crowd out health care when the two are integrated in a single system. On the other hand, in countries with a strong commitment to improving conditions, family planning can be combined successfully into an effective public health network. Unfortunately, the latter case tends to be the exception.

In many Third World countries today, and industrialized ones too, health care is the prerogative of the rich. Eighty percent of world health expenditures provide expensive curative care for less than 20 percent of the population. In the majority of Third World countries, scarce medical resources are concentrated in sophisticated urban hospitals, far from the villages where most people live.[28]

In response to this situation, 134 countries at a 1978 United Nations conference in Alma Ata endorsed Primary Health Care (PHC), which included family planning as one of its components, as the way to Health for All by the Year 2000.[29] Despite this noble pronouncement, however, few countries have made primary health care a priority. This is not simply a resource problem: A look at budget priorities often reveals that resources which could finance primary health care and other social services are not only diverted to high technology medicine for a small minority, but to the military. In Third World countries as a whole, almost as much is spent on defense as on education and health combined.[30]

Many members of the traditional medical establishment are also less than enthusiastic about primary health care, since it involves paramedical personnel and community volunteers trespassing on their territory. There are also problems with the way PHC has been conceived.

Typically primary health care programs tend to focus on a few select "cost-effective" interventions, such as child immunization, oral rehydration therapy for diarrhea, mother-child health, and family planning. Although these interventions are needed, the underlying causes of ill health—lack of food, shelter, clean drinking water, in other words poverty—tend to be ignored. In the process PHC can become another technical development exercise managed by those on top, with little input from those on the bottom.[31]

This technical view is reflected in an issue of the AID-funded *Population Reports,* which states: "Obviously, primary health care programs can address only health problems that can be solved with existing technology. . . . In contrast, malnutrition, while widespread and serious, is more difficult to prevent."[32] The issue then goes on to recommend family planning as one of the cheapest and most effective measures for improving mother and child health. This identification of family planning as a key, if not the key, PHC intervention has lately become a very popular way to justify giving priority to population control over other basic health measures. While it is true that good quality family planning services can improve health, it is equally true that badly designed population control programs have harmed the health of many women and children, a fact which *Population Reports* and other population interests seldom mention.

Population control actually dominates some primary health care programs. One such case is Indonesia, where the government's new PHC strategy is being introduced largely through the population control infrastructure, such as the contraceptive Acceptor Clubs. In the past, basic health care in Indonesia has not received nearly as much attention or resources as population control. According to AID, this is because:

> There is a strong consensus that progress in fertility reduction would have been far slower had family planning services been held back from the rural areas until it had somehow become possible to provide a general village-based health care package of which family planning was part.[33]

As a result, Indonesia has made slow progress on the health front. Its infant mortality rate of 90, for example, is significantly higher than in neighboring Southeast Asian countries.

Eventually, however, the Indonesian government recognized that the persistence of high infant mortality was acting as a constraint on family planning acceptance. It decided to "piggyback" some basic health measures on to the population program, in order, according to the government family planning organization, the BKBBN, to "strengthen the motivation of childbearing-aged couples to carry out family planning."[34] These measures include the monthly weighing of children to chart their growth, basic immunization, diarrheal disease control, nutrition education, and MCH services combined in an Integrated Family Health Package. The problem with this approach is that in terms of resource expenditure, the emphasis is still not on family *health*, but on family *planning*.

Dr. Henry Mosley, former program officer of the Ford Foundation's Southeast Asia Regional Office, describes a few of the drawbacks in a letter to an international consultant. On family planning versus health, he writes:

> I trust you know that the reason the FP [Family Planning]

program can do so much is that the BKBBN has about 75 cents per capita just to promote FP while the Ministry of Health [MOH] has only $1.30 per capita for the whole health system including all hospitals, clinics, drugs, doctors, nurses, etc. etc. . . .

To put the matter of communications in the rural areas simply—*money talks.* The MOH has hundreds of thousands of *volunteer* workers in the villages while the BKBBN has about 15,000 relatively *well paid* workers who are also well supervised and backed up. The difference in health information in the rural areas has been shown in numerous surveys. Over 95 percent of women know about FP methods while most surveys show only 15–25 percent of women have ever heard of oral rehydration or immunization.

Mosley points to the fact that delivering Primary Health Care "is far more difficult than is presently recognized by the international community. It cannot be done for 'nothing' using village volunteers. . . . PHC is a revolutionary concept that will involve fundamental power struggles if it is to be implemented effectively."[35]

Halfdan Mahler, director-general of the World Health Organization (WHO), has reached a similar conclusion. "In virtually all countries primary health care implies a very fundamental social revolution. . . ." he observes. "I believe that whatever resources you have, if they are being used in the spirit of social equity, then you have health for all."[36]

In the absence of equity, it is often extremely difficult to deliver primary health care. The economic and political roots of ill health can usually be traced to poor people's lack of productive resources, such as land, just as women's lack of control over reproduction can be traced to their basic lack of power.

The health connection thus goes far beyond formal models of health and family planning services to encompass the fundamental realities of poverty and power. If these realities are ignored, then the needs of the community for health care and safe contraception will not be met. But if ways of addressing these inequities are incorporated into health and family planning services then—as we shall see later—they can become positive forces for social change.

COMMUNITY PARTICIPATION

Within the population establishment, the new interest in community participation responds to the failure of top-down family planning programs. An IPPF publication cites the following shortcomings of the top-down approach: dependence on outside sources of funding and services, which when stopped bring the program to a halt; the inability to reach poor people because of the "social distance" between the providers and recipients of services; the insensitivity of outside officials toward local community needs; and the high financial costs of top-down systems. In contrast, the community participation approach is supposed to fit local perceptions and needs, fully utilize local resources, reduce costs, and contribute to a sense of "belonging and dignity."[37]

Problems arise, however, when one tries to define precisely what participation is. Is there not a basic contradiction between the desire of the donors to make community participation happen, and the fact that genuine community participation springs from the initiative of the local people themselves?

The question of funding reveals this contradiction. As a 1983 interagency working group acknowledged, donors tend to require "stated objectives" and "output targets" long in advance of funding a project, whereas the goal of participation is to let the community decide these for themselves over time.[38] The donor emphasis on quantifiable results also creates problems when the people participating are not skilled in or concerned about data collection.

The most glaring flaw in the community participation model of family planning, however, lies in the *concept* of community. In the West, communities are seldom homogeneous; even in the most middle-class of suburbs, variations in income, different political allegiances, personality, and power struggles divide people from one another. Yet most population agencies seem to have a romantic image of Third World villages as harmonious communities, where "natural" leaders come forward to work for the public good, in conjunction with benevolent government officials interested in bringing progress to their poorer brethren.

Instead, in many Third World villages scarcity of resources and their monopolization by a few lead to sharp conflicts among villagers, and "natural" leaders usually represent the interests of the rich, powerful minority. Cooperation between such leaders and local government officials is based on a well-understood traditional system of patronage, founded on mutual self-interest. Challenges to the local power structure, seldom tolerated, are often suppressed by brute force.

Familiar to those who have spent time working at the village level, these realities rarely enter into the peaceful picture of participatory projects painted by the donor agencies. Leafing through an IPPF description of such projects, one comes away with the impression that there are no real differences between the rich and poor, that local leaders enjoy the utmost confidence of the community, especially when promoting family planning, and that there is a well-functioning government social service network always ready and able to help.

Only occasionally is there a hint of tension. For example, the nutrition component of an Indonesian participatory family planning project ran into a snag when it tried to persuade people to diversify their diets, using the simple motto that four different types of food are healthy, and five are excellent. The IPPF reports:

> In areas where there had been problems with food production the motto irritated the local people who began to demand the fieldworkers should supply the five categories of food that they were so keen to promote. . . . As a result, however, greater attention was paid to consulting the local people in order to find out what their views were before putting new ideas into effect.[39]

In a genuinely participatory project, wouldn't local people be consulted about their views on the vital question of nutrition *in the first place?* The Population Council's study of Indonesia, in fact, points to "the present government's suspicion of virtually any spontaneous local organizing activity that is not within its control or directed towards its own program goals."[40]

Usually donors acknowledge that conflicts exist between different classes of villagers only when a participatory project carries "participation" too far. When poor people are truly involved in a project, to the extent of exercising power and control commensurate with their numbers, they invariably extend their demands beyond the narrow range of health and family planning to include broader issues, such as access to land. According to the interagency working group, the issue then is "how to channel participation in a positive way, i.e. leading to meaningful development *with the minimum of political friction* [my emphasis]."[41]

Steering clear of political friction may be a major concern of the donors, but such friction may in fact be a prerequisite to a project's success. One survey of participatory projects in Latin America concluded, "Where there is a history of struggle against the local landowners . . . community participation may be strong; then a good basis exists for the development of health activities."[42]

Participatory family planning projects that truly aim to meet the needs of poor people in general, and of poor women in particular, must be prepared to face conflict in the future. Otherwise "community participation" is little more than a smokescreen for business as usual, and just another convenient facade for population control.

THE USER PERSPECTIVE

The latest addition to the family planning lexicon is the "user perspective," a phrase coined by the Population Council. The user perspective emerged in response to low contraceptive continuation rates, when the more perceptive among the population community began to ask why.

Instead of blaming inefficient delivery systems, they stressed the long-neglected human factor in family planning, pointing out that people are more likely to use contraceptives on a sustained basis if services are geared toward meeting individual needs rather than toward maximizing acceptance rates in order to meet arbitrary targets. In the past, as Judith Bruce of the Population Council explains, "The individual's perspective and experience have often been viewed as discretionary and dispensable items, rather than as the determining factors in the effectiveness of a birth planning program."[43]

The user perspective challenges a number of underlying assumptions of conventional family planning programs. These include the views that the adoption of contraception is a one-stage, one-time event, that individual changes in methods are exceptions rather than to be expected, that intermittent use of contraception is unusual rather than normal, that lower overall fertility results more from birth limitation than from birth spacing, and that the theoretical effectiveness of a contraceptive method is a better guide to its performance than its actual use in the field.[44]

Instead, the user perspective argues that the widest possible range of contraceptives should be made available so that people can choose freely and can change methods if and when they want. Good counseling and follow-up should be a priority, rather than high initial acceptance rates which, in the absence of follow-up, tend to decline over time. Evaluation of family planning programs should shift from the preoccupation with "acceptors," "effectiveness," and "contraceptive prevalence" to "sustained use and use effectiveness," which judge a program's success by an individual's long-term satisfaction with the services delivered. The user perspective also acknowledges that family planning services do not necessarily result in sharp fertility declines, since people can use them to space a number of births, rather than to limit births absolutely.[45]

Although for some members of the population community, the discovery of the user perspective marks a genuine change in attitude, there is a danger that for others it may just be another catchy slogan that will go the way of all such trends. As a former IPPF official explained:

> The family planning world is one long succession of fads. It is very fashion conscious. . . . If you believe in "population control," then a truly voluntary program won't work, i.e. it won't reduce the population "sufficiently" because of the economic environment. Consequently, every new approach is doomed to fail and a new fad will be needed.[46]

Nevertheless, of all the new looks in family planning, the user perspective makes the most positive and decisive break with the past, for at long last it places individual needs for decent family planning services first, rather than the push for population control. Whether or not it is a fad that "sticks" depends above all on whether the population establishment in the future moves forward toward fundamental reform or backward toward more coercive policies. There is pressure from both directions. In the end that pressure could provoke a split, so that feminists and liberal family planners break definitively with the hard-line population control camp. Perhaps the Mexico City decade will be remembered not for consensus but for conflict. The next chapter looks at one of the present focuses of that conflict: the Chinese government's one-child policy.

8

China—One Child, One Too Few?

Today China has the most drastic population control policy of any country in the world. The goal is not just zero population growth but negative population growth through limiting births to one per family. The Chinese hope that in the next hundred years the population will come down to 700 million, from over a billion today.

The one-child policy has provided powerful ammunition to population control hard-liners, who argue that it proves once and for all that population control is not a Western-inspired plot against the Third World poor. China, after all, is a socialist country, as well as the largest nation in the world. If the Chinese are prepared to go to such drastic lengths to reduce population growth, then who dare dispute the need? Indeed, many argue that other countries should follow China's lead.

It is easy to forget that before the one-child family policy, China achieved substantial reductions in its birth rate through economic and social change, coupled with a highly effective family planning program.

Before accepting China's one-child family policy as the only alternative, it is important to place the current Chinese program in historical perspective.

THROUGH THE LOOKING GLASS

Before the 1949 revolution, China presented the world with a picture of impending apocalypse. The country had been ravaged by colonial powers and civil war, and the feudal land tenure system in the countryside had blocked agricultural development. The majority of China's people were impoverished peasants, living on the very margin of survival. A 1929–31 survey of rural farmers found dire conditions: Infant mortality was 300 per 1,000, life expectancy was only twenty-four, and the birth rate was over 41.[1] In the words of one Western observer:

> China quite literally cannot feed more people . . . the greatest tragedy that China could suffer at the present time would be a reduction in her death rate . . . millions are going to die. There can be no way out. These men and women, boys and girls, must serve as tragic sacrifices, on the twin altars of uncontrolled reproduction and uncontrolled abuse of the land and resources.[2]

The above prediction did not come true. Today, for the population as a whole, infant mortality is down to 67, life expectancy is 67, and the birth rate is around 20. With a population of 1 billion, over one fifth of the world's people, China's success in bringing down the birth rate means that the rate for the Third World as a whole is 33 instead of 37.[3]

Postrevolution reforms laid the basis for improved economic conditions and the subsequent decline in population growth. Land reforms and the accompanying shift to communal agriculture brought greater security to the peasants. Working collectively, rather than in a single family unit, reduced the need for children as a source of labor. Free health care and welfare funds organized by the commune or production brigade helped guarantee old age security.

In the cities, where 20 percent of the population live, labor and social welfare legislation ensured retirement benefits, and a policy of restricting migration into urban areas meant there was less pressure on employment than in many other countries. School enrollment greatly increased—today 90 percent of primary age children enter school—and the position of women improved. Changes in the marriage laws attempted to increase women's status within the family and substantially raised the marriage age, helping, along with education, to speed fertility decline.[4]

This decline appears to have begun in earnest in the mid-

1960s and proceeded rapidly in the 1970s. According to national statistics, the crude birth rate fell by almost half in the 1970s, from 33.6 at the beginning of the decade to 17.9 in 1979, a drop with few parallels in world population history. By the end of the decade, China was moving toward "replacement level fertility," the achievement of a two-child family norm.[5]

The process was no doubt aided by a vigorous but largely voluntary family planning program. In the thirty-five years since the revolution, China's population policy has fluctuated greatly, vacillating between the belief that a socialist economic system could benefit from and accommodate a growing population to fears that rapid population growth could slow and imperil the socialist transformation of the economy.

Though two brief birth control campaigns were launched in the 1950s and 1960s, it was not until 1971 that a national family planning program was institutionalized. Its motto was "Later, Longer, Fewer," meaning later marriages, longer intervals between births, and fewer children per family, ideally two in the cities and three in the countryside.

This campaign was built on the foundation of an impressive primary health care system, in which "barefoot doctor" paramedical workers provided basic health services to rural communities. Along with their other duties, these personnel were trained to provide contraceptives and to accompany people to commune health centers for birth control operations. In China health and family planning services were truly integrated.

The campaign was accelerated in the mid-1970s with the introduction of target population growth rates in each province and individual incentives for sterilization. Increasingly, the decision when to have children became a community affair, with local birth planning units giving permission to couples to become pregnant. In study groups, family planning workers described how birth control could help preserve the health of the married couple, allow better provision for a child's education, release time and energy for work and study, and liberate women.

Although in theory persuasion was the technique preferred, in practice there were incidents of coercion by overzealous party cadres.[6] Nevertheless, the program was a far cry from the drastic measures of today.

Given the country's impressive success in raising living standards and reducing birth rates, why did it feel compelled to adopt the one-child policy?

Certainly, China has good reasons for encouraging small families. With more than one fifth of the world's population on less than one tenth of the world's arable land, China does face concrete pressures on food production, including the potential ecological costs of intensifying and expanding cultivation. The country also has a bottom-heavy age structure. Today over half the population is below the age of twenty-one, and with many approaching marriageable age, there will be a sharp rise in the population, even if people have only two children. This rise, many argue, could put heavy pressure on social services and employment.[7]

Yet resource development has kept ahead of population growth. Grain output, for example, has increased faster than population, though not by a large margin. More impressive is the country's rate of industrial growth, over double the rate of other low-income countries during the past decade and higher than many middle-income countries as well.[8]

The decision to launch the one-child policy was prompted not by the specter of Malthusian disaster, but rather by the ambitious new economic strategy initiated by the post-Mao leadership, who, among other things, are opening the country up to Western investment. Today in China slogans proclaim "It Is Glorious to Get Rich," in marked contrast to the radical egalitarianism of the Mao era. The current regime wants to launch China firmly into the modern industrial era and aims to attain a per capita GNP of $1,000 by the year 2000—more than three times the level today.

To achieve this extraordinary target would require exceptionally high rates of economic growth and, in the Chinese leadership's view, very low rates of population growth. The Chinese have calculated that the country's optimal population size is between 630 and 700 million people, and hope to reduce the population to this level in the next one hundred years. This will require stringent enforcement of the one-child family in the beginning, followed by a gradual relaxation to a two-child norm.[9]

The Chinese government has resurrected Malthus in order to justify its population concerns. Both academic and popular publications now carry articles and essays revindicating the British clergyman-turned-economist, as part of a wider propaganda blitz. According to one recent visitor, "The revolutionary slogans and Mao quotes that once covered urban billboards and walls have been almost completely replaced by foreign commodity advertisements and birth control propaganda."[10]

The message sent to the people is simple indeed. "If the one-child policy is followed to the year 2000," said one rural brigade leader, repeating the party line, "it guarantees that food and industrial production will first double and then redouble."[11]

Even if these official calculations are correct and the one-child family policy will lead to a great leap in economic growth, important questions remain about how far the state should intervene in the regulation of fertility. Unlike many other governments, the Chinese leadership has consistently tried to meet the basic needs of its people, thereby setting the social and economic stage for a reduction in the birth rate. Thus the Chinese government, as the representative of the people, would appear to have more legitimacy in deciding that population growth rates must come down even further and that stricter individual fertility control measures are necessary for the greater public good. But just how far does that legitimacy extend?

The case of China today demonstrates the need for an ethical bottom line in population policies. By using punitive measures to impose its population policy, the government has trespassed too far into the personal lives of its citizenry, violating basic human rights.

THE ONLY ONE

Several years ago a documentary on China's one-child policy in the model city Changzhou appeared on public television in the United States and Great Britain. In one of the opening scenes, a young woman, Mrs. Chang Kang Mei, describes how she was "persuaded" by family planning workers to abort her second child when she was seven months pregnant. "I did want to have the baby," she tells the interviewer. "Yes, I did want it. But after they came and did their work, I agreed to the abortion."[12]

Despite her initial resistance, she was also persuaded to undergo sterilization several months later. The city's family planning program had scored yet another success in their drive to achieve complete compliance with the one-child policy, but at what human cost?

China's one-child policy is enforced by a system of strong incentives and disincentives. Couples who sign a single child pledge generally receive a cash health or welfare subsidy, priority in housing, and an additional old-age subsidy on retirement. The single child gets priority access to nurseries, schools, and clinics, and later on to employment. In the countryside a single child receives an adult grain ration and an extra large plot of land for the family's private use.

Parents who have additional children must pay an "excess child" levy, which can amount to a 5–10 percent deduction from their total income for ten to sixteen years, and even more if they have over two children. They must also pay all birth, medical, and educational expenses for the extra child, and are not eligible for additional housing space or private plots, or for promotion or bonuses for a number of years. If they have a second child after signing a single child certificate, they must pay back all the benefits they have received. Party cadres and local officials are also rewarded or punished on the basis of whether they fill their one-child family quotas.[13]

In places like Changzhou, the policy is also enforced by an efficient reproductive policing operation. In factories family planning workers carefully watch women to make sure they do not become pregnant. "We watch for women who start to eat less or who get morning sickness," explained one such worker. "If a woman isn't as active as she usually is, that's a sign of pregnancy. It's very difficult to escape the attention of us family planning workers. . . . No one has ever become pregnant without one of us finding out."[14]

In neighborhoods, elderly women called the Granny Police make frequent home visits to ensure women are using contraception, and sometimes even eavesdrop on private conversations. Women who use the IUD are subjected to periodic X-ray checks to make sure the coil is still in place.

The government says China's single-child policy is strictly voluntary. According to Family Planning Minister Qian Xinzhong,

> State guidance on birth planning and individual willingness to practice family planning are united in basic interests; they are not in conflict with each other. State guidance is by no means a compulsory command. . . . We absolutely oppose compulsory methods.[15]

Nevertheless, there have been many reports of forced abortions and some of compulsory sterilization. A reporter for a Hong Kong newspaper usually sympathetic to the Chinese government found on a visit to Guangdong province that pregnant women were dragged off the streets by vigilantes and taken to abortion clinics or hauled before mass rallies to secure their assent to abortion.[16] In March 1983 the Family Planning Minister himself excused the compulsory sterilization campaign in the southern province of Fujian as "understandable and reasonable."[17]

Force is often unnecessary, however, since the intense community pressure brought to bear on recalcitrant couples usually proves sufficiently "persuasive." In some cities, one-child benefits are withheld from *all* certificate holders in the production unit when any one member breaks the pledge to have only one child.[18] Throughout China, local leaders, party officials, family planning workers, neighbors, and colleagues join, according to economist Ashwani Saith, in "a barrage of propaganda and argumentation directed at the women, all aimed at making her revise the decision and to agree to an abortion."[19] The line between persuasion and coercion thus disappears.

Ironically, China's one-child policy was introduced at the

same time as agrarian reforms that have actually increased people's need for children. Greater private economic incentives in the countryside, where 80 percent of China's people live, are leading to a breakdown of the collective security system. Peasants are now opting for the "production responsibility system," in which a household or a group of households independently farms the land and turns over a fixed quota of the crop to the state. Any surplus produced belongs to the peasants, who are also allowed to pursue small-scale private entrepreneurial activities.

The new agricultural policy has had two major effects on the "demand" for children. First, now that agricultural production is based mainly on the family unit, children's labor is needed in the fields, especially as many peasant men are taking up commercial activities off the farm. Many families are even taking their children out of school so they can work on the land. Secondly, whereas before the agricultural commune had provided welfare and retirement benefits, now people are on their own again. Cooperative medical care, for example, has been replaced by a fee-for-service system, which especially threatens the elderly with no sources of cash income.[20] As a result, children are vital for old age support.

The new agricultural reforms may also be a setback for Chinese women. Under the collective system women worked outside the home as part of the waged labor force; now they are resuming their traditional roles in the household economy, with serious implications for their status in society at large. According to Elizabeth Croll, who has written extensively on Chinese women, "The current strengthening of the household as a unit of production" has already "further restricted the movement of women, reduced their visibility and lessened their independence."[21] The new system has also encouraged the resurgence of the traditional values and practices of prerevolutionary China, including the view that women's main purpose in life is to bear and raise children.[22]

Coupled with these factors, the one-child policy has already had very negative consequences for women. The most tragic is the dramatic increase in female infanticide. Son preference is still very strong in China, since daughters usually leave home after marriage to live with their in-laws, whereas sons help care for their parents in old age and carry on the family line. When the first—and only—child is a daughter, some couples resort to murder.

The Chinese press has carried a number of reports of parents drowning, suffocating, or abandoning their baby daughters so they will have another chance to try for a boy. The Anwei Women's Federation found that in Anwei and a neighboring province, the percentage of girl infants dropped significantly after the introduction of the one-child policy, from 48.4 percent in 1979 to 41.8 percent in 1981. In one village alone forty baby girls had been drowned in 1980–81.[23]

Overall, the 1982 Chinese census reported that there were 108.5 boys for every 100 girls.[24] Although the Chinese government and the Women's Federation have launched a strong campaign against female infanticide, it is likely to continue as long as son preference and the one-child family coexist. Indeed, even with a two-child limit, female infanticide remains a likelihood, since around one third of couples would not have sons.

If successful, the one-child policy could also cause serious imbalances in the age structure of the population, with a large proportion of old people and a small proportion of young people to support them. Labor shortages are also a possibility. Such a prospect has led Chinese economists to express serious reservations about the policy in private.[25] Many are also worried that the new generation of single children will be spoiled and self-centered, and that family life will suffer.

Not surprisingly, the one-child policy has met with resistance at all levels of Chinese society. "The single-child family is reckoned to be the most unpopular policy in contemporary China," writes Elizabeth Croll.[26] By 1983 only 10 percent of couples of childbearing age had signed the single child pledge, and they were concentrated in the cities where the incentive system functions more effectively, and there are institutional alternatives to children for old age security.

Compliance is made more difficult by wide variations in incentive levels. In poor enterprises, people are reluctant to sign up because the benefits are too low or may never materialize. In richer enterprises more people may sign up initially, but then the benefits are watered down to accommodate the high numbers. The growing number of people who are outside the formal economy also have little or no incentive to comply.

As a result, the policy has not been as demographically effective as originally envisaged. In fact, between 1979 and 1981 China's population growth rate actually *rose,* and it is highly unlikely that it will decline as fast as the government desires.[27]

Resistance to the policy sometimes takes the form of physical violence against government officials. In a village in Henan province, for example:

> The brigade cadre in charge of birth control implementation had called a village meeting to lay down the law in no uncertain terms, specifying strict punishments for families that had more than one child thereafter. Several families with expectant mothers were also named in the meeting and urged to get abortions or suffer the consequences, since the new birth would be the third or fourth child for some of them. Violent arguments were heard in the meeting by various sides, but the brigade cadre stuck firm to her responsibility to uphold the law. That night, after the meeting when everyone had long gone to bed, someone set fire to the cadre's wooden gate and fence, which half burned down before she and her family could get out to douse the flames [28]

Public resistance has led many local officials to take a more relaxed view of the policy, allowing families to have two children, for example, and there are wide variations between localities on how strictly it is observed. Many low-level cadres are said to tamper with data in order to meet quotas. From the beginning, ethnic minorities have been excluded from the policy, and couples who bear severely handicapped children or who get divorced and remarried are allowed a second child.

At the highest levels too there has been some softening of attitudes. In 1984 the Central Committee of the Communist Party adopted a more permissive approach toward second children in rural areas and called for more local discretion and sensitive work styles in carrying out the policy. In Guangxi and Guangdong couples whose first child is a daughter can have another child.[29]

Still the Chinese leadership insists that the policy will be necessary until the year 2010. They present their case to the Chinese people not by appealing to personal and family goals as in the earlier family planning campaign, but by stressing that this generation must make up for the mistakes of the past and sacrifice in order to develop the national economy.

But just who has determined that this sacrifice is necessary? China's one-child policy is clearly not the outcome of a grass-roots decision-making process, but emanates from above. Local cadres complain that they are carrying out the current line under tremendous pressure from the center; if they resist, their political careers will be ruined.[30]

A two-child policy would be much more acceptable. Says Madame Chen, the official in charge of Changzhou's one-child policy, "To be honest, my own opinion is if couples had two children, it would be quite all right. Two children is very desirable and people would easily accept it. . . . But we think of our country's future. We have to keep our population under 1.2 billion in the year 2000."[31]

According to demographers John Bongaarts and Susan Greenhalgh, a two-child policy could also yield similar demographic results, if accompanied by a delay in childbearing until at least the age of twenty-five and a four-to-six year interval between births. Even on narrow demographic terms alone, the one-child policy may be unnecessary.[32]

THE INTERNATIONAL RESPONSE

Deviating radically from the two-child norm advocated by most members of the population community, China's one-child policy has inevitably stirred much controversy. Population control hard-liners see it as a vindication of their view that drastic measures are required to check population growth and as a warning to countries who delay taking population control measures—in the end, they too may have no choice but to press for the one-child family.[33]

Others, however, have expressed concern over the coercive methods employed by the program. Dr. Joep van Arendonk of the United Nations Fund for Population Activities (UNFPA), for example, went to China to speak to officials about incidents of compulsion, since these are counter to United Nations human rights guidelines. Timothy King of the World Bank argues that the one-child policy violates the basic human right of each couple to bear two children. "It does not deny individuals their complete rights of reproduction or the joys of family life," he writes, "but it undeniably reduces them, both for parents and for children, and puts great strain on the emotional ties between the two."[34]

Nevertheless, there appear to be limits to how far critics within the population community are prepared to go. "The UNFPA is not a police organization, and it is impossible to prevent abuses from taking place," says van Arendonk.[35] The UNFPA, in fact, has been supporting the Chinese population program since 1980 with a $50 million grant. And in 1983 China's Family Planning Minister Qian Xinzhong, together with the late Indian Prime Minister Indira Gandhi, received the U.N.'s Population Award for "the most outstanding contribution to the awareness of population questions."

Today the UNFPA is under attack by Right to Life and conservative forces in the United States, who claim that the organization is helping to support forced abortion and sterilization in China. As a result of these pressures, in 1986 AID withheld its $25 million contribution to the UNFPA.

Many conservatives believe that ultimately China's socialist system is to blame for the abuses. "Countries with far higher population densities—such as Taiwan and South Korea—have prospered without such measures," says an editorial in the *Wall Street Journal*. "They've recognized that the best birth-control policy is an economic policy that produces rapid growth."[36]

Such a view ignores the tremendous strides China made in raising living standards and reducing birth rates *before* the one-child policy was instituted. The present Chinese leadership is more pro-Western than at any time in the country's postrevolutionary history. In fact, it may not be pure coincidence that when China opened the door to foreign investment, it let Malthus in through the window as well.

As for the left, there is a notable silence about the one-child policy. For many, China can do no wrong, while critics of the current leadership tend to focus more on its economic policies than on the implications of the population program. Even among reproductive rights activists, there is a reluctance to speak out against the policy.

China is different, some of them say. It has truly tried to meet its people's basic economic needs, and if despite this, it still feels that strong population control measures are necessary, well maybe then, in this particular instance, they are justified. Such logic runs perilously close to the kind of double standard adopted by many in the population establishment.

Today this double standard centers on the concept of "voluntarism." "As I see it, voluntarism is based on the idea that couples should have the right—the basic human right—to determine the number of its children," writes UNFPA's Bangladesh representative Walter Holzhausen. "But what is a human right in one country may not be a right in another." Or, in the words of his colleague, Dr. van Arendonk:

> Human rights is not the overriding issue in the population field. . . . You have to afford to be ethical first. You can't impose the ethics of a nice village in England on the ethics of a village in Bangladesh.[37]

There is a sense that Asian peoples, especially, are different, that they are more willing to accept authoritarian control over reproduction and are less concerned than Westerners with individual rights. "A growing problem in the future," predicts Dr. Sinding, former head of AID's Office of Population, "is likely to be the difference in perspective between Western voluntarism and the urgency Asian countries feel to bring down their population growth rates."[38]

But is the distinction really so much between cultures, as it is between the controllers and the controlled? Many Western members of the population establishment are more than ready to infringe on individual rights, even in their own countries, when it comes to population control, and they have exerted powerful pressures on Third World leaders. Asian countries "are taking the action we've urged them all along to take," admits Dr. Sinding. It is the people on the bottom who have the best appreciation of voluntarism, because they know what it means to be denied it.

Today population control—a philosophy that subordinates people's need for control over their own bodies and lives to dubious economic and political imperatives—knows no borders. Its very universality demands a universal response, a set of ethics that is not relative to race, class, sex, or nationality. Only through respect for basic human rights can family planning be liberated from the yoke of population control and play a liberating role in the lives of women, and men, around the world.

PART THREE

CONTRACEPTIVE CONTROVERSIES

Shaping Contraceptive Technology

Technological innovations are not "neutral"; instead, they embody the values of their creators. It is no accident that at the end of the twentieth century billions of dollars are spent every year on nuclear power and weaponry, while technologies that could dramatically improve people's lives—nonpolluting energy sources, sustainable agricultural systems, basic health and sanitation measures—receive minimal funding at best. Those who hold the reins of power exercise power over technological choice.

Contraceptive technology is no exception. The contraceptive revolution of the second half of this century has been influenced more by the pursuit of population control, prestige, and profit than by people's need for safe birth control. Millions of dollars have flowed into the development, production, and promotion of technically sophisticated contraceptives such as the pill and injectables, despite their health risks, while the improvement of safer and simpler barrier methods has been virtually neglected.

The misdirection of contraceptive technology begins in the research phase and culminates in its use as a destructive and even deadly weapon in the war on population. It is mainly women who bear the cost, many paying dearly with their health and lives.

THE SEARCH BEHIND THE RESEARCH

Prior to the midtwentieth century, the social stigma attached to contraception made the medical profession and the pharmaceutical industry shy away from research and development of new birth control methods. Before 1959, "the word contraceptive suggested rubber goods from a back street shop, not a tablet from a leading pharmaceutical company," commented a representative of the drug manufacturer G. D. Searle & Co.[1]

What then ignited the contraceptive revolution? The catalyst, to a large extent, was the powerful new philosophy of population control. In the search for a quick solution to rising birth rates, members of the population community began to press for the development of new contraceptive methods.

In 1950, at the age of eighty-eight, Margaret Sanger wrote in a fund-raising letter: "I consider that the world and almost all our civilization for the next 25 years is going to depend upon a simple, cheap, safe contraceptive to be used in poverty-stricken slums and jungles, and among the most ignorant people. . . ."[2] She raised $150,000 for Gregory Pincus, a reproductive scientist based in Massachusetts, to start research on a "universal" contraceptive. Pincus subsequently became a consultant to G. D. Searle, and the company marketed the first birth control pill in 1960. The contraceptive revolution was underway.

Searle's profits were substantial enough to entice other pharmaceutical firms into the contraceptive business, and the private sector dominated contraceptive research and development until the late 1960s. At the same time, however, the Ford Foundation, the Rockefeller Foundation, and the Population Council increased their funding for contraceptive research and urged the United States government to do the same. Much of the early impetus came from India, scene of the first government-sponsored family planning program, backed strongly by Ford. U.S. officials blamed the program's poor results on the lack of a "technological breakthrough." One U.S. Agency for International Development (AID) official went so far as to call for a crash program to develop birth control technology akin to the "intensive and coordinated research and development effort which solved the problem of controlled nuclear explosion."[3]

By the late 1960s, the United States government, through AID and the National Institutes of Health, had become a major funder of contraceptive research. During the next decade, it overtook the pharmaceutical industry in terms of investment in the field. By 1983 the United States government provided 59 percent of the $167 million in total worldwide expenditures in basic reproductive research, contraceptive research and development, and the evaluation of the long-term safety of existing contraceptive methods. U.S. pharmaceutical industries contributed another 21 percent and United States foundations another 4 percent, for a total United States contribution of almost 85 percent.[4]

Both United States government and foundation funds for contraceptive research and development are now channeled to six major institutions:

- the Center for Population Research of the U.S. National Institute of Child Health and Human Development.
- the International Fertility Research Program of Family Health International, based in North Carolina.
- the Program for Applied Research on Fertility Regulation (PARFR) at Northwestern University.
- the Population Council's International Committee for Contraceptive Research.
- the World Health Organization's (WHO) Special Program of Research, Development and Research Training in Human Development.
- the Program for the Introduction and Adaptation of Contraceptive Technology (PIACT), based in Seattle, Washington.[5]

There are several reasons why private industry's share in contraceptive research is now so much lower than that of public institutions. The costs involved in developing and testing new contraceptives are very high: To produce a totally new contraceptive for women requires an estimated investment of ten to seventeen years and up to $50 million.[6]

Companies are also worried about the risk of high product liability payments. Liability fears have already led two United States companies, Upjohn and G. D. Searle, to close down their fertility research operations, and only one U.S. company, Ortho Pharmaceuticals, is still doing extensive research in the field.

Even public sector contraceptive researchers are having trouble getting liability insurance, and as a result, the testing of many new contraceptives—from spermicides to hormonal implants—is being delayed.[7] The liability problem, of course, is not limited to the contraceptive field but plagues the entire U.S. medical establishment. Its resolution depends on safeguarding people's ability to seek effective redress against medical malpractice, harmful drugs, and dangerous contraceptives (the Dalkon Shield IUD, for example) at the same time that the liability system is overhauled, so that insurance rates and payments are kept within the bounds of reason.

Despite these obstacles, the fact remains that contraceptives are highly profitable items. The United States retail contraceptive market alone is estimated to be almost $1 billion a year; worldwide sales may be over twice this figure. Moreover, oral and injectable contraceptives are among the most lucrative of *all* pharmaceuticals.[8]

A more compelling reason for the public sector's domination of contraceptive research lies in the close relationship between the companies and the population establishment.

COMMON INTERESTS

In the contraceptive field, as well as in many other scientific endeavors, there is not necessarily a dichotomy between government and private research. In the United States legal provisions allow private firms to incorporate government-sponsored contraceptive research into their own product development activities, and in some cases public agencies will finance trials of drugs developed by private industry. The companies thus directly benefit from public research funds, and a number of them are strong supporters of the population lobby in Congress.[9] Public research institutions on the other hand need the companies to manufacture the contraceptives since they do not have an industrial capacity.

The common interest between the companies and the population establishment runs much deeper, however. As health researcher Cary LaCheen points out in a recent study, both are interested in maximizing the volume of contraceptives distributed worldwide and in reaching new consumers or acceptors in the Third World.

Population control programs represent an important market for a number of pharmaceutical companies. AID, for example, has spent an average of $15 million annually on birth control pills since the mid-1970s. From 1972 to 1979 most of this money went to one company alone, the Syntex Corporation, accounting in some years for 25 to 30 percent of Syntex's total oral contraceptive sales. Similarly, between 1982 and 1984, AID bought all of its $6.7 million worth of IUDs from Finishing Enterprises. According to an industry source, Ansell Industries, which produces condoms, would probably go out of business without AID contracts.[10]

Although not all companies rely so heavily on AID sales, the contraceptives they provide to population programs reach untapped markets where the companies would like to expand. Population agencies, in fact, play a vital role in advertising, promoting, and distributing industry products in the Third World.

This is particularly true in the case of Contraceptive Social Marketing (CSM) programs. In these programs, birth control pills, condoms, and sometimes spermicide tablets are sold at subsidized prices through existing marketing channels, typically small village shops. They are also advertised heavily, through, in the words of one organization, "the proven techniques used to sell soap, soft drinks and toothpaste in every corner of the globe."[11] AID and IPPF are among the main supporters of these schemes, which by 1980 operated in over twenty-seven countries. (On the health implications of this approach, see next chapter.)

According to LaCheen, "Contraceptive Social Marketing programs have whittled away the distance between population assistance programs and the contraceptive industry—and serve the industry's needs much more completely and directly than other types of population programs."[12] CSM schemes absorb the high costs of market research, advertisement, and distribution in remote rural areas. They accustom poor people to paying for contraception, albeit at reduced prices, and create a general awareness of modern contraceptive methods. In short, the industry gets a free ride down unpaved roads and dusty paths to thousands of Third World villages.

Today AID officials are talking of taking the CSM approach one step further: Population organizations will undertake research on the size of the straight (unsubsidized) contraceptive market, and hand over that information to private industry so firms can penetrate profitable Third World markets on their own.[13]

In order to maintain the profitable alliance between themselves and the population establishment, industry officials not only lobby Congress on the need for population appropriations, but give donations to population control organizations. According to LaCheen, the Syntex Corporation, for example, gives several thousands of dollars each year to the Population Crisis Committee.[14] Interlocking directorates further cement the alliance.

Take for instance Family Health International (FHI), whose population research is heavily funded by AID. Dr. William N. Hubbard, president of the Upjohn Company, the manufacturers of Depo-Provera, is on the FHI board of directors. In 1983 FHI president Dr. Malcolm Potts testified for the approval of Depo-Provera as a contraceptive before a U.S. board of inquiry.[15]

In a number of ways, then, the interests of the contraceptive industry and the population establishment converge. Many would argue that there is nothing intrinsically wrong with such a convergence, if the end result is that new and better contraceptives are developed and distributed widely around the globe. Before accepting such an argument, however, it is important to look at how these institutions have helped to bias the direction of contraceptive technology.

CONTRACEPTIVE BIASES

There are three basic biases in contemporary contraceptive research. First, research has focused overwhelmingly on the female reproductive system. In 1978, for example, 78 percent of public sector expenditures for the development of new contraceptives was for female methods, as opposed to only 7 percent for males.[16]

This is not only because women are the chief targets of population control programs but, according to Forrest Greenslade of the Population Council, "because of sexism."[17] From top to bottom, men dominate the contraceptive research field, and many of them hold the view that reproduction is basically a woman's concern. As R. J. Ericsson, an early pioneer in male reproductive research, complained:

> Male contraceptive research has a dismal past. It is almost an illegitimate specialty within reproductive biology. For the most part, the brightest workers avoid it and those who do work in the area are looked on as rather strange fellows.[18]

This is slowly beginning to change. In the 1980–1983 period, for example, male methods accounted for 12 percent of total contraceptive research and development expenditures.[19] However, even though organizations such as the Population Council are now devoting more resources to male reproductive research, people in the field say it will take at least fifteen to twenty years to catch up in building a knowledge base from which to develop male contraceptives.

A second persistent bias is toward systemic and surgical forms of birth control, as opposed to safer barrier methods. Thus hormonal, immunological, and surgical methods received almost 70 percent of total public expenditures for the development of new contraceptives in 1978, while barrier methods such as the diaphragm and condom received only 2.2 percent.[20]

Today, due to consumer and feminist pressure, resources devoted to barrier methods are slowly increasing, both in the public and private sector (see Chapter 13). From 1980 to 1983 they averaged almost 5 percent of contraceptive research and development expenditures. The overwhelming emphasis is on *female* barrier methods, however—the male condom has been almost totally neglected.

Female hormonal methods in particular have received a disproportionate share of research funds, accounting for nearly 30 percent of contraceptive research and development expenditures from 1980 to 1983.[21] They continue to appeal to many members of the population establishment who are still searching for a "miracle" contraceptive that will solve the world's population problem. Their preference, as we shall see, is for long-acting methods that require little initiative by the user and minimal interaction between the user and provider, reducing both the risk of accidental pregnancy and the need for counseling and support services.

The pharmaceutical industry has concentrated on hormonal methods not only because they are highly profitable, much more profitable than a diaphragm, which can be used for a year or more, but because public research funds have flowed in this direction. For their part, medical researchers are drawn to sophisticated systemic methods, incorporating the latest in biomedical science, since these are more likely to win recognition, prestige, and lucrative contracts.

A third bias, linked to the previous two, is a greater concern for contraceptive efficacy than safety.

SAFETY FIRST—OR LAST?

From 1965 onward less than 10 percent of total expenditures on reproductive research and contraceptive development has been devoted to safety.[22] This relative disregard for safety is the single most important factor underlying contraceptive abuse.

Safety expenditures also remain concentrated in the industrialized countries, which have more financial resources and trained personnel to test and investigate new contraceptives and where the media and consumer and women's groups play a key role in keeping up public pressure for regulation. In the United States, the Food and Drug Administration (FDA) is the government's main watchdog agency over the pharmaceutical industry. Since many Third World (and other) governments depend heavily on FDA rulings to formulate their own guidelines, its influence extends far beyond United States borders.

Just how effective is the FDA in protecting the consumer against contraceptive abuse? FDA approval of a new contraceptive typically takes eight and a half years. The tests are more stringent than for many other drugs, since contraceptives may be used regularly by healthy individuals for a period of up to thirty years. In the case of hormonal contraceptives, the FDA requires pharmaceutical manufacturers to undertake both short- and long-term animal tests and human trials.

Although on the surface regulations seem strict, experience has sometimes proved otherwise. Industry pressure can weaken FDA resolve. FDA officials often pass from public service to lucrative jobs with private industry, helping to ensure that pharmaceutical firms have clout within the agency. In 1974, fourteen FDA employees brought charges against the agency, claiming that because of industry pressure, they were removed from positions where they were either holding up drug approvals or preparing cautionary labeling.

Even when the FDA does not bow to industry pressure, the companies do not always play by the rules. An FDA investigation of G. D. Searle, for example, revealed that the company had consistently faked results in drug safety tests, including surreptitious removal of a tumor from a test dog in a study of the oral contraceptive Ovulen. In the aftermath of the investigation, the FDA commissioner conceded that the evidence cast doubt on the believability of all drug safety tests.[23]

Nevertheless, compared to the absence of regulatory procedures in many Third World and even some European countries, the FDA provides an important measure of protection against potentially harmful contraceptives. Theoretically, this protection was extended overseas by a law that prohibited United States pharmaceutical manufacturers from exporting drugs not approved for sale in the United States. However, the companies got around this restriction by using foreign subsidiaries to manufacture and export unapproved drugs.

There has also been considerable pressure on Congress to change existing legislation so that United States firms can export new drugs even if not yet approved for use within the United States, if the drugs meet certain minimal safety standards and the specifications of the importing country. In late 1986 Congress passed legislation that would allow such exports to twenty-one countries, mainly in Western Europe. As part of its policy of "regulatory relief," the Reagan administration is also talking of accelerating some of the FDA's "onerous" drug approval procedures.[24]

The eagerness of contraceptive manufacturers to circumvent United States regulations reflects a basic economic calculation: In contrast to the industrialized countries where near zero population growth has led to a saturation of the contraceptive market, the Third World presents a large, expanding market. Companies today are also shifting their initial research efforts abroad where drug regulations are not so rigid.[25]

In fact, in the contraceptive research business, the Third World has long been an important laboratory for human testing. From 1980 to 1983, at least one fifth of contraceptive research and development and safety evaluation projects were located in developing countries, with India, China, Chile, Mexico, and Brazil the major locations.[26] Not only can companies and research institutions get around Western guidelines by initiating or shifting their drug trials to the Third World, but Third World subjects are usually the prime target group for the new contraceptives.

The growing consumers' and women's movements in the West have led to increased public skepticism of the contraceptive industry, coupled with liability lawsuits that have cost the companies millions of dollars. Most Third World experimental subjects have little access to such information, much less to the courts. Their "informed consent"—consent to undergo drug tests with the full knowledge of potential risks—easily becomes a charade, because in a context of poverty and scarce health care, any attention from medical personnel is usually received with gratitude.[27]

Moreover, the protocol of drug trials often leaves much to be desired. For example, one variety of vaginal ring impregnated with hormones, pioneered by the contraceptive research wing of the Population Council, was studied for "field acceptability" among a poor target population in the Dominican Republic and Brazil. The premise of the study was, in the authors' words, that "the Contraceptive Vaginal Ring is a contraceptive method as effective and safe as the pill . . . which could be used in basic health systems *without direct medical supervision* [emphasis added]." In the course of the study, the users were not advised of any potential disadvantages of the method, since this would "confound the basic hypothesis." This, despite the fact that the rings have produced a number of worrisome side effects, including a high rate of vaginal discharge. Their long-term effect on the vagina and cervix also remains unknown (see Box: "Informed Consent" in India).[28]

"INFORMED CONSENT" IN INDIA

The Indian Council for Medical Research, which has one of the largest contraceptive research programs in the Third World, is currently testing the injectable contraceptive NET-EN on poor women in primary health centers around the country. At one center in Patancheru, near Hyderabad, the British medical journal *The Lancet* reported that women were not given information about the possible harmful effects of the drug:

> At Patancheru, it is reported, paramedical workers entrusted with the recruitment of acceptors for the trial said that if they were to tell women that this was part of a research programme, or that there were certain possible side effects, no one would have volunteered. Women who turned up for the "camp" were simply told:
>
> "If you take this injection, you will not conceive."
>
> A few Government doctors are said to have questioned the ethics of the trials, but they have not been outspoken because of the overall pressure to achieve targets for population control.[1]

Fortunately, a local women's group, Stree Shakti Sanghatana, challenged the lack of informed consent in the trial. Armed with petitions and placards describing the dangers of the drug, they asked the local government administrator to stop

continued

continued

the trials. He agreed that the group could present their views to the women participating in the test. Thirty village women attended the meeting and, after hearing from both the researchers and representatives of the women's group, 25 walked out. Visibly upset, the government administrator told the women of Stree Shakti Sanghatana that if they objected to NET-EN, they were morally bound to support the government's sterilization drive.[2]

Even those contraceptives approved in the West are often marketed in the Third World according to much looser standards. The printed list of side effects and precautions required to accompany each drug is often much more comprehensive in the United States than it is in Latin America, for example.

Take the case of G. D. Searle's oral contraceptive Ovulen. In the United States cautions against use included "tendency to blood clot, liver dysfunction, abnormal vaginal bleeding, epilepsy, migraine, asthma, heart trouble." In Brazil and Argentina, only blood clots. In the United States, adverse reactions publicized were "nausea, loss of hair, nervousness, jaundice, high blood pressure, weight change, headaches." In Brazil and Argentina, none.[29]

Many contraceptives are delivered to medical personnel in the Third World without any printed information on side effects. In Zimbabwe, a doctor reports that the packets of pills women receive do not even list the ingredients![30]

These practices imply a double standard: safety regulations for the West, but not for the Third World. Many members of the population establishment justify this double standard in terms of relative risks. They measure the risk of death from a given contraceptive against a woman's risk of dying in pregnancy or childbirth. In the Third World, where maternal mortality rates of over 500 per 100,000 live births are common in poor rural areas, contraceptive risks appear much lower than in the United States or Great Britain, for example, where the maternal mortality rate is roughly 10 per 100,000 live births.

This reasoning led the journal *Population Reports* to claim: "With all methods, family planning in developing countries is much safer than childbearing."[31] Indeed, this is the most common argument leveled against critics of indiscriminate contraceptive use in the Third World. But just how valid is the comparison between maternal mortality and contraceptive risk?

A close look at the logic reveals a number of very serious flaws:

1. The use of high rates of maternal mortality to justify higher contraceptive risk in effect *penalizes the poor for their poverty*. High maternal mortality rates result from inadequate nutrition, poor health care, and other effects of poverty. Addressing these problems first would not only alter the risk equation, but would establish a better foundation on which to build decent family planning services.

2. How can risk be precisely defined when the *long-term* risks of many contraceptives, such as the pill and injectables, will not be known for at least another one or two decades? Moreover, if a particular contraceptive increases the risk of cancer, a woman's life may be shortened, but the contraceptive will not be seen as the cause of death.

3. The measure of contraceptive risk is generally based on data from industrialized countries. *Third World women may actually be at greater risk from certain contraceptives* owing to their lower body weights, lack of sanitary facilities, poor medical care, etc. Moreover, they are rarely adequately screened before or followed up after contraceptive use.

4. *Why should the measure of risk center solely on women*, when there are male contraceptive methods such as the condom and vasectomy? As Judith Bruce and S. Bruce Schearer of the Population Council point out: "No attempt has been made to take into account the fact that whereas the health risks of *childbearing* are unavoidably sex-specific, the health risks of *contraception* can be assumed by either partner."[32]

5. *Many contraceptives have other harmful effects*, aside from death, which can have a profound impact on a

woman's life. For example, contraceptives like the IUD that carry the risk of impairing future fertility may be totally unacceptable to women, in spite of the risks they face from an unwanted pregnancy.

6. *Mortality risks in childbirth and mortality risks from a contraceptive do not necessarily belong in the same equation.* A woman may willingly assume the immediate risk of childbirth, while she may feel quite differently about the longer-term risk of death from the adverse effects of a contraceptive. Instead, the risk of a particular contraceptive should also be measured in comparison to other contraceptives, not only to giving birth. In health terms, barrier contraceptives, for example, are much safer than hormonal methods, even if they may be less effective in preventing pregnancy (a matter of dispute). Many women use contraceptives to *space* their pregnancies, not to end them altogether. An unplanned pregnancy resulting from the use of a barrier method might appear far more favorable to them than risking their lives on the pill.[33]

The acceptability of contraceptive risk is a personal decision as well as a scientific one. Many women are prepared to take health risks to prevent pregnancy, but each woman has a right to know all the risks and to make the decision for herself. Yet today, contraceptive manufacturers and population control programs are making that decision for millions of women.

A few members of the population establishment are beginning to challenge the maternal mortality/contraceptive risk comparison. George Zeidenstein, president of the Population Council, has expressed concern that "more often than not, important questions about safety and health risks of contraception are discussed by officials and professionals as if the only important issue raised was whether the mortality risk of using the particular contraceptive was lower than the mortality risk of pregnancy."[34]

And Judith Bruce and S. Bruce Schearer have pointed out the irony that the risks of modern contraception have given rise to a new public health problem in industrialized countries such as the United States: Although maternal mortality dropped by 75 percent between 1955 and 1975 in the United States, today about half that mortality is due to the adverse effects of new contraceptive technology, a cause that did not exist in 1955.[35]

Yet others argue that Third World people should be subjected to even greater risks to bring down birth rates. Dr. Carl Djerassi, one of the "fathers" of the birth control pill and a long-time consultant to the Syntex Corporation, called in 1983 for "heroic steps" in the next few years to speed the development of new contraceptives for the Third World so as to minimize the economic and political consequences of rapid population growth. These steps include expediting clinical research on humans, a priority rating system of studies with a "willingness to tolerate initially greater risks" in the case of especially promising contraceptives, and the establishment of a new international body to approve contraceptive research in order to bypass Western regulatory agencies, which are "currently not risk-oriented." Having called for a reduction in safety standards, Djerassi then says, "I take it for granted that 'informed consent' procedures are implemented rigorously and realistically—each country establishing its own."[36]

Today the forces shaping contraceptive technology—the population establishment, the pharmaceutical companies, and the scientific community—are far removed from the individual woman or man who uses birth control. As a result, the technology does not respond so much to individual needs as it does to the biases of its creators. Female contraception is emphasized far more than male, systemic and surgical methods receive much higher priority than barrier and natural methods, safety is a secondary concern. The next chapters look at the use and abuse of these technologies in more detail, focusing on their role in population control programs.

Hormonal Contraceptives and the IUD

To millions of women throughout the world, hormonal contraceptives and the IUD have been presented as liberating technologies. In the West they were heralded as the key to the so-called sexual revolution, and in the Third World as the answer to unwanted pregnancies and high birth rates. The enthusiasm which accompanied their introduction helped to obscure, and still obscures, their drawbacks. In population control programs particularly many women have been denied vital information about the risks of these contraceptives and have not received medical screening or follow-up care while using them. The result makes a mockery of informed consent.

PUSHING THE PILL

The Pill makes your breasts more beautiful and is good for everyone—including the tailors who have to make bigger brassieres.

> —*Slogan suggested by Dr. Malcolm Potts,*
> *director of the International Fertility Research*
> *Program, and colleagues at the 1977 Tokyo*
> *International Symposium on Population.*[1]

The birth control pill was the first and is still the most widely used of the hormonal contraceptives. Today over 60 million women take the pill worldwide, making it the most widely used *reversible* female contraceptive in the world. The pill undoubtedly has many advantages. Used correctly, it is very effective in preventing pregnancy and can alleviate menstrual disorders. It is relatively easy to use and does not interfere with sex. Moreover, it is under women's control—a woman must consciously decide to take the pill every day and can stop taking it if she suffers from side effects.

The most common type of pill contains the synthetic hormones, estrogen and progestin, similar to those produced in a woman's ovaries during the menstrual cycle. These affect the pituitary gland, altering the body's hormonal balance so that ovulation does not occur. The pill thus directly intervenes in one of the female body's most important reproductive processes.

Fears of the population explosion, the impetus behind the development of the pill, also determined where the first clinical trials of the method took place. The Caribbean island of Puerto Rico was chosen because, in the words of three pill researchers, it is a "region in which population pressure is a public health problem." In this particular study, undertaken in the late 1950s, one woman died from congestive heart failure and another developed pulmonary tuberculosis, but the researchers confidently asserted that "none of these effects could in any way be attributed" to the pill.[2] (The pill is closely linked to circulatory disorders.) The ethical and scientific standards of the early pill studies in Puerto Rico in fact left much to be desired. One study even blamed most occurrences of side effects such as nausea, vomiting, and dizziness on psychological factors.[3]

Nevertheless, the studies convinced the U.S. Food and Drug Administration (FDA) in 1960 to approve the first birth control pill, produced by Searle and marketed under the name of Enovid. By 1962, Searle had received reports of over one hundred cases of thrombosis and embolism (circulatory disorders, notably blood-clotting) associated with use of the Enovid pill, resulting in eleven deaths.

Yet despite such danger signs, the pill enjoyed "a sort of diplomatic immunity" throughout the early sixties. When the WHO organized a meeting of experts to study the pill in 1965, a member of the task force admitted to a reporter: "The people who were concerned with population problems had already decided that we were going to deliver a whitewash."[4]

By 1968 British studies firmly established the link between

the pill and blood-clotting, but the FDA was slow to act. The FDA Advisory Committee on Obstetrics and Gynecology concluded in 1969 that the pill's benefits sufficiently outweighed its risks to designate it "safe." According to the committee chairman, Dr. Louis Hellman, one of the pill's major benefits was that it "has made the problem of population control immeasurably easier."[5]

Following Senate hearings in 1970, U.S. feminists began to expose how little information on risks women had received. Through Congressional testimony, lawsuits, and other pressure tactics, they eventually forced the FDA to list possible adverse effects in a direct Patient Package Insert, separate from the insert to physicians.[6]

Today the estrogen content of the pill has been reduced, lessening the risk of circulatory disorders, and there is a progestin-only "mini pill." New biphastic and triphastic pills combine very low hormone doses with better menstrual cycle control. These modifications are definite improvements, but the pill still remains a very potent drug. Pill users run a greater risk of circulatory disorders—blood clots, heart attacks, strokes, and high blood pressure—than nonusers. The risk is higher among women over thirty-five, particularly those who smoke. The pill has been associated with nonmalignant liver tumors, which, though benign, are fatal if they rupture. These serious adverse effects mean that in Britain, for example, one out of every 500 pill users is hospitalized annually because of its effects. There is also ongoing concern about the pill's adverse effects on nutrition and lactation, and its possible link with cancer. Other "minor" adverse effects include nausea, headache, depression, and weight gain.[7]

While pill use in the developed countries has leveled off in the last five years, it is on the rise in the Third World, increasing from 14 million women in 1977 to 18 million in 1980. These figures exclude China, where an estimated 7 million women take the pill. In the United States, the percentage of pill users has actually *declined,* as a result of women's increased knowledge about risks and unhappiness with side effects.

Clearly, for the pill manufacturers, the growing market is

the Third World, where their sales are boosted by government and donor agencies' promotion of the pill. The U.S. Agency for International Development (AID) currently provides family planning programs, mostly in Asia, with about 100 million cycles of pills annually, enough to serve 7 to 8 million women; other donors provide another 20 million cycles.[8]

Since the beginning, population control has shaped the way AID and other agencies have promoted the pill in the Third World. Because of its efficacy in preventing pregnancy, they believe that the pill can have a dramatic demographic impact if distributed on a wide scale. Its adverse effects are shrugged off with references to high rates of maternal mortality, or hardly mentioned at all.[9] A 1979 AID-sponsored evaluation of family planning programs by Westinghouse Health Systems noted the "considerable pressure" AID has put on countries to accept the pill. The evaluation stated: "It is clear that political-administrative elites, and not the masses of acceptors, are deciding on the technology to be used."[10]

The use of the pill as an instrument of population control has passed through several stages (see Box: "Taking the Pill Is Good for Your Religion" for a particularly creative approach).

TAKING THE PILL IS GOOD FOR YOUR RELIGION

In Indonesia, the U.S. Agency for International Development (AID) prides itself on its ability to move fast in funding creative initiatives by local family planning officials. The following account of Dr. Haji Mahyuddin's Pill Ramadhan in West Sumatra, excerpted from an AID evaluation report, raises serious questions about the way modern contraceptives have been introduced into Third World settings. In this instance, certain religious customs (which arguably discriminate against women in the first place) were manipulated and religious leaders bribed in order to get women to take the pill.

continued

continued
The Pill Ramadhan

In 1971, while in private practice, Dr. Mahyuddin became interested in giving birth control pills to women in such a way as to prevent menstruation during the month of Ramadhan, when Muslims are to fast from sunrise to sunset. A menstruating woman is regarded as ritually unclean and thus may neither make the fast nor pray in the mosque. According to custom she may "pay back" missed days after Ramadhan is over but receives less *pahala* (grace from God) for days fasted after the month than during it. The people of West Sumatra are relatively devout Muslims, and thus many women among them would like to be able to fast straight through Ramadhan in order to receive the maximum amount of grace.

In about 1976 Dr. Mahyuddin discussed the feasibility of a "Ramadhan pill" with Dr. Malcolm Potts (then of IPPF) on the latter's visit to West Sumatra. Potts subsequently sent back information on a three-cycle pill being used elsewhere. Dr. Mahyuddin reasoned that many women would be attracted to use the pill to inhibit menstruation during Ramadhan and, having in this way overcome initial reluctance to use it, could be motivated to continue its use—or even switch to the IUD—after Ramadhan was over.

In May 1978 Dr. Mahyuddin took a Ramadhan Pill proposal to BKBBN [Indonesian National Family Planning Coordinating Board] headquarters. Headquarters approved it in principle but all agreed that support of the *ulama* [religious leaders] would be necessary before proceeding with the project—and before headquarters would agree to fund it.

Dr. Mahyuddin decided to hold a "consultation" for the *ulama*, using funds he would borrow from his DIP [budget] and then subsequently repay once the project had been approved by headquarters and AID funds for it made available to him.

A one-day consultation with the *ulama* and the *"adats"* was held on June 29. They were reportedly all pleased to be called to the provincial capital, to receive room and board, transportation, and a per diem, and all agreed to the Ramadhan Pill idea. . . . Headquarters received funding from AID in late July and funds were available for the project the first week in August.[1]

The "contraceptive inundation" approach was the brainchild of Dr. R. T. Ravenholt, former head of AID's Office of Population. He urged the vigorous promotion of the pill free or at minimal cost through house-to-house visits of nonmedical family planning personnel and through unrestricted sales in small cigarette stalls and shops sprinkled liberally throughout the rural and urban areas of the Third World in the belief that supply would automatically beget demand. "The principle involved in the household distribution of contraceptives can be demonstrated with Coca-Cola," he explained. "If one distributed an ample, free supply of Coca Cola into each household, would not poor illiterate peasants drink as much Coca-Cola as the rich literate residents?"[11]

However, as AID discovered, the relationship between supply and demand is not so straightforward, and the inundation strategy proved something of a disaster. In Pakistan, for example, it led to no significant uptake of contraception, but instead, in the view of the Westinghouse evaluation, to a waste of time, money, and effort, and to the "institutionalization of failure" in the country's family planning program.[12] "We were burned in enough places where that strategy was wrong," says Dr. Stephen Sinding, former director of AID's Office of Population. "Now there is greater sensitivity at AID to appropriate levels of supply." But is there greater sensitivity to the potentially harmful effects of the pill on women's and children's health?

Today, in a variation on the inundation theme, AID and other agencies such as the International Planned Parenthood Federation (IPPF) and the Pathfinder Fund are promoting the pill through various Community Based Distribution, Retail Sales, and Social Marketing schemes. In such programs, the pill is distributed or sold without a doctor's prescription and with very little, if any, screening or follow-up. This is not surprising since the overall goal, according to the Pathfinder Fund, "is to decrease the birth rate by increasing the level of contraceptive use,"[13] not to meet women's need for safe birth control.

Safety concerns are dismissed with assertions such as this

recent one in *Population Reports:* "Modern family planning methods are safe. Contraceptive products are not toxic even if used incorrectly—an important consideration for community-based or nonmedical supervision."[14] Social marketing schemes, in fact, have been designed with the explicit goal of avoiding the need for health services.[15]

A real concern for safety would dictate that potential pill users be adequately screened for history of heart disease and diabetes and for pregnancy, among other things, all of which call for the attention of trained medical or paramedical personnel. Yet population agencies insist, in the words of an IPPF publication, that "Women who should not try the Pill at all can be screened out by a simple set of questions which shopkeepers and nonmedical distributors can easily learn."[16]

In reality, however, these questions—and the interpretation of the answers—are not so simple for nonmedical personnel to learn. And *what incentive do they have to ask them when their goal is getting more acceptors or sales?* Moreover, cultural restrictions in many countries mean that the husband, rather than the woman herself, is the one who buys the pills at commercial outlets, and he often lacks knowledge of his wife's health or is reluctant to talk about it, especially when the sensitive issue of contraception is involved. Even when women do receive information about pill risks, it tends to be heavily biased. For example, the administrators of a Population Services International social marketing scheme in Thailand explained, "Women are told that the hormonal changes and related effects during pregnancy are 'the size of an elephant' while the changes and side effects of the pill are 'the size of an ant.' "[17]

Dr. Sinding admits that AID "can't guarantee screening through commercial outlets. There is a risk," he says, "but the health risk from unplanned pregnancy is worse. Each country must make its own decision about risk. It must be the country's policy to sell contraceptives without prescription, not our own." Country policy is subject to donor pressure, however, and that pressure has often proved instrumental in the deregulation of the pill.

Lack of screening and follow-up care are often justified on the basis that the serious side effects of the pill are associated with Western life-styles and health problems.[18] Yet there are very few studies of the pill's impact on Third World women. In fact, there is strong reason to believe that pushing the pill indiscriminately in the Third World actually *increases* its risks and the severity of its side effects. This can occur in the following ways:

The Risk of Circulatory Disorders It is commonly asserted that Third World women have a lower risk of developing circulatory disorders from the pill, since most do not smoke, overeat, or experience as much stress as Western women. Yet there is very little reliable comparative data on circulatory mortality rates. Moreover, chronic rheumatic heart disease, which often goes undetected but which is perhaps the most common heart disease among young Third World adults, increases the risk of blood clotting and other circulatory disorders, and thus could increase the risk of the pill.[19] One might also add that a life of poverty can be very stressful.

The Risk of Taking the Pill in Pregnancy In the United States an estimated 70,000 fetuses are exposed to oral contraceptives annually.[20] In the Third World the proportion is likely to be much higher, given inadequate screening and the absence of pregnancy tests. The possibility of the pill's link with birth defects—though not definitively proved one way or the other—raises questions about the wisdom of its indiscriminate promotion.

The Effect on Lactation This is one of the greatest dangers of pill use in the Third World. Lactating women on the combined estrogen-progestin pill frequently have a reduced supply of milk. Even a low estrogen pill, taken in the first few months after birth, can reduce the volume of milk by as much as 40 percent in three to six weeks. Since for millions of infants, breast milk is the main or only source of nutrition in the first one or two years of life, the pill can contribute directly to infant malnutrition and hence higher infant mortality rates. World Health Organization (WHO) guidelines recommend that women not be encouraged to use hormonal contraception for four to six months after birth,[21] but unfortunately many lactating mothers in the Third World are routinely given the pill. Since the long-term effects of infants' ingestion of hormones secreted in breast milk have yet to be determined, this is also a cause of concern.

Use of the pill while breast-feeding can also have another negative effect. Inadequate supervision in community distribution or retail sales schemes means that many women take the pill irregularly or drop it altogether after developing the first side effects. The WHO has found the incidence of irregular use to be over 50 percent in some parts of the Third World.[22] Dropout rates as high as 80 percent have been reported after only three months in Bangladesh.[23] As a result, although the pill is theoretically 99 percent effective in preventing pregnancy, the failure rate tends to be much higher in the Third World.

Ironically, these factors may be leading to what some observers have called a "pill-induced population explosion."[24] Breast-feeding, as noted in Chapter 1, is one of the world's most effective natural contraceptives because it suppresses ovulation. When breast-feeding women take the pill irregularly, they tend to resume ovulation sooner, and thus lose an important natural defense against pregnancy. A study in Bangladesh found that lactating women who used the pill had significantly shorter intervals to the next pregnancy than did lactating women who did not use it *or any other contraceptive.* The study concluded that women should not be given the pill while breast-feeding unless it can be ensured that they take it *regularly* for at least nine months after giving birth.[25]

The Effect on Women's Nutrition   Because the pill causes changes in the metabolism of important vitamins and minerals, some nutritionists fear it may help cause nutritional deficiency diseases in malnourished women. If so, it is a particularly inappropriate contraceptive for use in impoverished communities. There is a pressing need for more research on this subject.[26]

The Risk of Cancer   The most controversial question surrounding the pill is its relationship to cancer. It usually takes many years for a person to develop cancer after exposure to a carcinogen, but since the pill has only been in use for two and a half decades, it is impossible to evaluate the risks fully. The FDA concluded in 1984, however, that the pill may increase the risk of acquiring cervical cancer, and now recommends that women on the pill should be monitored carefully with physical examinations and Pap (cervical smear) tests, *at least yearly*. The FDA also recommends routine breast exams for pill users.[27]

Yet such monitoring is often difficult or impossible to obtain in the West, and virtually unheard of for women living in many rural areas of the Third World. Given that cervical cancer is the most common cause of death from cancer among both Latin American and African women, grave doubts arise as to the wisdom of promoting the pill in the Third World, with the almost certain lack of follow-up. Knowledge about the pill and cancer has been almost totally derived from studies in developed countries. Follow-up, even for research purposes, is extremely rare in the Third World.[28]

Many of the above risks increase with higher doses of estrogen, and thus the FDA recommends pills with the lowest effective amounts. The most common oral contraceptives in the West use 30 mcg. of estrogen, but Third World family planning programs often use higher amounts. In Zimbabwe, for example, the common pill distributed contains 50 mcg. of estrogen.[29] In the early 1970s, AID was accused of "dumping" high (80 mcg.) estrogen pills in the Third World, which were obtained from the Syntex Company at a very cheap price.[30]

What has been the response of the population establishment to such criticisms? "Critics of community distribution only think Anglo-Saxon gynecologists from Westchester [a rich New York suburb] are equipped to give pills to Third World women," says Richard Pomeroy of Family Planning International Assistance. According to Norma Swenson of the Boston Women's Health Book Collective, others go further, accusing women health activists of "imperialist arrogance" when they insist that the same safety standards be applied in the Third World as they have fought for in the West.[31]

Today there is a move on to "resell the pill." AID and others are encouraging the FDA to change pill labeling to stress its possible benefits in helping to prevent ovarian and endometrial cancers, ectopic pregnancy, and benign breast disease. Such a move would mark a major breach in the accepted practice of only listing a drug's benefits which relate directly to the reasons it is prescribed—in the case of the pill, these are preventing pregnancy and alleviating menstrual disorders.

The logic behind the reselling of the pill is dubious: What good is added protection against ovarian cancer when you run a higher risk of cervical cancer and circulatory disorders? Women take the pill as a contraceptive, not as a vaccine.[32]

It may be some time before the final verdict on the pill is delivered, but in the meantime, don't women *everywhere* deserve adequate information and medical supervision while taking this powerful drug? It is not imperialist arrogance to insist on equal rights when it comes to safety. It is ethical and humane.

DEPO-PROVERA: KEEPING AN EYE ON THE NEEDLE

For the average individual in a Western country, depot progestagen [Depo-Provera] preparations have a limited use because of the high incidence of irregular vaginal bleeding, and the slight risks of permanent amenorrhea. . . . Finally, depot progestagens provide an effective, acceptable and simple method of contraception for the underdeveloped world, which can be easily administered by paramedical personnel.

—D. F. HAWKINS AND M. S. ELDER
Human Fertility Control: Theory and Practice[33]

In recent years Depo-Provera, an injectable, hormonal contraceptive manufactured by the United States pharmaceutical firm Upjohn Co., has been at the center of contraceptive controversy. The Depo debate has raged in government hearings, among the medical community, population establishment, feminists, and health activists, and in the pages of the popular press. Supporters of the drug have challenged the very foundations of the USFDA regulatory process, while detractors condemn its use in the Third World as a particularly dangerous example of the contraceptive double standard.

Available since 1963, Depo-Provera is now approved for use in over eighty countries, though in some instances, notably

Sweden, West Germany, and the United Kingdom, its use is theoretically restricted to a small percentage of women for whom other methods are inappropriate. An estimated 11 million women have used Depo-Provera at some time, and up to 2.3 million may be taking it today. The highest rates of use are in Jamaica, Thailand, New Zealand, Mexico, and Sri Lanka.

Like the pill, Depo-Provera has been heavily promoted in population programs, with the IPPF and the UNFPA the main suppliers.[34] AID has been unable to supply Depo-Provera directly to family planning programs because it is not approved for contraceptive use in the United States. Upjohn has manufactured and exported it from a Belgian subsidiary.

Unlike the combination pill, Depo-Provera contains only progestin. It is usually administered in a single 150 milligram injection, effective for at least three months. Another widely marketed progestin injectable, produced by the West German Schering Co. under the brand name NET-EN, is usually given every two months. Both work primarily by inhibiting ovulation through effects on the pituitary gland, and are highly effective when used at regular intervals, resulting in a pregnancy rate of less than 1 in 100 per year.[35] Depo is much more widely used, but Depo's notoriety may mean that NET-EN is more heavily promoted in the years ahead. This is already occurring in India. A number of other injectables have also come onto the market recently, several of which contain estrogen to induce menstrual bleeding. Estrogen of course can cause other serious side effects.[36]

Depo-Provera's advantages lie primarily in the way it is administered. A single shot protects a woman from pregnancy for three to six months, freeing her from the need for continued responsibility for birth control, unlike the pill, which must be remembered every day, or barrier methods which require application before intercourse. For women whose husbands object to their using birth control, Depo can be given surreptitiously, during a quick visit to or by a family planning worker.

Depo also enjoys the so-called injection mystique. In many areas of the Third World, people associate injections with safe, effective, modern medicine, and are thus eager to receive them. As a Thai study notes: "A contraceptive to be taken by injection seems to make the dreams of most women come true, and has a tremendous initial psychological advantage over other methods."[37]

From the standpoint of population control, the drug is ideal: The injection mystique reduces the need for motivational efforts; it is easy to administer, long-acting, and effective in preventing pregnancy. And once a woman has had an injection, there is no possibility of user failure.

These advantages can actually be disadvantages when viewed from another perspective. Freedom from responsibility can also mean loss of control: If a woman suffers adverse effects from Depo, there is nothing she can do until the injection wears off. For some women this can mean months of intense suffering, since the side effects of the drug can linger beyond three months. The injection mystique can also lead to abuse, since if people inherently trust injections, it makes it easier to administer Depo without explaining its side effects.

The most common—and noticeable—side effects of Depo-Provera are menstrual disorders. Over two thirds of women using Depo have no regular menstrual cycles in the first year of use.[38] Many stop menstruating altogether, while others experience heavy or intermittent bleeding. Heavy bleeding can be particularly serious for undernourished women, who can ill afford the iron and blood loss. Because menstrual blood is considered unclean in many Third World cultures, women who experience intermittent bleeding suffer not only physical inconvenience but social ostracism.

Other side effects include skin disorders, tiredness, headaches, nausea, depression, hair loss, loss of libido, and delayed return to fertility. These are often dismissed as "minor," but as health writer Gena Corea notes, "Depression is a minor side effect which merely destroys the entire quality of a woman's life." She also points out how loss of libido can turn intercourse into a distasteful ordeal for women. Ironically, Depo has proved an effective male contraceptive, but has not been promoted because of complaints of loss of libido. Although women complain of the same thing, it supposedly does not matter in their case.[39]

As for weight gain, researchers hypothesize that Depo

stimulates the hypothalmic appetite control center in the brain, causing women to eat more. "In undernourished women this effect would be beneficial if they can obtain more food," states *Population Reports*. But of course if they could obtain more food, they would not be malnourished in the first place![40]

Depo's possible long-term adverse effects are similar to those of the pill: the possible risk of birth defects as the result of women taking the drug during pregnancy, the potentially negative impact on infant development of ingesting the hormone in breast milk, and a possible link to breast, endometrial, and cervical cancers.[41] These possible risks have led feminists, health activists, and many members of the medical community to fight against the approval of Depo-Provera.

Despite these concerns, the medical boards of both the WHO and IPPF have approved the drug for widespread use, with only a few minor precautions. WHO recommends administration of Depo within the first five days of a woman's menstrual cycle to ensure that she is not pregnant. But according to *Population Reports*, "In some programs, particularly where access to family planning services is limited, women are given injections at any time during the menstrual cycle."[42] In considering the perils of fetal exposure to synthetic hormones during pregnancy, it is worthwhile remembering the women who took the synthetic estrogen DES during pregnancy, whose daughters developed vaginal cancer and cervical abnormalities twenty years later.[43]

Both the WHO and IPPF do not discourage the use of Depo by lactating mothers, despite the fact that, in the words of the IPPF, "to date no proper, thorough follow-up studies of children breast-fed by mothers using injectable contraceptives have been carried out."[44] WHO does recommend delaying the injection for six weeks after birth, however, displaying some recognition of the potential risk.[45]

As for cancer, the findings of FDA-mandated animal studies that Depo caused a significant incidence of breast tumors in beagle dogs and endometrial cancer in rhesus monkeys are downplayed as being irrelevant to humans since the test animals are inappropriate.[46] Depo supporters argue that so far there is no evidence linking the drug with human cancers.

Given that cancer often takes many years to develop, it is far too early to be so complacent. Moreover, very few follow-up studies have been performed on long-term users of Depo, and the few that have taken place are seriously flawed. Nevertheless, Upjohn's Gordon Duncan, who coordinates the company's international research program in fertility, has said categorically, "There's no evidence of a cancer risk potential in any women. That's a flat statement. The studies are negative."[47]

In the autumn of 1984, the findings of a public board of inquiry on Depo-Provera, convened by the USFDA, took a very different view of the matter. After a two-year investigation of the evidence, the board recommended that the FDA not approve Depo's use as a contraceptive in the United States because the drug had not yet been proved safe. Studies of Depo's effects on humans, the board found, are both "insufficient and inadequate" to confirm or refute the risk of cancer. The development of cancer in Depo-injected beagle dogs and monkeys could not be dismissed as irrelevant to humans without conclusive evidence to the contrary. The board also pointed to the need for more research on Depo's effects on breast-feeding infants before the risks of malformations could be dismissed, and expressed some concern about the risk of birth defects.[48]

What emerges most strongly from the board's report is the poor quality of the human studies conducted on Depo-Provera. "If I learned one thing from our review, it is to check every document," said one member of the board. "We were told 'the experts say this, the experts all agree.' Our review tells me that we experts had better be careful what we say." The board's verdict was that Upjohn and others had not adequately proved their case.[49] It thus upheld the basic principle that a drug should be considered dangerous until proved safe.

Why have the studies of Depo-Provera been so poorly done? As Gena Corea points out, they largely reflect the underlying values of Depo's proponents:

> If you regard women as interchangeable members of a sex class; if you believe their reproduction ought to be controlled

and curtailed; if you have different standards of safety for poor women and women of color and "socially irresponsible" women than for women of your own race, social class, and high level of "responsibility," then this affects the way you design studies and evaluate their results.[50]

Today WHO is undertaking more rigorous human studies of Depo-Provera, including a study of cancer risk in Thailand, Kenya, and Mexico. Preliminary findings released in 1985 indicate that Depo users have not experienced an increased risk of cancer of the breast, endometrium, ovary, or liver. However, there appears to be a small elevation in the risk of acquiring cervical cancer, similar to that reported for young, long-term users of the pill. WHO is careful to point out that these findings cannot be viewed as conclusive, since any effect of Depo on cancer incidence may not appear until after a delay of many years.[51] In the same vein Judith Weisz, chair of the FDA Board of Inquiry, has noted that the data on Depo and breast cancer relate almost exclusively to premenopausal women, whereas in the United States breast cancer occurs mainly in postmenopausal women.[52]

Depo's short-term side effects and long-term risks make it questionable whether it should be used at all, but the ways it is administered, both in industrialized and Third World countries, raise further doubts. In the West, Depo is often used on ethnic minorities and working class women, with little or no explanation of its effects.

"It's no use explaining about beagle dogs," said one British doctor who had just injected a Bangladeshi immigrant, "she's an illiterate peasant from the bush."[53] Britain recently gave Depo a long-term license (with certain restrictions), raising fears that such abuses may become more widespread. In Australia, Depo is often used on aboriginal peoples, and although Depo use is widespread among white women in New Zealand, a greater proportion of ethnic minority Maori women are injected. Upjohn is currently financing a major study of the drug's safety in New Zealand, which reproductive rights activists argue has serious design flaws guaranteed to give Depo a clean bill of health.[54]

Though not approved for contraceptive use in the United States, Depo is available as a cancer treatment, and thus individual doctors can and do give it to patients as a method of birth control. Low-income black women in the South and Native American women have been special targets.[55] Dr. Malcolm Potts, head of the International Fertility Research Program, has recommended Depo's use on "minority populations in the U.S.A.," such as Mexican immigrants, who "have the same problems as people in the Third World."[56]

Mentally retarded women, incarcerated women, and drug addicts are also Depo targets. In fact, one of the members of the FDA's board of inquiry, Dr. Griff T. Ross, recommended that the drug be approved for limited use on retarded women and drug addicts, though he admitted its safety was not sufficiently proved for use on "human subjects."[57]

The same logic which justifies giving Depo to these women in the West underlies the drug's promotion among the poor majority in the Third World. Their safety is somehow more expendable—they count, more often than not, mainly as demographic statistics.

Thailand has one of the longest experiences and highest percentages of injectable contraceptive use in the world. Seven percent of women of reproductive age use injectables, making them the third most popular form of contraception. Although Depo-Provera is a popular drug, it is unclear how many women using it are actually aware of its potential risks. Thai consumer activist Weena Silapa-archa writes, for example: "The long-acting injection is widespread among people in the rural areas. This is not only because the people don't know the adverse effect of the drug, but also because they are told the drug is good, safe and effective."[58]

In Thailand, Depo has been actively promoted by donor agencies—the country has been the largest recipient by far of donor supplies of injectables, receiving over half of all such supplies between 1978 and 1981. Now, with encouragement and loans from the World Bank, Thailand is starting to buy Depo commercially.[59]

Like the pill, Depo is often given without adequate medical supervision. In Mexico it is sold over the counter in pharmacies and given by "injectionists," practitioners with little or no formal training.[60] Many medical personnel in Third World countries have reported that they never saw any physician package insert accompanying the drug, and thus were unable to communicate adequately the risks and side effects to women.[61]

Coercive use of Depo in the Third World is not uncommon. In Thai refugee camps, for example, an official of the International Committee of the Red Cross found that Cambodian women were required to have the injection before being allowed to marry.[62]

In South Africa the situation is particularly severe. Black women have been the victims of mass Depo-Provera campaigns, at the same time as they have virtually no access to decent health care. In fact, family planning is the only free health service available to blacks, and Depo-Provera is the most commonly used contraceptive. According to Dr. Nthato Motlana, one of the country's leading black physicians, "The agencies are administering Depo-Provera shots to young black girls without even asking their consent."[63] In some regions, family planning workers travel to white-owned factories and farms to give injections to black employees. In order to apply for a job, many black women have to present family planning cards documenting their use of birth control to prospective employers. Meanwhile, white women are encouraged to have a large number of children.

As justification for its population control efforts, the South African government claims that black people are putting too much pressure on the environment, especially on water supplies. "The statistics show that we must drastically cut the population growth, whether it is in the black man's nature to do so or not," warned South Africa's Minister of Environment Affairs and Fisheries in 1984, "otherwise we are all going to die of thirst."[64] The real fear, of course, is that a growing number of blacks and a shrinking number of whites will speed the demise of the apartheid system.

In its 1986 report on population growth and policies in sub-Saharan Africa, the World Bank urges African governments to relax restrictions on injectable contraceptives and claims that they can be delivered safely by nonmedical personnel outside of a clinic system. In fact, according to the Bank, the only major disadvantages of injectables are "minimal side effects"![65] The same report endorses the use of incentive and disincentive schemes in Africa, although it notes that they are not likely to be effective until contraception is more readily available. Given such attitudes, it is not hard to imagine a future scenario where many African women will be pressured into "accepting" Depo-Provera and other injectables.

These cases do not mean that Depo is always misused. There are examples of family planning programs where women are adequately screened, informed of risks, followed up, and offered other options. Indian feminist doctor Hari John defends her use of Depo in rural South India (she explains the risks and uses the drug herself) on the basis of women's powerlessness and male opposition to contraception: "Using Depo-Provera is the only way these women can have any control over any aspect of their lives."[66] For this reason, Depo may be the choice of some Third World women.

Many feminists and health activists, however, disagree with Dr. John's position. "In my opinion the use of Depo could not improve the unjust situation of the women in rural South India," writes Weena Silapa-archa.[67] Judy Norsigian of the Boston Women's Health Book Collective points out that the widespread availability of Depo could actually undermine efforts to change the basic social and economic conditions that produce women's powerlessness in the first place. "It's the old Band-Aid approach," she says, "which does nothing to prevent the cuts."[68] Moreover, although Depo may free women from the burden of pregnancy, it does nothing to free them from the pressure to have unwanted intercourse. Others believe that the severity of the drug's side effects and risks means its use is never justified.

Even supposing the drug is used responsibly, in the hands of people whose first concern is women's welfare not population control, another important question remains: Do a few good programs justify Depo's general approval, given its great potential for abuse?

The board of inquiry findings make it improbable that the FDA will approve Depo-Provera's use as a contraceptive in the United States, although Upjohn is now planning to bring its case before the FDA once again. Lack of FDA approval has sorely disappointed the company, for it had hoped that if the ban was lifted, 4 million U.S. women would use the drug. But more importantly, a positive FDA decision would have meant a greater market in the Third World, since countries such as India and Egypt usually abide by FDA decisions in formulating their own drug regulations.[69]

Even if the FDA continues the ban on the drug, however, changes in United States drug export laws may eventually make it possible to export Depo directly from the United States. This would constitute an important landmark in official acceptance of the contraceptive double standard. Already in 1978 the FDA, in rejecting Upjohn's request for a license to market Depo in the United States, added this sweetener: "Benefit-risk considerations are not the same in all countries of the world." Depo may be appropriate "for nations with higher birthrates, lower physician–patient ratios, and less readily available contraceptive methods."[70]

Sweden, however, has turned the contraceptive double standard on its head. Although Depo is licensed for domestic use in Sweden when other contraceptives have proved unsuitable or caused adverse effects, the Swedish International Development Authority (SIDA) has decided "not to deliver or finance purchase of Depo-Provera to any of SIDA's projects or programs in developing countries." The reasons cited by SIDA are worth quoting:

> SIDA is of the opinion that the use of Depo-Provera needs continuous medical follow-up by health staff in a well functioning health system. We know this is lacking in many of SIDA's program countries. Without a good health infrastructure there are risks that the clients are not given enough information to make an informed choice of contraceptive methods. We know of several occasions where Depo-Provera has been abused. SIDA further thinks that more research is needed on the effects of the injectable on suckling and unborn infants. SIDA is also of the opinion that there are other aspects than medical ones that should be taken into consideration, e.g., regarding menstruation disturbances. These include

psychological and social aspects of the use of the injectable in various cultures.[71]

It is a pity that these same basic concerns for health and safety do not influence decisions by other agencies on the use of Depo-Provera in the Third World.

AND NOW NORPLANT . . .

I believe that the latest Council-developed method, Norplant® contraceptive subdermal implants, is the most important new contraceptive system since the pill.[72]

—GEORGE ZEIDENSTEIN
President of the Population Council

In the winter of 1984, the population community was abuzz with the news of Norplant, encapsulated hormones inserted under the skin of the arm which prevent pregnancy for at least five years. In almost every office I visited in Washington and New York, people expressed the hope that Norplant might prove a much needed technological breakthrough, a long-acting but reversible form of contraception, which could serve as an alternative to sterilization.

At the Population Council, where Norplant was developed, one of its promoters was a walking advertisement for the drug. He had me feel the capsules, minus the hormone of course, inserted in his arm. "The evidence to date indicates that this new method will have significant personal and demographic impact," says the Population Council, "now that it is ready to be introduced into family planning programs worldwide."[73] The demographic objective is obvious in the very design of the drug: It is effective for five or more years. One wonders why a one- or two-year option was not developed first.

Norplant is the council's trade name for six capsules (Norplant I) or two rods (Norplant II) containing the progestin levonorgestrel, which is commonly found in oral contraceptives. Insertion and removal of the implants requires local anesthesia and medical skill. Norplant has a very low failure rate and has the advantages over the combined pill and Depo-Provera of a smaller hormonal dose (similar to the minipill) and a relatively constant hormonal release, which could cause fewer side effects. Studies show no adverse effect on fertility; after Norplant is removed, women return to normal hormonal levels within twenty-four hours.

Norplant has not yet been approved by the FDA, although clinical trials are underway in the United States. It is approved in Finland, however, where it is manufactured by Leiras Pharmaceuticals, who as part of their contract with the Population Council, must provide it at a low price to Third World governments and family planning organizations. Sweden, Thailand, Indonesia, and Ecuador have also licensed the drug, and in 1986 IPPF added it to its list of available contraceptives.[74]

Norplant has been tested on over 30,000 women in twenty-five countries. Like Depo-Provera, its most common side effect is disruption of the menstrual cycle, resulting in prolonged bleeding, intermittent spotting, or amenorrhea. Other adverse effects are also common to progestin contraceptives: headache, depression, loss of libido, weight change, nausea, and acne. It is not recommended for use by lactating women. In regard to long-term effects, the risk of cancer is not mentioned in the literature, though both the pill and Depo's possible link with reproductive cancers suggests this should be an area of concern.[75]

In clinical and field trials, Norplant has shown high continuation rates, which has prompted great optimism on the part of the Population Council about its acceptability to Third World women.[76] Ecuadorian researchers, however, have pointed out that high continuation rates may result from women's fears of having the implants removed:

> In our view, it would be wrong to be content with the low termination rate due to menstrual problems. We believe that the rate would have been much higher if it had been easier to remove the implants. In other words, there is a balance between distress caused by the menstrual problems and the fear of the removal procedure.[77]

These fears are well-grounded, for both insertion and removal are far from simple procedures. If sterile conditions are not maintained, infections can result. During insertion special care must be taken not to drive the capsules into the underlying muscles, since they can migrate in muscle and be difficult to remove. Removal is more difficult than insertion, since once capsules are in the body, a layer of fibrous tissue forms around them, which must be cut away. According to one clinical manual:

> Occasionally all capsules cannot be removed readily at the first visit. *Do not take heroic measures to remove the last one or two.* Send the woman home and ask her to return in two weeks, after the area is fully healed. The remaining implant(s) will probably be readily located and removed at a second visit.[78]

The way Norplant is administered may in fact make it a particularly inappropriate contraceptive technology in many areas of the Third World where health systems are poorly developed. Even in closely monitored trials, under direct medical supervision, infections have resulted, requiring the removal of the capsules, and these are likely to be more widespread and potentially more dangerous in clinics with inadequate antiseptic standards.[79]

The greatest problem with Norplant, however, is the almost total loss of user control, despite the fact that people at the Population Council like to call it "user soft," i.e., easy to use. Although it is billed as a reversible method, Norplant should only be removed by trained medical personnel if a woman decides to terminate use early because of side effects or the desire to become pregnant. Given the inadequacies of many Third World family planning programs and general lack of access to health care, one would expect that many women would find it difficult, if not impossible, to get the capsules removed without significant delays.

In past Norplant trials, people moving out of the area have been advised to have the implants removed "as no other clinics were trained in the technique of removal." Nevertheless, even under such artificial study conditions, many women have been "lost to follow-up," including 238 women out of a total of 813 participating in one recent trial in Indonesia.[80] Some women have also experienced difficulties in getting the implants removed because of resistance from trial investigators, who, according to the Population Council, "may be hesitant to remove the implants out of concern that the scientific data may be rendered incomplete."[81]

The drug's promoters are not blind to these problems and are advising that Norplant should be introduced only under certain conditions. The Population Council is taking great pains to stress that if a woman wants the capsules removed, the procedure should be scheduled without delay, and is trying to enforce informed consent guidelines in clinical trials.[82] According to the council, Norplant is essentially a clinic-based method, requiring "careful training, supervision, information dissemination, logistics and follow-up." That said, the council has suggested, however, that Norplant could possibly be used in mobile clinics or contraceptive camps, where follow-up is far more problematic.[83]

Ironically, some Third World officials are enthusiastic about Norplant precisely because of the lack of good health and communications infrastructure in their countries. In Bangladesh, for example, a 1981 draft government proposal for a Norplant trial stated: "Bangladesh, with a largely illiterate and conservative population, together with poor communication facilities . . . is unsuitable for short-term contraceptive techniques, which demand a continuous motivation on the part of the client and a continuous supply of material on the part of the program managers."[84]

The solution: long-acting Norplant. In fact, this proposal views Norplant not as a reversible contraceptive but as a drug which "has got the potential for becoming nearly as effective as sterilization," and which can complement the government's drive to perform at least 100,000 sterilizations a month. Norplant is currently being tested in Bangladesh, and already there are reports of women having difficulty getting the implants removed.

In Indonesia the government family planning program is interested in using Norplant in "remote areas," particularly the Outer Islands, where education, communication, and transportation systems are poorly developed. This is because

Norplant "is easy to use, requiring only one insertion for five years of protection" and "easy to supply."[85]

There is also another worrisome feature of the drug, should it be used as an instrument of population control. In thin women, especially, the capsules are visible under the skin, which would allow a coercive population control program to identify nonusers easily. China is currently testing the drug at eight provincial centers. Given the nature of the Chinese population control program, where IUD users are routinely X-rayed to make sure the devices are still in place, fears arise as to how voluntary Norplant acceptance and continuation there will be.

Despite these potential problems, the Population Council is vigorously promoting the drug for use in Third World family planning programs. It naively assumes that its own good guidelines regarding informed consent and easy access to removal will be carried out in practice. It is currently trying to "facilitate the international regulatory process" by informing "regulatory officials in countries throughout the developing world of the advantages of the Norplant system."[86] There is a great danger that this drug, like the pill and Depo-Provera, will be used indiscriminately, without proper medical screening, supervision, and follow-up.

THE IUD STORY

They [IUDs] are horrible things, they produce infection, they are outmoded and not worth using . . . [but] suppose one does develop an intrauterine infection and suppose she does end up with a hysterectomy and bilateral salpingo-oophorectomy? How serious is that for the particular patient and for the population of the world in general? Not very. . . . Perhaps the individual patient is expendable in the general scheme of things, particularly if the infection she acquires is sterilizing but not lethal.

—DR. J. ROBERT WILLSON
at the First International Conference on Intra-Uterine Contraception, sponsored by the Population Council, New York City, 1962.[87]

The IUD (or intrauterine device) is typically a small coiled, looped, or T-shaped plastic or copper device inserted inside the uterus with a tail reaching down into the upper vagina. It is used by an estimated 60 million women worldwide, but over two thirds of them are in China alone.[88] The IUD is believed to prevent pregnancy primarily by causing inflammation or infection of the uterus, which in turn leads to expulsion of any fertilized eggs. As a form of contraception, it is almost as effective as hormonal varieties, without the disadvantage of altering the body's hormonal balance. The IUD is by no means hazard-free, however.

The story of the IUD, in fact, presents yet another example of the exposure of women to unnecessary risks in the name of population control and corporate profit. Although modern intrauterine devices date from the 1920s, they were considered dangerous by many members of the medical profession because of the risk of infection.

In 1962, at the First International Conference on Intra-Uterine Contraception sponsored by the Population Council, the IUD was suddenly embraced with an almost missionary zeal, as a way to stem overpopulation and as one participant put it, to "change the history of the world."[89] The participants were impressed by clinical evidence that two IUD rings—neither of which had tails—had caused very few side effects.

When U.S. researchers set about to make IUDs, however, they added tails, since these would make it easier for paramedical personnel in the Third World to insert and remove IUDs and would allow women to check that their IUDs were still in place and had not been spontaneously expelled. The possible increased risk of infection from the tails was passed over in view of the main goal, a technical solution to the population problem. (Recent research indicates that single nylon thread tails do not pose an increased infection risk.)

The most common IUD complications are heavy bleeding and cramps, which are more likely to occur with women who have never borne a child. Faulty insertion can lead to perforation of the uterus, and in some cases to the eventual escape of the IUD into the abdominal cavity, where it can cause serious damage. Women who become pregnant while using the IUD

run a higher risk of potentially life-threatening ectopic pregnancies or septic abortions, so that although the method has a
low failure rate (3–5 pregnancies per 100 users), each IUD
pregnancy is not only a contraceptive failure, but a medical
complication. The device is not recommended for use just after
childbirth, since it can more easily become embedded in or
perforate the uterine wall.[90]

The most frequent serious long-term effect of the IUD is
infertility caused by pelvic inflammatory disease (PID), an infection of the upper reproductive tract. Women who use the
IUD run a significantly higher risk of developing PID (anywhere
from 1.5 times to 9 times, or even more, the normal risk),
possibly because bacteria enter the uterus during insertion or
move up the IUD tail, and then grow rapidly because of IUD-
related inflammation or increased bleeding. The Dalkon Shield
IUD is the worst offender—Shield users face a fivefold increase
in the risk of PID compared with women wearing other IUDs.[91]
The body fights severe PID by laying down scar tissue, which
can eventually block the fallopian tubes connecting the ovaries
to the uterus, leading to infertility. In especially serious cases
of PID, hysterectomy (removal of the uterus) is necessary. Because of the risk of infertility, the FDA recommends that young
women who have not had children should not use the IUD.[92]
It is most suitable for women who do not intend to have any
more pregnancies and have only one sex partner.

As with the pill, the IUDs side effects were virtually ignored
in the United States until Congressional hearings in 1971 finally
brought them into the open. At the hearings, Dr. John Madry,
an obstetrician-gynecologist from Florida, charged IUD advocates with excluding "uncertainties and minimizing complications in their reports." He stated: "The philosophy of most
IUD advocates is more impersonal and population-control oriented, and a high complication rate may be more readily acceptable if their goal of reducing pregnancy on a global basis
is accomplished."[93]

The hearings led to the withdrawal of the Majzlen Spring,
a particularly dangerous IUD variety, but the IUD scandals
were only beginning.

As the hearings took place, U.S. women were already falling

victim to another IUD, the Dalkon Shield. The device could rip through the uterine wall, and its wicklike tail, which physically and chemically erodes in the uterus, was an excellent conduit for bacteria. But what attracted the most attention was the number of septic abortions (abortions accompanied by toxic infection) caused by the Shield. By 1974 the FDA had recorded 287 septic abortions from IUDs, 219 of them caused by the Dalkon Shield. Fourteen Shield users had died.[94]

A. H. Robins Co., manufacturer of the Dalkon Shield, was alerted to these dangers as early as 1971, a few months after the product went on the market, when reports of adverse reactions began to come in. The company, in fact, covered up the negative results of its own studies of the Shield. A former Robins' attorney recently testified that he was ordered to burn hundreds of potentially incriminating documents in 1975, including a number relating to the wicking action of the tail string.[95]

In the expectation of declining United States sales, Robins decided to diversify its markets in 1972. According to Barbara Ehrenreich, Mark Dowie, and Stephen Minkin's exposé in *Mother Jones* magazine, one of its first initiatives was to contact the Office of Population at AID, offering a 48 percent discount on bulk packages of unsterilized Shields. Ravenholt accepted, and the Dalkon Shield was on its way to the "prime target," the women of the Third World.

Although AID maintains that it did not know of the Shield's dangers at the time, its distribution of unsterilized IUDs alone is damning evidence of the contraceptive double standard. In the United States, IUDs are sold in individual sterilized packages, along with a sterile disposable inserter. AID's unsterilized Shields were supposed to be soaked in disinfectant before insertion, but whether this procedure was rigorously followed in poorly equipped Third World clinics is open to question, especially since *only one set of instructions was attached to every 1,000 Shields.* Moreover, these were printed in only three languages—English, French, and Spanish—though the Shield was destined for distribution in forty-two countries.

Field reports from the Third World added to the mounting evidence against the Shield in the United States, but AID and the Robins Company stood firmly behind the product. Then, in 1974, FDA hearings pressured Robins to withdraw the Shield voluntarily from the U.S. market, where an estimated 2.3 million devices had already been sold.

The next year AID issued a recall. By this time 440,000 women were already using the AID-supplied device, and the thousands of Shields in remote family planning clinics were virtually irrecoverable. Ravenholt later admitted that AID "had been hearing about infections" before Robins' withdrawal of the Shield, but he shrugged them off. "Women who frequently change sexual partners have these intercurrent low-grade infections," he explained. "The IUD can't cause an infection. The body tolerates anything that's sterile."[96]

The United States courts did not agree. Spurred by publicity and the educational efforts of the National Women's Health Network, almost 10,000 Shield users filed lawsuits, which forced Robins and its insurers to pay $520 million in damages. In 1984, the Honorable Miles Lord, chief U.S. District Court judge of Minnesota, issued a powerful indictment of the company's representatives:

> Mr. Robins Jr., Mr. Forrest, Dr. Lunsford: You have not been rehabilitated. Under your direction your company has in fact continued to allow women, tens of thousands of them, to wear this device—a deadly depth charge in their wombs, ready to explode at any time. . . . The only conceivable reasons you have not recalled this product are that it would hurt your balance sheet and alert women who already have been harmed that you may be liable for their injuries. You have taken the bottom line as your guiding beacon and the low road as your route. This is corporate irresponsibility at its meanest.[97]

Robins was pressured into launching a campaign in 1984 to locate Shield users in the United States and overseas. In 1985 the company filed a controversial bankruptcy petition in order to limit its liability and set an April 1986 deadline for women filing claims. Over 300,000 claims were made from the United States and fifty other countries.[98]

The Dalkon Shield's notoriety has drawn attention away

from the way other much more common IUDs, such as the Lippes Loop, have been misused in Third World population programs. In the late 1960s, for example, with advice and financial assistance from AID and other international agencies, the Indian government promoted the Loop, which can cause heavy blood loss, as *the* mass contraceptive method in a major expansion of the country's family planning program. (The 1967–1968 Indian family planning budget was almost as large as the sum of the budgets of the previous fifteen years!)[99] In the mass campaign little effort was made even to tell women about side effects, much less to treat them, and most women were not given a medical examination before IUD insertion. While the drive was initially successful in recruiting acceptors, the Loop soon lost popularity as thousands of women developed adverse effects. The Indian Health Secretary later said: "As regards the loop, it is correct that under pressure of our foreign advisers, the program was formulated and put into operation without thinking of the effects it would have on women."[100]

Today IUD abuse persists in India. An Indian health journalist reports that in one clinic outside Bombay, women are told that their uterus is being "cleansed" when they suffer from heavy bleeding. Women face difficulties getting the IUD removed on their own request, but if their husbands complain that the bleeding interferes with intercourse, the device is promptly removed.[101]

In China not only are women X-rayed to check that their IUDs are in place, but the varieties used, especially the Mahua ring, are associated with high failure and expulsion rates, as well as a high incidence of excessive bleeding, PID, and back and pelvic pain. The Chinese varieties also do not have tails—perhaps because the government is worried that women would withdraw them. The Chinese government, with UNFPA assistance, is now shifting over to copper IUDs, which are believed to have fewer health risks.[102]

Whether the IUD is purposefully abused or not, the poor health conditions prevailing in many Third World countries exacerbate its risks and complications. The mortality rate from IUDs in the Third World is roughly *double* that in the West because of increased risk from infections, septic abortions, and untreated ectopic pregnancies.[103] Recent studies also indicate that in countries where malnutrition and anemia are common, the increased menstrual blood loss associated with IUDs leads to iron depletion in many women after twelve months of IUD use.[104]

And what about infertility? PID caused by sexually transmitted diseases is already a major health problem in many countries, and a chief cause of infertility. In parts of Africa, for example, as many as 40 percent of all women suffer from infertility. The decision to introduce the IUD into such a setting is dubious to say the least, for it can only be expected to worsen the problem.[105] While for most women infertility is a deep personal tragedy, in many societies it can also cause social ostracism, abandonment, and ultimately destitution.

Despite these risks, the IUD continues to be promoted heavily in many Third World family planning programs, not only because of its efficacy in preventing pregnancy, but because women lack control over the device. Getting the IUD removed safely requires a visit to a health clinic, which many women may find difficult to make, and once there, the doctor will not necessarily take it out. Thus, high IUD continuation rates, says the journal *Family Planning Perspectives*, "are probably a reflection of involuntary continuation."[106] This, incredibly, is considered one of the IUDs main *advantages*.

Today IUD use is declining in the West. It is now the *least* popular contraceptive in the United States, used by only 7 percent of contraceptive users. In 1986 fears of high liability suits and insurance rates led G. D. Searle and Co. to take the Copper-7, one of the most common IUDs, off the United States market; the Lippes Loop had already been withdrawn by Ortho Pharmaceutical Corporation in 1985. Now only one brand— the hormone-containing Progestasert—is still being marketed in the U.S.[107] In the future, it will be interesting to see if the absence of a U.S. market leads to an even heavier IUD hard sell in the Third World.

In conclusion, an overall pattern emerges from the history of hormonal contraception and the IUD:

- In the development of these contraceptives, the overriding goal of preventing pregnancy has led to a neglect of potential health risks.
- Safety studies have often proved less than rigorous, if undertaken at all.
- When they finally come to light, adverse effects and long-term risks such as cancer are trivialized by population agencies.
- Typically, women are not fully informed of health risks.
- In population control programs, women are not adequately screened or given follow-up care, compounding the dangers of these contraceptives. A double standard is at work that allows the pill, for example, to be distributed freely in Third World village shops, while it is available only by prescription in the West.

This pattern was not predestined. The history of hormonal contraception and the IUD might have been very different if women's welfare had been the primary concern. The time is long overdue to challenge the prevailing mentality that the womb of the individual woman is expendable in the general population control scheme of things.

▌▌

Bangladesh—Survival of the Richest

Soon after my arrival in the Bangladesh village of Katni in 1975, I experienced firsthand what the population establishment calls the "unmet need" for contraception. The village women were extremely curious about why I had no children at the ripe old age of twenty-four, and I told them about my use of birth control.

Within a few days, women who had already borne a number of children started approaching me for help—many were desperate to avoid another pregnancy. I succumbed to the pressure and visited the government family planning office in the nearby town, setting in motion a chain of events that dramatically altered my perception of Bangladesh's "population problem."

Three days after my visit to the family planning office, a government jeep sputtered down the path toward the village. Inside were two young women, who were later ushered into a small, dark house, where they were handed bamboo fans and seated in wooden chairs as a gesture of respect. About fifteen village women assembled, not only to learn about birth control but also to see the strange town women with their educated accents and fine clothes.

The family planning workers spoke about the concept of birth control but did not encourage the women to ask questions. They promised they would return in a few days with IUDs and pills for any women who wanted them. After they left, the villagers asked me if they were my sisters from America.

A week passed, then two, then three. There was no sign of the family planning workers. "When will they come back?" women asked. "We want some pills. All government officers care about is their salary. They sit in their offices and drink tea. What do they care about us?"

In response to the women's pleas, I again visited the family planning office. A few days later two women extension workers came to the village. The younger one wore a silk sari and expensive jewelry; the other was an older woman, the wife of a wealthy merchant. Another meeting was called, and this time even more women attended. The family planning workers began by insulting the village women, asking me how I could stand to live in the village "where everything is dirty and inconvenient." They chided the women for not wearing blouses, unaware that most of them could not afford them.

After this dismal start, the meeting finally turned toward birth control. The family planning workers showed the women pills, told them how to use them, and spoke about the IUD and sterilization. They neglected to tell the women about the side effects of any of these methods or how they actually worked. The village women were confused, but they took the pills the workers distributed.

Then a woman spoke up. "There's a Hindu woman in the next neighborhood who has one of those coils inside her. It hurts, and she bleeds all the time. She got it four years ago, but no one has come to see her since. She wants it taken out."

"Go and get her," the older woman commanded.

Ten minutes later a frail young woman appeared in the company of her mother-in-law. Shaking with fear, she pulled her thin white sari around her bare shoulders. There was a commotion as everyone was moved out of the house, and stray men and children lingering on the outside were driven away. After five minutes the Hindu woman emerged, clearly in pain, covering her face with her sari.

The older of the family planning women laughed. "Well, it was in for a long time," she said. "But she didn't get pregnant. Now she will, and she'll be sorry."

On that note, the family planning workers left Katni. They left behind several cartons of pills for me to distribute and promised that they would return to replenish the stock. "Are these women really Bengalis?" several women asked as the officials pulled away in a rickshaw. "They speak such a strange language."

When I returned to Bangladesh for a visit in 1982, the women to whom I had given the pill jokingly held up their newest offspring. I learned that the family planning workers had never come back. The Hindu woman who had the IUD removed was dead—no one knew the exact cause.

Despite the millions of dollars flowing into the country for population control, women's unmet need for contraception was still not being met. Should I return today, however, I would probably find that things have changed—and not for the better. Under intense international pressure, especially from AID and the World Bank, the Bangladesh government has considerably stepped up its population control efforts. Whereas before village women were neglected by Bangladesh's family planning program, now they are the targets of an aggressive sterilization drive that uses incentives and intimidation to produce results. Meanwhile, access to safe and reversible methods of fertility control is still very limited.

Today Bangladesh is a population control battlefield. Not only are poor women pitted against a powerful bureaucracy, but even the international donors are fighting among themselves.

PRIORITY NUMBER ONE

The initial pattern of population control interventions in Bangladesh is a familiar one. It began with the formation of a private Family Planning Association in the 1950s, founded by a senior police officer and funded largely from abroad, followed by a 1960 Population Council mission and culminated in the establishment of a government National Family Planning Board in the midsixties, which launched a village-level IUD and vasectomy campaign. Bangladesh's bloody 1971 war of liberation from Pakistan led to a temporary lull in these activities, but the aid money that flowed into the country after the war also washed in a new wave of population advisers.

The new government's First Five Year Plan (1973–1978) set an ambitious fertility decline goal and established a National

Population Council, which pursued a variety of strategies: integrating family planning and health services, women and development activities, social marketing schemes, and a misconceived contraceptive inundation campaign.[1]

In the end, none proved particularly effective. Administratively, the program was weak, and family planning workers lacked adequate training, motivation, and supervision. Moreover, economic conditions in the countryside were hardly conducive to a substantial reduction in the birth rate.

Nevertheless, the government's Second Five Year Plan (1980–1985) aimed to reduce the crude birth rate from 43 in 1980 to 32 by 1985, primarily by increasing the number of sterilizations through the lure of incentives.[2] Although international donors viewed this target as overly ambitious, they applauded the government's growing commitment to population control.

Unfortunately, this commitment did not extend to improving the lives of the target population, the rural poor. In fact, the acceleration of population control efforts in Bangladesh has taken place against a backdrop of declining living standards for the vast majority. Landlessness is on the rise, real wages of agricultural laborers are decreasing, and per capita food consumption is dropping year by year, so that today more than 60 percent of the population has an inadequate diet.[3]

As poverty has deepened for the majority, a small urban elite and their rural allies—the landlords, rich peasants and merchants—have tightened their control over the country's land and other resources. Billions of aid dollars, coming to Bangladesh since independence (aid currently finances three quarters of the government's development budget), have primarily benefited this wealthy minority. Outside resources have also strengthened the hand of the Bangladesh military, which has ruled the country since 1975, stifling attempts to restore democracy and initiate positive social change.[4]

Blind to their own role in bolstering the inequity that perpetuates poverty—and hence high fertility—in Bangladesh, the main international donors have opted to push full steam ahead with population control.

In March 1983, concerned that the government's population performance was not yet up to snuff, donor agencies, including AID, the World Bank, and UNFPA, circulated a position paper calling for a "drastic" reduction in population growth, the creation of an autonomous National Population Control Board with "emergency powers" and frequent visits by "high-ranking government and Army personnel" to promote family planning in the villages.[5] It also recommended increasing sterilization incentives.

Pressure intensified several months later when World Bank Vice President W. David Hopper sent a letter to Bangladesh's Minister of Finance and Planning, A. M. A. Muhith, instructing him to "outline necessary measures to strengthen the program so that agreed national population objectives could be met on time."[6]

In January 1984, the UNFPA's Dhaka representative, Walter Holzhausen, circulated an even stronger letter, implicitly endorsing compulsion. He wrote UNFPA headquarters in New York:

> Most donor representatives here greatly admire the Chinese for their achievements; a success story brought about by massive direct and indirect compulsion. . . . Talking privately to Bangladesh top officials associated with population control . . . you hear the almost unanimous view that drastic action is needed and that a new dimension needs to be added to the current "voluntary" program. . . . It is time for donors to get away from too narrow an interpretation of voluntarism and certain governments in Asia using massive incentive schemes, including disincentives and other measures of pressure, still deserve international support.[7]

Heavily dependent on foreign aid, the Bangladesh government responded quickly to these pressures, instituting a "crash program" for reducing the birth rate. It enhanced incentives for sterilization and introduced punitive measures against family planning personnel who failed to meet monthly sterilization quotas. Today President Ershad, the country's martial-law ruler, considers population control the country's number one priority, more important than boosting agricultural production, increasing literacy, improving health care, or feeding hungry children.[8]

STERILIZATION AT STARVATION POINT

The capital city of Dhaka rises from the flat, fertile river delta of Bangladesh like an oasis of affluence. The latest Japanese cars drive along its wide, smooth boulevards, the hum of their air conditioners merging with the beat of stereo cassette recorders. The rich residential areas of Gulshan and Dhanmondi, home to high government officials, businessmen, diplomats, and aid agency personnel, boast sprawling houses maintained by retinues of servants. If you travel in the right circles, foreign wine and whiskey flow freely, and if you have a color TV, you can watch the latest "soaps" from the United States. Dhaka, in fact, is making itself in the image of Dallas. It is a city on the make.

Twenty-year-old Rohima has never been to Dhaka, even though her village is only a few hours' bus ride away. She has just made one of her longest journeys ever, to a government hospital in the nearby town where she was sterilized yesterday. She is hungry—they gave her no food during her twenty-four hours' stay—but at least she now has 175 *taka*, a new sari, and a card which says that, as a sterilization acceptor, she is eligible for relief wheat. The doctor has given her a prescription, and before returning home, she goes to the pharmacy.

The medicines cost 80 *taka*, so she is left with only 95, which she spends on rice and eggs. She is eager to see her four-month-old son, her only child. When she was seven months pregnant, her husband divorced her and sent her back to her mother's house. She worked for a wealthy family husking rice, but when the floods came, there was no more work, and she had nothing to eat. Her breast milk dried up, and she had to feed her son on barley water.

When she approached the Union Council chairman for food relief, he told her, "If you have the operation, you will get wheat." Family planning workers told other destitute women in the village the same thing. No sterilization, no wheat.[9] Rohima's sterilization effectively ends her chances of remarriage, for in Bangladesh few men will marry a sterile woman.

Although Rohima has probably never even heard of the

World Bank, she has indirectly made her way onto page 22 of a 1985 Bank confidential report.[10] On that page the Bangladesh government's new population targets are matched with present and projected contraceptive "mix."* Today 34 percent of contraceptive users, or 1.6 million people, have been sterilized in Bangladesh, and the government aims to increase this percentage to 41 percent, or 3.5 million people, by the end of the decade. (So much for free contraceptive "choice.") According to the World Bank, this goal is "achievable." Achievable, its critics might add, only through the use of incentives and at the expense of poor women like Rohima.

Under the government's incentive system, each person—man or woman—who agrees to be sterilized receives 175 *taka*, equivalent to several weeks' wages. In addition, women receive a sari worth 100 *taka* and men a sarong worth 50 *taka*. Doctors and clinic staff get a special payment for each sterilization they perform, and government health and family planning workers, as well as village midwives and members of the public, receive a fee for each client they "refer" or "motivate" to undergo sterilization. The emphasis is on recruiting women clients. Until the summer of 1985, family planning workers who failed to meet monthly sterilization quotas could have their salaries withheld and ultimately lose their jobs. Lesser incentives are also offered for IUD insertions.

AID finances 85 percent of these incentives and referral fees as part of its more than $25 million annual contribution to the country's family planning program, the agency's largest bilateral population commitment in the world. AID's funding of incentives contravenes Section 104(f) of the 1982/83 U.S. Foreign Assistance Act, which prohibits the use of United States funds "to pay for the performance of involuntary sterilizations as a method of family planning or to coerce or provide any financial incentive to any person to undergo sterilization."

In Bangladesh, AID skirts the law by calling the incentives "compensation payments." It maintains that the money is intended to cover transportation, food costs, and wages lost due

---

* Contraceptive mix refers to what contraceptives are used in a program, and in what proportions.

to the operation. The free saris and lungis are justified as "surgical apparel," since the peasants' clothing is considered unhygienic. "Just look at these people, they're so dirty," said Jack Thomas, AID's deputy chief of family planning in Bangladesh.[11] In fact, the clothing is often handed out *after* the operation, giving the lie to the surgical apparel argument. Moreover, free clothing is not handed out after other forms of surgery.

In Bangladesh, where chronic hunger and unemployment are realities for much of the rural population, the distinction between compensation and incentives is no more than a semantic sleight of hand. A hungry person can buy many meals for 175 *taka*, and a new piece of clothing is a powerful inducement for a man or woman who owns only one worn-out garment. In fact, the documents of other donors, as well as of the Bangladesh government itself, freely call the payments "incentives" since they do not have to worry about complying with United States law.[12]

Not surprisingly, government figures show that the number of sterilizations have tended to increase dramatically during the lean autumn months before the rice harvest, when many landless peasants are unemployed and destitute.[13] Village surveys by Bangladeshi researchers have found that the incentives, coupled with continuing pressure from family planning workers, are instrumental in persuading many poor people to undergo sterilization.[14] Today sterilization rates are starting to fall, suggesting that the saturation level may have been reached or that disillusionment with the quality of sterilization is starting to spread.

Under what conditions are the sterilizations carried out? A 1983 study of the program by the World Bank, WHO, the Swedish International Development Authority (SIDA), and the Bangladesh government raises a number of serious concerns.

Informed consent is, officially, the basis of the sterilization program, but the reviewers found that "consent forms are not adequately filled in at most of the centers." In more than 40 percent of the centers observed, clients were "not adequately informed about the permanent nature of the operation" or about surgical procedures. The reviewers also discovered shocking standards of hygiene, and felt compelled to prepare guidelines on such basic procedures as "how to scrub the hands for operation."[15]

Under such conditions one would expect a high rate of complications from the operations, but the review team found that "case records are often not written up and complications are not recorded."[16] A Western health adviser put it more bluntly: "If people die during the operation or there is a complication, their records cards will be torn up."[17] As a result, the official death rate from sterilization operations in Bangladesh is below that of the United States, a finding the review team diplomatically calls "surprising."

Other reports suggest that complications are quite common. A survey of 950 sterilized persons in villages scattered throughout Bangladesh, undertaken by the Catholic Commission for Justice and Peace in 1985–86, found that it took over a third of the women forty-five days or more before they could resume normal work. Eighty percent of males and females had to seek some form of medical treatment after the operation, for which most of them had to pay. A fifth of them could not afford the cost. The survey also found that over half the men and a third of the women said they did not know of other methods to avoid pregnancy besides sterilization. Although under government guidelines families are supposed to have three children before undergoing sterilization, over 10 percent of the respondents had only one or two children. One man had no children at all and "accepted" because of the incentives; one woman sterilized was sixty-six years old![18]

Another recent survey by a Bangladeshi social science research organization found instances of both husband and wife being sterilized in order to collect the incentives. Many sterilization clients suffered side effects and were denied follow-up treatment. A family planning worker told the interviewers how some of her clients have been mistreated during the operation itself:

> During the operation, she [my client] felt pain and started screaming. The doctor was annoyed and asked the woman to keep quiet. But the woman kept screaming in pain and attempted to get up from the bed several times. The doctor

became very angry and hit her with his elbow on her face. He did it one more time. The woman started screaming more and more. Soon all the family planning staff entered the room and found the woman crying. Her face had marks of injuries. This kind of incident happens quite often.[19]

A 1984 investigation by the United States-based Program for the Introduction and Adaptation of Contraceptive Technology (PIACT) revealed further adverse consequences of the system. According to the study, sterilization and IUD referral fees have led to "unhealthy competition" between different categories of health and family planning workers, who vie for clients. Moreover, the lure of the fees means that other contraceptive methods are neglected; family planning workers spend half their time finding sterilization and IUD clients, local midwives virtually all of their time. They do not provide information on sterilization side effects for fear that clients might then refuse to have the operation, and they would lose their money. Aftercare services are neglected as well. PIACT also reports the existence of male agents, with no family planning background, who scour the villages for sterilization clients, sometimes "selling" them to family planning workers who need to fill monthly quotas.[20]

These official studies represent only the tip of the iceberg of sterilization abuse in Bangladesh. In 1983 the Bangladesh Army launched a campaign of compulsory sterilization in the northern district of Mymensingh. Villagers whose names had been listed by local leaders as having more than three children were forcibly rounded up by military personnel and taken in trucks to a local clinic where they were made to sign "informed consent" papers. In the space of a few weeks, over 500 people, mainly poor women including many from a minority tribal community, had been sterilized against their will. AID officials eventually exerted pressure on the Bangladesh government to halt the Army campaign. "The government knows it won't work with the Army in the long run," said AID's Jack Thomas. "There'll be a backlash."[21]

A year later such overt compulsion gave way to a more subtle strategy. In the course of monitoring flood relief in the autumn of 1984, field workers of British voluntary agencies discovered that emergency food aid provided by the U.N. World Food Program had been withheld from destitute women unless they agreed to be sterilized. Rohima was one of these women.

Cases were reported from Barisal, Jessore, Comilla, and Pabna districts. A pattern emerged of local officials issuing special cards authorizing food relief to women who were sterilized, then reneging on their promises (see Box: Sterilized for Food). Meanwhile, older women and widows, who should have been eligible for the relief wheat, received none, since they were not deemed suitable for sterilization.[22]

Official statistics would seem to substantiate these unofficial reports. According to government figures presented by the *Bangladesh Observer*, an "unprecedented" 257,000 sterilizations were performed in the flood months July–October 1984, almost one quarter of the total performed in the entire decade 1972–1982.[23]

AID, which is supposed to monitor the sterilization program closely, was not aware of the food aid abuses until alerted by outside parties. It then undertook an investigation, which suggested that "some incidents may in fact have occurred but were not widespread."

The World Bank meanwhile maintained that any abuses were probably due to "overzealous local officials" taking "undue advantage of food shortages to improve their family planning records." These agencies did, however, bring the matter to the attention of senior Bangladesh government officials, who responded by issuing a memorandum prohibiting the use of "unapproved inducements for sterilization acceptance," such as "food/grain supply."[24]

While the linking of sterilization and food aid is not official government policy, it is a logical outgrowth of the incentive/disincentive system. In Bangladesh, where millions go hungry every day, food—or the cash to buy it—is the ultimate weapon. Local officials were bound to add food aid to their arsenal sooner or later, especially since *they are under pressure themselves* to meet sterilization targets. Recent surveys indicate that not only food has been used as an inducement, but the promise of free tin roofing, medical treatment, ration cards, cows and even meat donated by Saudi Arabia, all of which never materialize.[25] And despite government pronouncements, food continues to be used as an incentive: "50 sterilized women are given wheat and money at a ceremony by the chairman Abdus Salam and doctors," reads a photo caption in a Bangladeshi newspaper on January 21, 1986.[26]

New community incentives instituted by the government reinforce this kind of behavior. For instance, local administrations who meet or exceed targets for sterilizations, the IUD, and injectables are now eligible for an award of 50,000 taka (approximately $2,000), a hefty sum by Bangladeshi standards.[27]

The incentive system also tempts officials to tamper with statistics, by, for example, listing false sterilization cases in order to receive fees. At least one donor agency has noted that this fiddling of data generates "serious management problems," which are hardly conducive to the establishment of an effective family planning program.[28]

Within the donor community, deep divisions are now emerging over the incentive system. AID and the World Bank are its main defenders. These agencies deny that abuses are inherent in the system and instead maintain that better monitoring and management are the answer. The Bank's senior population adviser, Dr. K. Kanagaratnam, goes so far as to deny that aid agencies bear any responsibility for abuses in sterilization programs which they fund. "It's not the donors' responsibility to supervise government programs," he argues. "If you buy a car from me and then run someone over, is it my fault?"[29]

Other agencies, however, are more critical. A 1985 position paper of the Swedish International Development Authority (SIDA) expresses concern that the incentive/disincentive system may lead to "indirect coercion" and contravene the principle of "free and informed choice as to contraceptive methods" universally endorsed in the U.N. World Population Plan of Action. It also warns that local elites are likely to take advantage of community incentives, increasing the risk of coercion and discrimination against the rural poor. "The more people or institutions that have economic or prestige interest in the regulation of an individual's fertility," says SIDA, "the more . . . free and informed choice will be jeopardized."[30]

SIDA, as well as other European donors, is also concerned that the incentive system detracts from the provision of basic health services. The question of health, in fact, has widened the divide between these donors and the population hard-liners.

HEARTS OF DARKNESS

In Bangladesh the shadow of disease and premature death falls especially on the young—one in every four Bangladeshi children dies before the age of five. The main cause of death is malnutrition combined with diarrheal disease. Yet Bangladesh has no national nutrition program.

The shadow also falls disproportionately on mothers. Maternal mortality rates are extremely high in Bangladesh. Unhygienic birth practices and septic abortions are leading killers, helped along by generally high levels of female malnutrition and anemia. Over half of maternal deaths could be prevented by better care. Yet most health facilities are inaccessible to poor women, and traditional midwives now spend most of their time recruiting sterilization and IUD acceptors.[31]

The result is human tragedy on a massive scale, less newsworthy than drought in Africa, car bombs in Lebanon, or war in Central America, but just as devastating.

While this tragedy is enacted in the villages, government offices in Dhaka are the venue for a bureaucratic farce. In Bangladesh's short life as an independent nation, the uneasy relationship between health care and population control has resulted in five major reorganizations of the health system, causing, according to the World Bank, "a legacy of program disruption and staff demoralization."[32] Under the current system set up in 1983, both are joined in the Ministry of Health and Population Control, with family planning and Mother and Child Health (MCH) services forming one wing and broader health services the other. At the local level health and family planning are functionally integrated, with various health personnel theoretically assuming aspects of both duties.

The shift toward greater integration of the two stems in part from the growing emphasis on sterilization and the IUD, which require clinical infrastructure.[33] While the population program has benefited from the use of medical facilities and personnel, basic health care has suffered. Spending on population control now absorbs over one third of the country's annual health budget, and its share is growing. The incentive system also lures health workers away from their basic duties. "It's virtually impossible to interest government health workers in primary health care when they stand to gain so much from sterilization fees," explained one aid official in Dhaka. The government frankly admits that family planning is the more important priority, and that MCH services especially have lagged behind.[34]

Foreign aid finances nearly half of the health budget, giving donors considerable influence over the program's direction. What has been their response to the government's emphasis on population control at the expense of health?

AID, by far the largest single donor, is in basic agreement—in fact, pressure from the agency probably helped shape government policy. According to the 1983 AID Emergency Plan for Population Control in Bangladesh, the integration of family planning with MCH services

> . . . requires unnecessarily costly and long term efforts to establish a PHC [Primary Health Care] system instead of focusing on a quick delivery of birth control services to meet the unmet demand. . . . A population control program does not depend on a functioning primary health care system.[35]

This paper rejects the proved positive association between reductions in infant mortality and increased use of birth control on the basis that Bangladesh cannot afford to wait for infant mortality to come down. This view is echoed by UNFPA's Dhaka representative, Walter Holzhausen, who writes that no one seriously believes that "Bangladesh has the money or the time to establish better MCH services and better educational facilities as a precondition for making voluntary family planning more successful."[36]

A second perspective, embodied in the World Bank approach, holds that selected MCH services can be very useful in conferring "credibility" to population control efforts. The Bank recognizes that many villagers distrust health and family planning workers because they rightly suspect that these workers are less concerned with improving human welfare than with maximizing their income from incentives, etc.

The Bank places great stock in research undertaken by the International Center for Diarrhoeal Disease Research in Bangladesh (ICDDR) on this issue. The ICDDR introduced select MCH interventions, such as oral rehydration, immunization, and basic child care measures, to its family planning program in different "packages" to see which ones have the greatest effect on increasing contraceptive prevalence rates and enhancing worker credibility. Through a series of regression equations, researchers concluded that only a minimal MCH package achieved the desired result and that further expansion of the health services was not essential to increase family planning use.[37]

The implications of the ICDDR study are chilling. For example, when oral rehydration therapy was introduced for diarrhea, the study found that this had the "negative" effect of diverting "attention away from family planning to new and complex health education and community organization activities."[38] This was especially true when the locally available salt and molasses rehydration mixture was promoted, because more training and motivation were required for this method than if villagers were simply given manufactured and more expensive rehydration packets.

In other words, a local and affordable solution to the serious problem of diarrhea is likely to be passed over because it is "disruptive" of family planning. In the end, there is not much difference between this view of health and AID's position. Concern for women and children's well-being extends only so far as MCH services help to reduce population growth. In fact, there is evidence that some private health and family planning agencies in Bangladesh are being instructed by donors to scale *down* their MCH activities in order to better concentrate on recruiting family planning clients.[39]

Fortunately, there is a third perspective among foreign officials, including representatives of the Dutch, Swedish, and Norwegian aid agencies and UNICEF, who believe that health care is a basic human right, and that curing a suffering child takes precedence over averting a brother or sister's birth. They are not against family planning; on the contrary, they believe it must be included as a voluntary part of improved and expanded health services. They are deeply worried about the present system of population control. For example, SIDA's position paper states:

> The incentives and disincentives system is likely to compete with other health services. . . . Health workers are likely to favor the activities which bring money and are set by target. . . . From the consumers' perspective, the emphasis on sterilization to the detriment of associated health objectives may result in doubts about the objectives of Government health policies and personnel.[40]

Similarly, within Bangladesh itself there are many doctors, health and family planning workers, and government officials who disapprove of the single-minded emphasis on sterilization to the neglect of basic health and the provision of a broad range of birth control choices. They have made positive moves to reform the health system, including a courageous Drug Ordinance, which bans dangerous and useless drugs and curbs the power of multinational pharmaceutical companies in the country.[41] Their influence, however, is restricted by the budgetary and political priority of population control.

In 1985 the protagonists of these three perspectives found themselves locked into battle over a World Bank-sponsored population project for Bangladesh.

DAYS AND KNIGHTS AT THE ROUND TABLE

In the bitter cold month of February 1985, representatives of the World Bank, the Bangladesh government, UNICEF, and the official aid agencies of Australia, Canada, Germany, the Netherlands, Norway, Sweden, and the United Kingdom met in Paris. Each carried a copy of a confidential World Bank draft Staff Appraisal Report, which described in detail a five-year proposed population and family health project for Bangladesh, known as Population III. The sums involved were not insignificant—the total project budget was over U.S. $270 million.

Usually such meetings serve as a rubber stamp of approval. A few concerns are raised, discussed, and incorporated so that by the end of the day donors can comfortably make their pledges and return home secure in the knowledge that the aid machine will roll forward, lubricated by a fresh infusion of funds.

This meeting was different. Politely, but in no uncertain terms, a number of the prospective donors, including the Dutch, British, Scandinavians, and UNICEF, withheld their final pledges because of concern over the incentive system, reports of sterilization abuses, and the neglect of MCH services. Both the World Bank and the Bangladesh government came under fire. These donors asked if the Bangladesh government had any plans to phase out the incentive system, and demanded assurances that disincentives, such as the withholding of salaries of family planning personnel who failed to meet targets, would be abolished soon.

For the World Bank representatives the end result of the meeting must have been a painful headache. Months of effort and thousands of dollars of consultancy fees had gone into preparing Population III. Now the multimillion dollar project was hanging in the balance, and in the months ahead anything could tip the scales.

A month after the Paris meeting, Christopher Allison, population adviser to the British Overseas Development Administration, wrote the World Bank that the British government was concerned that the Bank's controversial Staff Appraisal Report "may be intepreted as providing a tacit endorsement" of the incentive system, which he argued "has potentially greater negative than positive effects on worker attitudes, practices and performance." Allison bluntly stated that the United Kingdom "would like to see the entire system of incentives and disincentives abolished altogether."[42]

Then in May 1985 UNICEF definitively rocked the boat.

It decided not to become formally involved with the World Bank project because of reservations about the strong emphasis on sterilization. Meanwhile, the date of the next pledging meeting was postponed again and again, as all parties sought room to maneuver. According to one concerned official, donors were using the negotiations as the only way to wrest improvements in the project from the Bangladesh government and World Bank.[43]

Only days before the meeting was finally scheduled for mid-September 1985, the Swedish government pulled out of Population III because of its long-standing concern about the sterilization system. The remaining European donors meanwhile demanded more assurances that the sterilization program would be monitored and reformed. The Bangladesh government and the World Bank were in for another rough ride.

Finally, at the beginning of 1986, European donors gave their approval to the project, although most negotiated separately with the Bangladesh government and steered clear of directly funding sterilization. According to the Bank, significant reforms have been made in management and supervision systems to guard against sterilization abuse, and the Bangladesh government will undertake a comprehensive study of the incentive system to assess its effects. But for now the incentive system remains in place, and in a new twist, the World Bank project itself will finance the cost of the free clothing distributed as "surgical apparel."[44]

The issue is not likely to die, however. In Europe, Bangladesh support groups, development activists, and feminists have launched a campaign against the sterilization incentives, and the issue has been aired widely in the press. In the United States, too, pressure is beginning to mount from women health activists, including the National Women's Health Network.[45]

Meanwhile, far away in the villages of Bangladesh, malnutrition and disease continue to claim their victims, and the government responds with the same callous logic attributed to Marie Antoinette: "Let them be sterilized." This perversion of priorities is reinforced by pressure from abroad. In Bangladesh population control is a matter of life and death.

STERILIZED FOR FOOD

This is the kind of card issued to poor women who were forced to undergo sterilization in order to receive relief wheat. It was copied down by independent researchers, who omitted the woman's name and location for fear she might suffer retribution at the hands of local authorities.

CERTIFICATE

This is to certify that Mrs _____ w/o _____ vill _____ union _____ dist _____ was sterilized in the health centre today the _____ 84. She is given necessary medicines, sari and money.

She can be given the food under government relief.

Thana Family Planning Officer
_____ 1984

Sign.
Chairman
1984

Sign.
Member
1984

12

Sterilization and Abortion

Sterilization and abortion are the most controversial of birth control methods—sterilization because of its finality, abortion because it terminates pregnancy. While arguments rage over the ethics of both methods, this does not prevent their widespread use by women all over the world. This chapter looks at the crucial question of why these methods are chosen—and who makes the choice.

BARREN POLICIES

If some excesses appear, don't blame me. . . . You must consider it something like a war. There could be a certain amount of misfiring out of enthusiasm. There has been pressure to show results. Whether you like it or not, there will be a few dead people.

—DR. D. N. PAI
Harvard-educated director of family planning in
Bombay, commenting on his plans for compulsory
*sterilization (*The New York Times*, 1976)*.[1]

Today sterilization is the world's most widespread form of birth control, used by an estimated 100 million couples in 1983. In most countries female sterilization is more common than male, even though it is a more complicated and riskier operation. In the United States, the death rate from the tubal ligation operation (tying or severing the ends of the fallopian tubes) is 25–30 per 100,000 women sterilized, which compares unfavorably with almost every other form of contraception. The figure is likely to be much higher in many areas of the Third

World, and there may be long-term side effects such as heavier menstrual periods or lower back pain. Nevertheless, new female surgical methods are often billed as easy and safe—Planned Parenthood, for example, calls the "minilap" technique "Band-Aid surgery"—although they all require a high degree of technical competence.[2]

By contrast, male sterilization, called vasectomy, is relatively risk-free, yet it is common in only four countries: the United States, Great Britain, India, and China. The mortality rate from vasectomy is virtually zero in the United States, though in those Third World countries where vasectomies are performed in large "fairs" or "camps" under less than sanitary conditions, deaths from infection are not unknown. Bangladesh and India in particular have poor records in this regard[3] (see Box: Sterilization Side Effects: Unanswered Questions).

**STERILIZATION SIDE EFFECTS:
UNANSWERED QUESTIONS**

While doing field work in a village in the Indian Punjab, social anthropologist Joyce Pettigrew discovered that almost every village woman who had undergone sterilization complained of persistent pain in the pelvic area and lower back region. "After this operation we suffer so much," said one woman. "And then when we cannot work the husbands say 'go and die.' "[1]

Such complaints led Pettigrew to the tentative conclusion that the side effects of sterilization are worse for poor laboring women, whose daily tasks involve bending and stretching for long hours and who subsist on an iron-deficient diet. Because they do not have time to take rest or the facilities to bathe properly after the operation, their incisions appear to take longer to heal. The spinal anesthesia used during the operation could also contribute to lower back pain. Only one woman, the wife of a better-off farmer who was allowed to rest, had no complaint of side effects.

The conditions under which village women were sterilized also left much to be desired. In visits to government health clinics, Pettigrew found that "innumerable premises had dirty sheets over which flitted a liberal number of flies." One junior official in the health department confided that in one year alone there had been fifty deaths in the Punjab sterilization program. Other village-level researchers have reported similar findings. In South India, the Caldwells note:

> *The majority of those who have been sterilized report that they have in fact suffered debilitating effects. In their private capacity, all members of the family planning program know this but it is never reported partly because it would be regarded as non-constructive and partly because the doctors do not believe there can be a physical basis for it.*[2]

Similar reports have come from places as far afield as Bangladesh and El Salvador.[3]

Yet there appear to be no official studies of the phenomenon, perhaps for the same reasons Pettigrew found in India: "After effects were not their [the Health Ministry's] business because the government's overall aim was a restricted one—control of the birth rate at all costs."

Although vasectomy is much safer than female sterilization, there are many prejudices against it. Many men fear vasectomy will somehow affect their virility and potency, while many doctors find female sterilization more "interesting," not the least because they receive higher fees for it than for vasectomy. Most family planning programs ignore male responsibility for contraception—and hence vasectomy—an attitude that reflects the basic unequal power relationship between the sexes. Nevertheless, there are examples of successful vasectomy programs, where a real effort has been made to educate and communicate with men.[4]

Because of its permanence, sterilization has frequently been employed as a method of population control. However, there is considerable debate over its demographic effectiveness. Couples who opt for *voluntary* sterilization (in the true sense of the word) tend to have completed their family size, and in many cases already have more children than would be commensurate with a reduced rate of population growth. Thus a number of population agencies favor birth spacing methods, such as the pill, which appeal to younger couples, who ideally will have fewer children, farther between, with a more pronounced impact on birth rates.[5] Of course, there is a way to make sterilization more demographically effective—that is, to make it *involuntary*—through targeting people who have not completed their family size by means of incentives/disincentives or force.

The United States has played a major role in the introduction of sterilization into Third World family planning programs. In a 1977 interview, Dr. R. T. Ravenholt made his now famous statement that the United States was seeking to provide the means by which one quarter of the world's fertile women could be voluntarily sterilized.[6] The U.S. Agency for International Development (AID) funds the Program for International Education in Gynecology and Obstetrics, which brings foreign medical personnel to the United States to learn sterilization techniques, and the greater part of the Association for Voluntary Sterilization's (AVS) international programs budget of about $10 million.

AVS, formerly linked with the eugenics movement, works in over sixty countries. "To begin with, the philosophy of AVS had more to do with population control," says International Programs director Terrence Jezowski, "but now sterilization is viewed primarily as a human rights issue." He admits, however, that the leadership still represents "all points of view," and indeed the 1982 annual report warns strongly of the dangers of rapid population growth.[7]

Both AID and AVS insist that they support only *voluntary* sterilization programs, and ones in which other contraceptive methods are also offered in order to ensure freedom of choice. By law, AID is prohibited from financing incentives for sterilization, and AVS has a similar policy, although it can provide other forms of support for projects that use incentives. Both also insist that rigorous informed consent procedures must be part of any projects they fund. Such is the theory—but what about the practice?

As in the Bangladesh case, these agencies are often directly or indirectly involved in the support of sterilization incentives, even if they choose to call them compensation payments.

In Sri Lanka these "compensation payments" have fluctuated dramatically since 1980, from a low of 100 *rupees* to a present high of 500. Not surprisingly, each time the payment goes up, so does the number of acceptors. Despite AVS's expressed reservations about incentives, it has continued to support the Sri Lankan sterilization program after determining that higher payments were "reasonable" and did not seriously compromise the "voluntariness" of the program. The main conclusion it draws from the Sri Lankan experience is that governments should be prepared to finance incentives at the highest rate offered "in order to sustain desired levels of performance."[8]

A recent study by the Sri Lankan Family Planning Association found, however, that for almost three quarters of the acceptors, the actual compensation required in terms of lost income was less than 150 *rupees*. According to *People* magazine, this calls "into question the voluntary acceptance which should be the basis of all contraceptive sterilization."[9]

Meanwhile, AVS justifies sterilization incentives paid to medical personnel on a per case basis with the logic that they "reward personnel better for their time and energy and thus more will be willing to participate in the program."[10] In practice, however, these payments encourage personnel to neglect counseling and rush through operations, performing as many as possible within a given amount of time, in order to earn more money. This piecework approach to sterilization, in fact, lies behind abnormally high rates of complications in mass campaigns in countries such as India and Bangladesh.

Incentives are not the only means of restricting individual choice in sterilization programs. As the following Latin American case studies reveal, there are other important social dimensions to the problem.

L'Operacion: Sterilization in Latin America   The history of United States involvement in sterilization abroad began on the Caribbean island of Puerto Rico. In the 1930s, as poverty and unemployment fueled social unrest, United States colonial officials labeled overpopulation as a main cause of the "Puerto

Rican problem," conveniently ignoring their own role in generating the economic crisis. After the United States seized control of the island from the Spanish in 1898, United States sugar interests quickly moved in, evicting farmers and cattle ranchers to make way for large plantations. By 1925, less than 2 percent of the population owned 80 percent of the land, and 70 percent of the people were landless.[11]

In the 1940s, in another wave from the mainland, United States manufacturing industries began to locate in Puerto Rico, attracted by tax-free investment incentives and the prospect of cheap labor. Women were an important part of that cheap labor force, and sterilization was perceived as a way to help "free" them for employment, as opposed to, for example, providing good child-care facilities.

Both private agencies, including the International Planned Parenthood Federation (IPPF), and the Puerto Rican government, with United States government funds, encouraged women to accept sterilization by providing it at minimal or no cost. By 1968, one third of women of childbearing age had been sterilized on the island, the highest percentage anywhere in the world at that time.[12]

Many women undergoing *l'operacion,* as it is commonly called in Puerto Rico, were no doubt eager for birth control, but as Rosalind Petchesky points out, their choice of sterilization was voluntary only in a narrow sense. Not only were many women unaware that the operation was permanent, but other forms of contraception were either unavailable or prohibitively expensive. Moreover, the Catholic Church's opposition to sterilization was relatively weak compared to its outright condemnation of abortion and other birth control methods. The Puerto Rican medical establishment favored sterilization because, in the words of demographer J. M. Stycos, they "thought and still think that contraceptive methods are too difficult for lower class Puerto Rican women."[13]

Today contraceptive options are still extremely limited. The choice is between sterilization and the pill: Barrier methods and abortion are virtually unavailable.

Colombia is currently the scene of Latin America's most vigorous sterilization drive. Female sterilization is the second most popular family planning method after the pill, not surprising since these are the two methods most heavily promoted. Sterilizations are largely promoted and performed by the private Profamilia family planning organization, supported by AID, AVS, and IPPF, among others. Profamilia's executive director, Dr. Miguel Trias, famous on the population scene, has lectured the U.S. Congress on the dire consequences of rapid population growth. Trias justifies his organization's accent on female sterilization on the basis that its side effects are "negligible," the cost to the acceptor is "extremely low," and "its irreversibility puts the patient safety beyond any possible social, religious, or marital conflict."[14]

In Colombia, where illegal abortion rates are extremely high and complications common, sterilization is also presented as an antidote to abortion. "If we reduced our surgery program," says Dr. Trias, "we would stimulate an epidemic of illegal abortions."[15]

Do such factors form a solid foundation for a *voluntary* sterilization program? As in Puerto Rico, Colombian women are not outright coerced into sterilization, but their acceptance must be viewed in context. The view that the side effects of the operation are negligible means that women are not well-counseled about them. According to a British researcher who visited Colombia, "The information given about the operation is very brief; no mention is made about possible side effects or problems. The main emphasis is the economic advantages to be gained by having fewer children."[16]

Because sterilization is heavily subsidized, the cost to the acceptor is low, but this raises the question of whether the poor would prefer other methods, if they were available and low-cost as well. As Dr. Trias notes: "Any attempt to increase the recipient's cost brings about an immediate and substantial diminution in demand among the poorest people who are precisely those who need sterilization most."[17]

Not-so-subtle pressures are sometimes exerted on women to undergo the operation, especially right after giving birth. The British researcher found that women in state hospitals were told that if they consented to sterilization after delivery, they could stay in the hospital for three days instead of the normal twenty-four hours, "a great temptation to an exhausted woman with other children at home."[18]

As for abortion, is sterilization really the cure? As health activist Dr. Rodriguez-Trias points out, "Abortion is a principle cause of maternal mortality in Colombia, but instead of providing safe, legal abortion, the population people promote sterilization."[19] This is not to argue that sterilization should be eliminated from the Colombian family planning program, but its aggressive promotion raises serious questions.

The phenomenon of sterilization regret, long unrecognized and understudied, is starting to command attention. A recent WHO study of sterilized women in India, Colombia, Nigeria, the Philippines, and the United Kingdom found that from 1 to 6 percent of women regretted having the operation in the twelve month follow-up interview. (One would expect the percentage to rise as women's circumstances change, children die, etc.) The highest figures were in Colombia and India.[20] Sterilization's irreversibility, instead of placing the patient safely beyond conflict, thus may instead engender deep conflict, if the decision, made in haste or under pressure, leads later to regret.

Fortunately, in Colombia today public concern is mounting over Profamilia's methods. In 1984 reports that Profamilia contraceptives and sterilization equipment were mysteriously disappearing led the Colombian Ministry of Health to launch an official investigation into the family planning organization.

According to reliable sources, the investigation discovered lax management standards: Oral contraceptives, lost from storage at the Ministry of Health, were being sold in private pharmacies; in the process of distribution laparoscopes were landing in the hands of private physicians; and a number of seminars that had received funding had never taken place. The investigation also found definitive evidence of sterilization incentives.

Profamilia claims that doctors receive payments, not for performing sterilizations per se, but for recording each case and providing the information to Profamilia. However, when other clinical personnel demanded the payments as well, Profamilia began to give them money too. Records clearly showed that the number of sterilizations fluctuated according to whether incentives were offered or not.

Concerned about these practices, the investigatory team drew up a resolution making the Ministry of Health responsible for overseeing the country's family planning program, so that all procedures, contraceptives, and sources of finance would be carefully reviewed. Then the pressure from international agencies—IPPF and the Pathfinder Fund among them—began. They lobbied Colombian officials not to support the resolution, but despite their attempts, the resolution passed.[21]

The situation in Brazil reveals another important aspect of the sterilization debate in Latin America. There religious and official prohibitions on sterilization have forced many women to resort to unnecessary cesarean sections in private clinics in order to obtain discreet tubectomies.[22] (In general, there are many unnecessary cesareans in Brazil due to the overmedicalization of childbirth.) Poor women are paying from $10 to $50 for a sterilization, when the minimum wage is only $60 a month.[23]

Why are these women so desperate for sterilization? According to Sonia Corrêa, member of SOS Corpo, a reproductive rights group in the northeastern city of Recife, many women seek sterilization because they lack other birth control options.[24] The only contraceptive widely available is the pill, and that has typically been handed out by BENFAM, the Brazilian IPPF affiliate, without adequate counseling or follow-up care as part of population control efforts.[25]

In a survey of Recife slums, SOS Corpo found that women as young as eighteen were getting sterilized; 15 percent of the women were less than twenty-five. A number later regretted their decision, for they were unemployed and missed the company of small children or wanted to start another family if they changed partners.

Today population control efforts are intensifying in Brazil, partly as the result of pressures on the debt-ridden country by the International Monetary Fund. According to Corrêa, population agencies, in an attempt to escape regulation by the Health Ministry, are pushing for the establishment of an independent family planning program, that would emphasize sterilization over other methods. The logic is that the clinical infrastructure for sterilization is already in place. Doctors are also in favor of such a course, since they benefit financially from sterilization fees. The Brazilian Health Ministry is resisting, however, fighting instead for the integration of family planning and health services and the provision of a broad range of contraceptives.

Whatever the outcome of the struggle, sterilization is likely to become more widely available in Brazil in the years to come. If sterilization is provided within the context of the health services, as only one birth control option among many, then Brazilian women will have scored a victory. If it is promoted as the main means of population control, then the country may be headed down the same narrow road as Puerto Rico and Colombia (see Box: Is El Salvador Next?).

IS EL SALVADOR NEXT?

Journalists' reports from war-torn El Salvador point to increasing pressure on poor women to be sterilized, as part of an intensive campaign to bring down birth rates. According to British journalist Hugh O'Shaughnessy, writing in the *Observer* in 1984, "This new pressure comes at a time when social workers report an increasing unwillingness of women to be sterilized which they put down to the fears aroused by the growing death toll" in the country's civil war.[1] The sterilization campaign's organizers are the government health ministry, with the support of AID, and the Salvadorean Demographic Association, a private IPPF affiliate. Official United States population aid to El Salvador doubled between 1984 and 1985, as part of AID's new concentration on Central America.[2]

In El Salvador hospital, clinic, and field workers must now meet monthly targets of sterilizations performed. As the Demographic Association's director of information and education explained, "We expect each nurse in the field to sign up one woman for sterilization a day, and if a nurse doesn't find 300 women a year for sterilization, she falls below what we consider average."[3]

Relief workers charge that in some areas food aid is offered to poor women as an inducement to undergo sterilization, and there have been accounts of women sterilized without their knowledge after giving birth in hospitals. O'Shaughnessy interviewed one mother in a refugee camp in Tiangue who told him, "When I went to the social security hospital in San Miguel last year to have my young child the staff threatened not to give me my baby and to cut down my food if I did not agree to sterilization."[4] The woman resisted, despite these threats.

In London, IPPF has publicly responded to these charges with the claim that there is not evidence of coercion in the program, though privately staff members admit that it is virtually impossible to monitor the situation in El Salvador.

India: Something Like a War   Nowhere in the world is the continuum between restriction of choice and outright physical compulsion more dramatically exposed than in India. From the introduction of targets and incentives in the mid-1960s to the mass vasectomy camps of the early 1970s, India's family planning program, one of the first and largest in the world, consistently treated the poor recipients of its services as second-class citizens. Lack of respect translated into lack of results. Despite massive infusions of foreign and national funds, India's birth rate stubbornly refused to come down.[26]

Then in 1975 Prime Minister Indira Gandhi declared Emergency Rule. Encouraged by her son Sanjay, she decided to take action once and for all to solve the country's population problem. Civil liberties had already been suspended in 1975, and in 1976 a variety of laws and regulations on sterilization were enacted, as the central government put pressure on the states to meet sterilization quotas. Public employees' salaries were made contingent on the number of acceptors they brought for sterilization. Fines and imprisonment threatened couples who failed to be sterilized after three children, and food rations and other government services were withheld from the unsterilized.

In some cases, state governments resorted to brute force, with police raids to round up "eligible" men for forcible sterilization. In at least one case, *all* the young men of one village were sterilized.[27] It was the poor who were most often the victims of both the regulations and police violence, since the wealthy were able to buy their way out either with bribes or substitution of poor men in their places.

In the last six months of 1976, 6.5 million people were sterilized, four times the rate of any previous period. Meanwhile hundreds, if not thousands, died from infections associated with the operation, and in riots and protests against the program.[28]

Although the compulsory sterilization campaign received critical coverage in the foreign press, many members of the population establishment were slow to condemn it. When World Bank President Robert McNamara visited India during Emergency Rule, he paid tribute to "the political will and determination shown by the leadership at the highest level in intensifying the family planning drive with a rare courage of conviction." Paul Ehrlich, author of *The Population Bomb*, criticized the United States for not supporting a proposal for mandatory sterilization of all Indian men with three or more children: "We should have volunteered logistic support in the form of helicopters, vehicles and surgical instruments. We should have sent doctors. . . . Coercion? Perhaps, but coercion in a good cause." UNFPA's Dr. Joep van Arendonk, who went personally to India in 1976 to investigate the situation, still maintains that compulsory sterilization did not exist "except for a few abuses."[29]

These "few abuses," however, were enough to bring down Indira Gandhi's government in 1977 in a dramatic electoral defeat. There followed a predictable backlash against family planning: The number of sterilizations dropped to 900,000 that year.

Today India's sterilization program is back in swing. Although direct coercion is rare, other forms of pressures are brought to bear on the poor.

Carrying out research in rural South India, demographers John and Pat Caldwell and P. H. Reddy saw some of these pressures firsthand. Although the rural elite preferred to use the IUD, poor villagers were offered no other birth control alternative but sterilization in the belief that they were too ignorant to cope with anything else and that their fertility had to be controlled at all costs. According to the research team, when health workers, drawn from the elite, suggest

> the operation for the first time to a young woman with two or three children, there is little overt pressure on her or her family, but rejecting such advice . . . perhaps 20 or 30 times over a two-year period is much more difficult. This is particularly so in the Hindu society with its concepts of elite leadership and of religious virtue arising from proper social behavior. This moral pressure partly explains the rapidity with which sterilization decisions are often made. . . .[30]

Such pressure is also exerted on India's tribal minorities, even those who are in danger of extinction. While visiting a Rabha tribal village in the Indian state of West Bengal in 1982, I witnessed a government development officer putting pressure on village leaders to send women "10 to 15 at a time" to the hospital to be sterilized. I later learned that the entire Rabha tribe only numbers 2,500 people, out of a total population of 55 million in West Bengal.

Added to these pressures is the added inducement of incentives—a woman now receives the equivalent of $22 for submitting to sterilization, a man $15.[31] This differential reflects the government's policy of concentrating on female sterilization after the politically costly vasectomy abuses of the emergency. As analyst Alaka Basu explains: "What better way then than to turn to another target group—that of women—which lacked the individual and group capability to protest and which in any case was beginning to display a demand for *some* form of birth control even if tubectomy was still not its first preference?"[32] Since 1977–1978, female sterilization has accounted for 80 percent of total sterilizations, despite the fact that it is a much riskier operation than vasectomy.

More than 70 percent of the sterilizations are performed in camps, where hygienic standards are appalling. In the autumn of 1985, India was rocked by yet another sterilization scandal: In a Maharashtran sterilization camp one woman died and seventeen others were in serious condition after being given an antidiabetic drug mistaken for a pain killer. During the sterilization operation itself, the woman who died had screamed with pain since the anesthetic had not taken effect. The doctors had paid no attention. "The family planning program is beginning to resemble a giant, over-developed and hyperactive limb growing out of an inefficient health system which is incapable of supervising and controlling it," comments an editorial in a prominent Indian weekly.[33]

Today there are ominous signs that India's new Prime Minister, Rajiv Gandhi, may embrace the population cause with the same zeal as his mother and brother. He has declared population control India's Priority Number One, and his government is considering implementing significantly higher incentives for couples who agree to be sterilized after having two children. Funding for population control is due to triple.[34]

Is there no alternative? One wonders what would happen if the Indian government simply took the sensible and humane step of providing decent health and voluntary family planning services to its people, instead of herding poor women like cattle into sterilization camps. Not only might human suffering be greatly alleviated, but the birth rate might actually come down.

The United States Parallel   Today sterilization is the most widely used method of birth control in the United States,[35] but, as in many parts of the Third World, sterilization "choice" often takes place in a restrictive context. This is especially the case for poor white, black, Hispanic, and Native American women who lack access to other birth control methods and/or who are the victims of racially motivated designs to limit their numbers. Their choice was further restricted in 1977 when public funding of abortion was virtually eliminated, although sterilization continues to be covered in Medicaid programs for up to 90 percent of the cost.[36]

Poor women and women of color are frequently subjected unnecessarily to hysterectomies, a much more dangerous form of sterilization, with mortality risks fifteen to twenty times higher than those for tubal sterilization and significant long-term ill effects.

Why are these women given hysterectomies? "In most major teaching hospitals in New York City, it is the unwritten policy to do elective hysterectomies on poor black and Puerto Rican women, with minimal indications, to train residents," explained the director of obstetrics and gynecology at a New York municipal hospital.[37] Doctors are also paid more for hysterectomies than for tubal ligations.

Compulsory sterilization also has a long history in the United States, with the focus on the mentally retarded, prison inmates, and ethnic minorities. In the famous Relf case in the early 1970s, when two young black teenagers in Alabama were sterilized without their consent or knowledge, a federal district court found that there was

> uncontroverted evidence in the record that minors and other incompetents have been sterilized with federal funds and that an indefinite number of poor people have been improperly coerced into accepting a sterilization operation under the threat that various federally supported welfare benefits would be withdrawn unless they submitted to irreversible sterilization.[38]

In 1976, the U.S. General Accounting Office revealed that the federally funded Indian Health Service had sterilized 3,000 Native American women in a four-year period using consent forms "not in compliance . . . with regulations."[39]

These and other abuses led feminists and health activists to campaign for more stringent sterilization regulations in the United States. The first victory was won in New York City in 1975, when stricter guidelines were enacted, which later formed the basis of federal sterilization reform. These include more rigorous informed consent procedures, a thirty-day waiting period between consent and the actual operation, a prohibition on hysterectomies for sterilization purposes, and a moratorium on federally funded sterilizations of minors, the involuntarily institutionalized, and the legally incompetent.[40]

These measures have met harsh opposition not only from medical quarters, where doctors fear loss of control, but from population agencies. In seeking to relax regulations for the sterilization of the mentally handicapped, AVS, for example, states, "protection against involuntary pregnancy is as much an individual right as is protection against involuntary sterilization."[41] But to weigh these two rights against each other is highly misleading. There are other ways to avoid pregnancy besides sterilization, and even if an unwanted pregnancy does occur, there are the alternatives of abortion and adoption. Sterilization ends forever the capacity to bear children.

There is a place for sterilization, without pressure or incentives, with full knowledge and informed consent. In the right hands it can be a powerful tool of reproductive freedom. In the wrong hands it is an intrusive act of physical violence, no matter how clean the surgeon's gloves or the consciences of the donors from abroad.

A WOMAN'S RIGHT TO HER LIFE

Abortion is murder.
　—*slogan of the antiabortion movement in the United States*

A woman's life is a human life.
　—*slogan of prochoice activists*

Despite the controversy surrounding it, abortion should not be viewed in isolation from other contraceptive methods, since it is ideally a complement to them. No contraceptive method is entirely effective. The backup of safe abortion—the termination of a pregnancy by extracting the fetus—provides an important insurance against contraceptive failure and allows women to use safer but sometimes less effective methods such as barrier contraceptives and natural family planning. If all women were guaranteed access to safe, cheap, legal abortion, the profile of contraceptive use might very well shift from riskier but more effective varieties.

Denying women the right to abortion makes women bear all the hardship and blame for unwanted pregnancies, ignoring the fact that men bear responsibility too, and that many unwanted pregnancies result from unwanted intercourse. For many women, and especially for the young, an unwanted pregnancy can alter irrevocably the course of their lives, closing off options, forcing them into marriages they do not want, or making them raise a child without social and material support. No woman wants an abortion if she can help it, but sometimes it is the only way out.

Legal abortion performed within the first three months of pregnancy is relatively safe, with a lower death rate than from the use of oral contraceptives or even from a simple tonsillectomy.[42] Nevertheless, it is not entirely risk-free, and possible complications, especially infection, are likely to be higher where antiseptic conditions are not maintained.

The vacuum aspiration method in particular has a good safety record and appears to have no adverse effect on fertility, for the first or even second such abortion. To avoid the word "abortion," vacuum aspiration is euphemistically termed menstrual regulation (MR) when its use is limited to the first few weeks after a missed period. MR has become very popular in a number of Third World countries, where, strictly speaking, abortion is illegal.[43] Although it is the safest of all methods, MR is not mentioned in most medical textbooks in the United States and is unavailable in most hospitals.

The controversy surrounding abortion is a relatively recent phenomenon. In most societies, abortion has been used for centuries as a common fertility control method, tolerated implicitly, if not explicitly, by social custom and law. Traditional European, British, and United States common law, for example, allowed abortion before "quickening," the noticeable movement of the fetus usually during the fifth month of pregnancy. Even the Catholic Church was relatively tolerant of early abortion—not until 1869 did Pope Pius IX declare all abortion to be murder.[44]

Historically, society's view of abortion has reflected changing perceptions of the medical profession and the role of women. In the United States, for example, as medical practice became more institutionalized in the late nineteenth century, doctors sought to secure a monopoly over the practice of medicine and medical technology through an attack on irregular practitioners, such as midwives and women healers, who provided abortion services. At the same time Victorian morality was gaining ground: Middle-class women were relegated back to the home, where their main mission in life was to produce children. Abortion became criminalized, separated from its original context of birth control.[45]

Today as a conservative backlash sweeps many Western countries, women are once again being told that their place is at home with their families, though "home" is hardly the safe refuge it is made out to be. Denying women access to abortion is part of that process; even where abortion is legal, women are made to feel it is a crime. There are many people, of course, who have sincere moral and religious objections to abortion, but it is important to point out that not all of them are Right to Lifers. Many feel that, although they would not choose abortion personally, it must be up to each individual woman to make that choice.[46]

On the international stage, the United States government is leading the attack against abortion, despite its legality in the United States. All foreign nongovernmental organizations that receive funds originating from AID must sign an infamous clause certifying that they will not perform or actively promote abortion as a family planning method. This extends to counseling and referral services as well. Many pro-choice family planning officials jokingly refer to abortion as that "unmentionable word." Indeed, agencies receiving U.S. funds have even had to clear their libraries of any books on abortion, and AID-funded journals are noticeably silent about this common form of fertility control. The Reagan adminstration's attack on abortion resembles the book burning of the 1930s and reflects a deep political cynicism. In order to win the domestic anti-abortion vote, the White House and conservative congressmen are willing to deny Third World women access to desperately needed safe abortion facilities.

In many countries, illegal abortion is a leading cause of death for women in their childbearing years. Could it not be said that denying women the right to safe abortion is itself a form of murder?

Abortion and Fertility Control Despite the development of social sanctions against abortion, it continues to play a major role in fertility control the world over. Abortion has been an important factor in the initial stages of most demographic transitions, in countries as diverse as the United States, the Soviet Union, and Korea. In fact, according to one text on abortion, "No human community has ever shown a marked fall in its birth rate without a significant recourse to induced abortion."[47]

In many countries its incidence declines over time as other contraceptive practices become more widely available, though it remains an important recourse in the event of contraceptive failure or lack of access to alternatives. In some areas, notably Japan, the Soviet Union, and Western Europe, it continues to be a chief means of fertility control.[48]

Today 10 percent of the world's population live in countries where abortion is prohibited without exception and another 18 percent where it is permitted only to save the life of a pregnant woman. These include most of the Muslim countries of Asia, two thirds of the countries of Latin America, and much of Africa. Only 39 percent live in countries where abortion is freely available on request during the first trimester of pregnancy.[49]

Whether or not abortion is legal has remarkably little to do with its incidence, however. Half the annual 30 to 50 million abortions worldwide are estimated to be illegal, and many of these are in conservative Catholic countries. Women have traditionally sought abortion when they need it, regardless of the law. The crucial difference legality can make is in *safety*.

In some places, such as South Korea and Hong Kong, high illegal abortion rates appear to have resulted in very few casualties,[50] but in general legalization of abortion leads to significant reductions in mortality. In the United States, for example, prior to legalization in 1973, an average of 292 women died per year from induced abortion. In 1973 the figure fell to 36.[51]

Legalization does not automatically guarantee access to safe abortion for all sectors of the population, however, because of geographical, political, and financial constraints. In many Third World countries, and in the West, abortion facilities are few and far between. Many hospitals and physicians refuse to provide them, and even if they are available, poor people often cannot afford them. In the United States abortion, which costs over $200, was put beyond the reach of many women with the passage of the Hyde amendment to health appropriation legislation prohibiting federal Medicaid funding of abortion. Just one month after the amendment went into effect in 1977, a young Mexican American woman, Rosie Jimenez, died with her Medicaid card in her purse from a cheap illegal abortion performed in Mexico.[52]

Legalization is thus only the first step in making safe abortion a real option; spreading low-cost services is the other.

Although most women choose voluntarily to have an abortion, like other contraceptives, it too can be used as an instrument of population control. The most dramatic case is China, where women have been pressured to abort unsanctioned pregnancies even at very late stages. In England and the United States, poor women seeking abortion are sometimes sterilized at the same time, without their full informed consent. "Unless we get those tubes tied before they go home," said one U.S. doctor, "some of them will change their minds by the time they come back to the clinic."[53] Rates of sterilization regret and physical complications are typically higher in post-abortion sterilization.

In some Third World countries, IUDs are inserted in women appearing in hospitals as the result of complications from illegal abortion. Although at such times, contraceptive counseling would no doubt be useful, inserting an IUD, with its high risk of uterine infection, is a very questionable procedure to say the least. In India women have been denied abortions in clinics unless they first agreed to the IUD.[54]

In Bangladesh the general liberalization of abortion has taken place within the context of coercive government population control policies. While welcoming the liberalization, some members of the health community worry that abortion could be misused, and caution that successful abortion services require "good practical training, motivation of the workers, and careful continued supervision—qualities which have been lacking in government programs to date."[55]

In a model clinic set up by the Pathfinder Fund and in several other facilities in Bangladesh, menstrual regulation has proved very popular, more popular in fact than any other contraceptive method. Given its apparent acceptability to women, it is a sad irony that this method is now under attack. The Pathfinder Fund no longer supports abortion services in Bangladesh, or anywhere, because of the threatened cutoff of AID funds.

In the present conservative climate, those family planning agencies which are heavily dependent on United States government funds are doing the best they can to disassociate themselves from abortion. Their position is that they offer contraceptives as an *alternative* to abortion. Even the IPPF, which (aside from its Western Hemisphere office) has suffered a cutoff of United States funds because of its refusal to deny funding of abortion services, takes an extremely cautious public stance toward abortion.[56]

Several major private foundations are now defending and supporting abortion services, however. Hewlett, Ford, and Mellon, for example, provide financial support to the International Women's Health Coalition, which aids women-run reproductive health care and abortion services overseas. The Swedish government is also stepping into the breach to support abortion services in Bangladesh and elsewhere.

Population "Quality" Control Today the abortion issue has taken on a new dimension with the development of reproductive technologies that can identify sex and certain genetic defects such as Downs Syndrome and spina bifida in the early stages of pregnancy. This has already led to the selective abortion of female and disabled fetuses. The Chinese, for example, have developed a method of determining the sex of the fetus from cells removed by suction after only seven weeks. In the first Chinese tests, of thirty women who chose to have abortions, twenty-nine aborted female fetuses, at which point the procedure was stopped.[57]

In India, amniocentesis, commonly used to screen for a number of genetic abnormalities, is instead being used to determine sex. As in China, the fetus is aborted if it is a girl. Such a procedure must be seen in the context of "son preference" and the widespread oppression of Indian women of all classes.

India is the only country in the world where the ratio of women to men has been declining, down from 972 females per 1,000 males in 1901 to around 935 today. Despite the fact that the female child is biologically stronger at birth, in India female infant mortality is higher than male, because daughters tend to receive less food and health care than sons. Female infanticide is also practiced in certain localities, mainly because poor parents fear they will not be able to afford high dowry payments.[58]

The selective abortion of female fetuses is simply a "cleaner" method of female infanticide. The women who decide to undergo it usually do so because they are under intense pressure themselves, threatened by the ongoing hostility of their in-laws or the prospect of divorce if they bear yet another daughter or fail to conceive a son. Outrage over the procedure has mounted in India since the exposé of a clinic which publicly advertised sex selection, but it nevertheless continues throughout the country. Even poor villagers are saving up money for the procedure.[59]

There is a very real danger that in countries like India sex selection could become an established method of population control. In a 1984 seminar in Bombay, one family planning official stated that "desperate measures" were needed to address India's "explosive" population problem, and condoned sex-selective abortion. And even as far back as 1974, Dr. D. N. Pai, Bombay's former family planning director of compulsory sterilization fame, gave his approval to sex selection.[60] One shudders at the implications of such views.

Although instances of sex selection are not unknown in Western countries, amniocentesis and other new reproductive technologies are more typically used to identify genetic defects, with the expectation that women will abort any defective fetuses. These technologies pose very difficult ethical dilemmas.

As women with disabilities have pointed out, the decision to abort a disabled child is influenced by a number of factors besides purely personal ones. In a society like the United States, for example, where the media sells an image of health that only the affluent young can hope to fulfill, fears about raising a disabled child may be way out of proportion to the facts, or far greater than they would be in a more compassionate environment. As one disabled woman describes:

> There is tremendous pressure upon us to have "perfect babies." Do we want a world of "perfect people?" I really wonder what are the human costs of attempts to control our differences, our vulnerability. I believe that if women are to maintain our "choice" we must include *the choice to have a disabled child.*[61]

In the years ahead, the new reproductive technologies and medical advances in prenatal and neonatal care are likely to bring the issue of eugenics back into the population arena.

In the last analysis, today's controversy over abortion is misplaced. Whether or not abortion should occur is really not the issue. It will occur, no matter how many bombs are thrown at abortion clinics, how many dollars the United States government withholds from family planning organizations, how many times the Pope condemns it, or how widely other forms of contraception are distributed. Unwanted pregnancies may decline, but they will not vanish altogether.

Instead, the vital questions regarding abortion are these:

- whether it is legal, safe, and accessible, or illegal and dangerous.
- whether it is abused as an instrument of population quantity or quality control, or used as a tool of reproductive choice.

Properly performed, abortion is a woman's safety net and one of the most important reproductive rights of all.

13

Barrier Contraceptives and Natural Family Planning

The contraceptive revolution of the 1960s and 1970s brought the pill, the IUD, the injectable, and the implant, all extremely effective forms of reversible contraception if used correctly. Yet despite the millions of dollars poured into research, that revolution did not bring real improvements in contraceptive safety. On the contrary, the health risks of these methods are considerable and are compounded by their misuse in population programs.

Today there is a need for a second contraceptive revolution. "Without giving up the high effectiveness, convenience, and relatively low cost of today's contraceptives," write Judith Bruce and S. Bruce Schearer, "tomorrow's contraceptives must be safe in both the short and long-term; fully reversible and free of effects on future fertility . . . on breast-feeding infants and on lactation."[1]

The irony is that such methods *already* exist, in the form of barrier contraceptives—spermicides, condoms, diaphragms, cervical caps—though there is great need and scope for their improvement. Yet these safe, simple, reversible contraceptives are unavailable in many, if not most, Third World family planning programs, and in Western countries also people are often discouraged from using them.

Such was my experience in Bangladesh, where I myself used the diaphragm, brought from abroad. Despite the diaphragm's drawbacks, I would have felt more comfortable if I had been able to offer it, or spermicides, as an option to the village women, instead of just distributing the pill. But the choice was not there.

In neighboring India it was the same story. If you were

rich and lived in a big city, then you might be able to find one or two pharmacies that stocked female barrier methods such as the diaphragm or cervical cap. But even if you did, as one Indian author writes, "It is doubtful if doctors here would even know how to fit a woman with one of these devices. . . ."[2]

The same complaint was voiced over and over again at the 1984 Women's International Tribunal on Reproductive Rights in Amsterdam. The tribunal was told, for example, that while the IPPF vigorously promoted the pill and sterilization in Costa Rica, there was not one diaphragm to be had in the country.

Within the population community, the prejudice against barrier contraceptives runs deep. "The diaphragm was useful in the Western world when services had to be based in clinics and before IUDs or pills were invented," wrote Dr. Malcolm Potts, one of the most prominent researchers in the field, in 1976. "It is a Model-T Ford, still running in a few places, but insignificant at a world level."[3]

Are barrier methods really so anachronistic and insignificant—or could they be the foundation of a second contraceptive revolution, in which health and safety come first?

BARRIER METHODS REVISITED

The needs of millions of men and women throughout the world are being neglected because of a one-sided concentration on high technology birth control methods.

—JUDITH BRUCE *and* S. BRUCE SCHEARER, 1984[4]

Unlike antique cars, barrier methods are still used by many people today. During the first half of the twentieth century, the diaphragm and condom were the most common forms of contraception in the United States. Although their use declined with the development of the pill and IUD, barrier methods are on the rise again, as more and more people grow wary of the side effects of modern methods and want to protect themselves against sexually transmitted diseases (STDs). A survey in the United States found that among couples who wanted children later, the use of the pill had fallen from 61 percent of such couples in 1973 to 45 percent in 1982, while in the same period diaphragm use more than doubled, from 16 percent to 34 percent. Nevertheless, the diaphragm and other barrier methods continue to be discriminated against in U.S. family planning programs. A recent study found that when giving information to clients, family planning staff overrate the pill and IUD in terms of effectiveness and underrate barrier methods, thus biasing people against them.[5]

In Third World countries, knowledge and use of female barrier methods remains very low. Sample surveys reveal that typically only 1 to 5 percent of women contraceptors use them, except in rare exceptions such as Trinidad and Tobago, where the figure is 10 percent. The condom, however, is more widely used. In Fiji, Korea, Pakistan, Singapore, Barbados, Jamaica, and Trinidad and Tobago, for example, over 15 percent of contraceptors use the condom. In Japan the figure has reached as high as 75 percent, in part because condoms are readily available throughout the country, and male responsibility for contraception is a cultural norm.[6]

What are the advantages of barrier methods? Unlike hormonal contraceptives and the IUD, they cause no known major side effects. When used with the backup of legal abortion, *they are the safest by far of all reversible contraceptives in terms of mortality risks.*[7] They do not cause any delay in or risk to fertility after cessation of use and, in addition, help to protect users from a number of sexually transmitted diseases, which are a primary cause of infertility and morbidity in many parts of the world. They may also reduce the risk of acquiring cervical cancer, while hormonal methods may increase it (see Box: AIDS and Barrier Methods).

AIDS AND BARRIER METHODS

There is still no cure for AIDS, acquired immune deficiency syndrome, the deadly sexually transmitted disease that destroys the body's immune system. In the United States the two groups most at risk of acquiring AIDS are homosexual men and intravenous drug users, but new research indicates that the virus is also being spread through male-female sexual relations. In Africa the primary means of AIDS transmission is believed to be heterosexual contact. The disease has already reached epidemic proportions in Zaire, Zambia, Rwanda, and Uganda.[1]

While there is still no cure for AIDS, barrier contraceptives may help prevent its sexual transmission and could potentially be one of the most important means to contain the AIDS epidemic. It is highly likely that the simple condom prevents the transmission of the AIDS virus. Under laboratory conditions, the condom has already proved impenetrable to two other viruses of similar dimensions, herpes simplex virus type 2 and cytomegalovirus.[2] In the United States fear of AIDS and other sexually transmitted diseases has led to a boom in condom sales. Forty percent of the buyers are women.[3]

However, given the condom's documented failure rate of 1 to 2 percent, it alone cannot provide full protection against AIDS. Instead scientists believe that better protection may be attained if condoms are used together with spermicides. In one study, nonoxynol-9, one of the most common spermicidal agents, has inactivated the AIDS virus in vitro.[4] Other in vitro studies of spermicides indicate that they may be effective against a broad range of sexually transmitted diseases, including gonorrhea, trichomonas, herpes, and candida.[5]

The Contraceptive Evaluation Branch of the U.S. National Institute of Child Health and Human Development is currently planning to sponsor a clinical trial where a group of people at high risk of contracting AIDS will use condoms, diaphragms, cervical caps, and lubricants and spermicides containing high concentrations of nonoxynol-9 to see if the combination of these methods prevents transmission of AIDS. The trial will also study if barrier contraception plays a role in retarding the development of AIDS in an already infected person by limiting reexposure to the virus.[6]

If barrier methods do prove effective against AIDS, the profile of contraceptive use could change dramatically in the United States. Whether the population establishment will reverse its long-standing prejudice against the use of these methods in the Third World is another matter, however. In Africa particularly, promoting barrier methods may make eminent sense in terms of public health, but will the methods still be considered too ineffective in terms of reducing population growth?

The WHO has endorsed barrier methods as particularly suitable for lactating mothers, since they do not affect either milk quality or quantity. They may also be especially appropriate for the increasing numbers of sexually active unmarried young people throughout the world, who are either unwilling or unable to get contraceptives through formal channels and who face a high risk of sexually transmitted disease.[8]

And the disadvantages? Recently there has been some concern that spermicides may cause a higher rate of miscarriage and birth defects among women who continue to use them after conception, though studies suggesting such links have been found to be flawed.[9] There have also been incidences of toxic shock syndrome in women who have left the diaphragm or new contraceptive sponge in place for extended periods of time. According to a recent study, diaphragm users experience a higher rate of urinary tract infections.[10]

The primary criticism leveled against barrier methods, especially from population control quarters, is their high failure rate. According to *Population Reports,* for example, female vaginal methods "are less effective than oral contraceptives, IUD's, and voluntary sterilization."[11]

Yet, in reality, the clinical data on the performance of barrier methods varies widely, ranging from a pregnancy rate of 2 per 100 users per year, comparable to the pill and IUD, to a high of 30. What accounts for such a difference?

Most studies show that long-time, experienced users of barrier methods have more success in preventing pregnancy. According to Bruce and Schearer, successful use also depends on "full information, competent instruction and follow-up support."[12] Because barrier methods must be used with each act of intercourse, their efficacy requires cooperation between partners.

When comparing how effective barrier methods are in relation to other reversible contraceptives, it is important to remember that in many Third World countries high pregnancy rates result from improper use of the pill. And in terms of continuation rates, the side effects of the pill, IUD, and injectables cause from 40 to 70 percent of users of these methods to abandon them within two years. In fact, fear of adverse effects prevents from one third to one quarter of married women of reproductive age from using any contraceptives at all![13] Even in population control terms, the modern "miracle" methods are not that effective, so why, then, are barrier methods the subject of so much scorn?

The prejudice against barrier methods has several roots. First, poor people, especially the illiterate, are alleged to be too embarrassed and ignorant about their bodies even to attempt to use them. Second, the methods are deemed "inconvenient," "awkward," and "intrusive." In many settings they may be difficult to wash, store, and dispose. Third, their use requires that the couple be willing and able to cooperate with each other; a woman cannot use barrier methods surreptitiously, like Depo-Provera. Last, but not least, many population people argue that it takes too much time and resources to educate people about them and to provide adequate follow-up.

Do these arguments really add up to a decisive case against barrier methods? Many problems could be overcome if the methods were introduced with sensitive instruction and follow-up and a stress on joint male-female responsibility for contraception. Sanitation, storage, and disposal problems, though difficult, are not insurmountable. As for costly education and follow-up, shouldn't family planning programs devote resources to these crucial activities in the case of *all* contraceptives?

To the limited extent that barrier methods have been introduced in Third World family planning programs, it is not surprising that they have sometimes proved less effective than the so-called modern techniques. As Bruce and Schearer explain, biases against barrier methods tend to be self-fulfilling:

> The policymakers' prophecies of the incompetence of poor women are confirmed by the results that occur when barrier methods are introduced with little or no understanding of rural women's culture, and without thorough education and follow-up.[14]

More often than not, barrier methods are simply not made available or are promoted with far less enthusiasm than the pill, IUD, or sterilization. *Population Reports* notes that negative "providers' attitudes" are instrumental in restricting access to them, and that their popularity might well increase if their benefits were stressed.[15]

Indeed, there are a number of encouraging examples of the successful promotion and use of barrier methods in Third World settings. A Bombay clinic achieved an effectiveness rate of 90 percent for the diaphragm among women who maintained contact with the clinic, and success was not correlated with variations in income level, education, or availability of tap water. The foaming spermicidal tablet, Neosampoon, which requires no special application, is heat-resistant, and can be sold individually, has proved effective and popular in studies in Bangladesh and Egypt.

In a number of countries, among them Thailand, Jamaica, Indonesia, Korea, Colombia, Sri Lanka, India, and Bangladesh, the vigorous promotion of condoms through both commercial channels and family planning programs has led to a significant increase in use.[16] Unlike the pill, condoms and spermicides are well-suited to mass distribution schemes, since they do not require medical supervision.

Even if barrier methods were to prove only moderately effective or personally acceptable, they could be an important option for women who want to space births, who have access to safe abortion, or who are disillusioned with other contraceptives. At the very least, people should have the *choice*.

Donor agencies have played an important role in restricting that choice. For example, while AID has provided an average of 8.5 *million* women with oral contraceptives every year since 1974, it gave an average of only 25 *thousand* diaphragms per year between 1978 and 1982. In 1978, in fact, it provided *no* diaphragms at all.

AID's record is better on the condom (144 million per year) and foaming tablets, though their supply too falls way short of the pill.[17] The rationale given for this bias is that AID and other agencies are simply responding to requests from Third World family planning programs, and if there is not much demand for barrier methods, then why should they provide them?

As we have seen, however, contraceptive demand is heavily

influenced by the donor agencies themselves. If barrier methods were promoted with the same determination as the pill, IUD, injectable, and sterilization to governments and family planners, the contraceptive experience of many people might be very different indeed.

The bias against barrier methods in family planning programs is matched by their neglect in contraceptive research. Two United States agencies, the Contraceptive Development Branch of the National Institute of Child Health and Human Development and the AID-funded International Fertility Research Program, have made the greatest public sector investments in barrier research. However, neither of the two major international research programs, those of the WHO and the Population Council, is devoting *any* resources to barrier R&D.[18] As a result of systematic exclusion from research programs, barrier technology has stagnated; many of its current drawbacks reflect what Bruce and Schearer call an "unnecessary obsolescence."[19]

Yet in the field of barrier technology, even minor improvements could make a major difference in terms of acceptability. Says Dr. Gabriel Bialy, head of contraceptive development at the U.S. National Institutes of Health (NIH), "We feel that if we can make the techniques easier to use, women will take to them."[20]

Despite the low level of resources, there are already several promising new developments:

Spermicides Research has been underway in recent years to develop more effective spermicidal chemicals and better and more convenient ways to apply them. In 1984, AID began purchasing a new foaming tablet manufactured by Ortho under the trade name Conceptional.[21]

The Diaphragm Current areas of research include spermicide-impregnated, disposable diaphragms, which reduce messiness and which are effective for up to twenty-four hours, a one-size-fits-all diaphragm, and a diaphragm with a thick, compressible outer ring which could reduce the need for costly spermicides. New devices should be available within the next several years.[22]

The Sponge   In 1983, the Today vaginal sponge, impregnated with spermicide and effective for twenty-four hours, was released on the United States market by a small company in California. Despite its disadvantages—a relatively high pregnancy risk, several cases of toxic shock syndrome associated with its use, and fears of the carcinogenic potential of the heavy dose of spermicide—it is now the leading over-the-counter female contraceptive method in the United States, with sales four times greater than the company had originally anticipated.

Sponge research was funded in large part by AID and the National Institutes of Health. However, in 1984 AID's chief of contraceptive research, James Shelton, was not enthusiastic about its application in the Third World, not only because of efficacy and safety concerns, but because "the cost is high and the product bulky." Yet mass production could bring the sponge price down, and as one Indian health writer asks, "If the pill and injectable can be subsidized for mass use, why shouldn't a safe and noncontroversial sponge be subsidized to reach the same masses?"[23]

High hopes accompanied the introduction of the sponge, and even though it has not turned out to be the perfect product, it shows the great demand for new female barrier methods. It is ironic that it took until the late twentieth century to apply modern research to a method that was in existence thousands of years ago.

The Cervical Cap   The cervical cap, a thimblelike device which stays in place by suction, has suffered years of neglect by contraceptive researchers. In the 1920s and 1930s more then fifty types of cap were marketed in Europe, but now only several exist. Until recently, the cap was not approved for widespread use in the United States; instead it was imported from Europe as an "investigational device." When author and health activist Barbara Seaman approached the Ortho Company about reviving cap manufacture in the United States, the company told her it was out of the question since it "is a low-profit item, which might cut spermicide sales."[24] Indeed one of the cap's advantages is that it requires less spermicide and can be left in place for longer periods of time than the diaphragm.

Pressure from U.S. women health activists led the FDA to undertake studies of the cap, with thirty women's clinics and health projects participating. According to Rebecca Chalker, author of the *Complete Cervical Cap Guide*, 40,000 women in the United States have used the cap over the last nine years. The studies indicate that the cap is as effective as the diaphragm and many women prefer it over that method. The FDA is expected to approve the Prentif Cavity Rim Cap in the summer of 1987, after which it should be available in Planned Parenthood clinics.[25]

The implications for Third World family planning programs are unclear, since up to now the cap has not figured at all in the contraceptive mix offered by donors. However, the case of the cervical cap illustrates that feminists and health activists can have an impact and that there are possibilities not only for confrontation but for cooperation with the contraceptive research establishment.

The Condom Today there are virtually *no* public or private sector research projects to improve the condom, despite the fact that it is one of the most widely used forms of contraception and the only reversible method available to men. The technology could greatly benefit from the development of a membrane that would provide better heat and tactile sensitivity to users, but what little research there is concentrates only on cosmetic changes.[26] More variation and sizes are available in Europe and Asia, however.

There has also been hardly any research on enhancing the ability of barrier contraceptives to prevent sexually transmitted diseases, by incorporating effective antibacterial agents into spermicides, for example. Such a development could bring major public health benefits for men and women everywhere. Moreover, most research on barrier methods has focused on their use in industrialized countries; almost no work is being done on making them more suitable to Third World settings by, for example, improving their ability to withstand heat and humidity.[27]

In the past few years, public pressure and consumer demand have helped to increase funding for barrier research from a few isolated drops to a slow trickle. Within the population establishment too attitudes are slowly beginning to change. In a 1981 article, Malcolm Potts reverses his negative attitude toward barrier contraceptives, recognizing the "positive health implications" of their use, especially with the backup of legal abortion. He and his coauthor criticize the emphasis contraceptive researchers and family planning providers have put on contraceptive "effectiveness" and point out that in the case of the pill and IUD a high degree of effectiveness is associated with serious side effects. Higher continuation rates on barrier and traditional methods also mean that their effectiveness compares favorably with the pill and IUD when viewed over the long term.[28]

Although these are hopeful signs, much more positive action is needed now, if the tide is to be turned and barrier methods are to occupy the prominent place they deserve in contraceptive technology.

THE NATURAL WAY

Like barrier methods, natural family planning (NFP), or periodic abstinence as it is also called, provides an important alternative to hormonal and surgical forms of birth control. Natural family planning involves a woman identifying the fertile and infertile periods in her monthly cycle by employing the following techniques: the calendar or "rhythm" method, which charts the time of ovulation according to the pattern of a normal menstrual cycle; the temperature method, which identifies ovulation by a rise in body temperature; the mucus or Billings method, which both predicts and identifies ovulation by changes in the consistency of cervical mucus; and the symptothermal method, which combines elements of the other three and which in several studies has proved the most effective.[29] Because all these methods help to pinpoint the fertile period, they can be used to increase the chances of getting pregnant as well as to prevent pregnancy.

An estimated 10 to 15 million couples worldwide employ some technique of natural family planning. In only six Third World countries—Haiti, Mauritius, Peru, the Philippines,

South Korea, and Sri Lanka—are more than 5 percent of married women of reproductive age known to use the method. Ireland and Poland are the two industrialized countries with the highest use.

NFP has been promoted primarily by the Catholic Church, which sanctions the method as the only acceptable form of contraception, stressing the moral value of abstinence during the fertile period. The two main international organizations that teach and promote NFP are the International Federation for Family Life Promotion (IFFLP) and the World Organization of the Ovulation (Billings) Method (WOOMB). WOOMB only promotes the mucus method and is hostile to the others.[30]

NFP's success in preventing pregnancy largely depends on training, motivation, and cooperation between partners. Failure rates are quite high in some studies—up to 30 percent—whereas in others they are comparable to the more effective contraceptives. In one project in India where close follow-up was top priority, only three pregnancies were reported among 813 women in the first year.[31] Among the advantages of the method are that it is cheap, demands no regular source of supply, causes no side effects that require medical supervision, and encourages active participation by both partners.

If used without any contraceptive backup, NFP has the major drawback of requiring abstinence during the fertile period. Many of the pregnancies that do occur result from couples deciding not to abstain, or husbands forcing their wives to have intercourse. Audrey Bronstein describes some of the "sexual politics" which emerged in an NFP training course she attended in El Salvador:

> A number of women said that abstinence didn't work, because the husbands often came home drunk and would beat them if they didn't agree to have sex. They also said that if the women tried to refuse too many times, the men would go off, and find other women. On the positive side, they felt that where there was a small understanding between the couple, practicing abstinence increases the man's respect for his wife, and will help create a "dialogue" between the two.[32]

In Kenya a missionary teaching the method reported, "Women

show up by the hundreds, but the men do not want to make the effort to keep the rules, even if they see the need to limit their families."[33] To some extent, the problem of abstinence can be overcome by the use of barrier methods on fertile days (especially the condom which does not interfere as much with mucus symptoms). However, many NFP promoters are against these "artificial" methods for religious reasons, just as they are against abortion in the event of method failure.

Like barrier methods, NFP has been neglected by population agencies, though NFP organizations have received small amounts of funding from AID, UNFPA, WHO, and the British, Canadian, and West German governments. Recently, AID has increased its support of NFP, mainly under pressure from Right to Life forces in the United States. In FY 1985 AID devoted over $7 million to NFP activities, as opposed to only $400,000 in 1980.[34]

Population agencies typically base their case against NFP on three main grounds: effectiveness, the need for careful counseling, and cost. "Where competition for scarce government family planning dollars and an urgent need to promote fertility control require strict attention to cost—and time—effectiveness," writes the Population Crisis Committee, "experts usually assign NFP a lower priority than other, more effective methods."[35]

As we have seen, however, the more "effective" contraceptives also have high failure and low continuation rates when introduced improperly. NFP's success does depend on careful counseling, but so do the effectiveness and ethical use of almost all contraceptives. According to the WHO, the once-a-month follow-up required by NFP "is greater than could be provided in national family planning programs," and the cost often prohibitive.[36] Yet otherwise natural family planning is *free*, aside from the cost of a thermometer or charts.

Surely, when everything is added up, teaching one woman NFP is not more costly than providing that person with many cycles of pills, the IUD, or sterilization and treating their side effects. One wonders if the issue is not really costs, but *profit*, for NFP is the one contraceptive method where no profits accrue to either the pharmaceutical industry or the medical profession.

NFP research also suffers from lack of funds. From 1980 to 1983 it received only 0.6 percent of expenditures for contraceptive research and development.[37] However, research is underway on more accurate ways of determining ovulation, through better thermometers, tests on urine, mucus, and saliva, and even a way to monitor temperature changes in the hands.[38] The development of a foolproof, convenient way to identify the fertile period would greatly enhance both the acceptability and reliability of natural family planning.

The attitude of the population establishment is not the only obstacle to more widespread promotion of natural family planning. Since many of NFP's advocates oppose other forms of birth control, they are against NFP's inclusion in comprehensive family planning programs. Affiliates of WOOMB, for example, have issued this declaration:

> A fundamental concept of the philosophy of WOOMB is the acceptance of periodic abstinence and the rejection of artificial contraception, abortion and sterilization, each member [of WOOMB] undertaking not to counsel for or dispense such methods of birth control.[39]

In 1985, under pressure from politically powerful Right to Lifers, AID endorsed this position in a major policy shift. It announced that the agency was prepared to make an exception to its "informed choice" policy and to give grants to natural family planning organizations who oppose all other forms of contraception. These groups would no longer be required to provide information on or referral for other birth control methods, formerly a prerequisite for AID family planning funding. Fortunately, Congress objected to the new policy and AID was forced to retract it.[40]

This approach to NFP not only limits its availability but ultimately restricts women's choice. Many women, for example, might be willing to use natural family planning *with* the backup of barrier methods and/or abortion, but in their absence are worried about high failure rates. Others may choose NFP only at certain times during their reproductive years, when they are more concerned with spacing births and are willing to accept an earlier than expected pregnancy. At other times they may well want access to other contraceptives.

Fortunately, in addition to more traditional advocates of natural family planning, today support is building among women disillusioned with the side effects of other contraceptives and interested in a more holistic approach to birth control, in which a woman's knowledge of her own body and male cooperation are key. Such advocacy could help change the tenor of natural family planning, so that it is both more acceptable and accessible in the future.

ON THE HORIZON

Although public pressure has led to some shift in direction, the pattern of contraceptive research, development, and promotion we have witnessed in recent decades seems likely to continue, at least in the short run. Today the primary emphasis remains on female hormonal contraception, despite the health risks that it entails. The latest versions include injectables with lower doses of hormones steadily released in minute, biodegradable capsules, combined estrogen/progestin injectables, hormone-releasing vaginal rings, hormone-impregnated IUDs, and a second generation of implants which do not require surgical removal and are effective for one year.[41]

Other new frontiers include an antipregnancy vaccine, effective for one to two years, which "immunizes" women against the pregnancy hormone human chorionic gonadotrophin, thereby interrupting the reproductive process before the fertilized egg has been implanted in the womb. The first human trial of the vaccine is already underway in Australia. Population agencies are enthusiastic, since they believe that vaccines, like injectables, are especially "suitable" for Third World countries.[42] Research is also underway on new ovulation inhibitors such as analogs of the brain hormone LHRH, which could be administered, for example, by nasal spray.

The search goes on for improved and reversible surgical sterilization techniques, as well as for a chemical sterilant. The chemical methylcyanoacrylate is already being marketed as a sterilant in the United Kingdom and Canada, although it has not been found highly effective with a single application. According to a recent article on contraceptive research, the main motivation behind the search for a chemical sterilant is that it "is still needed in many developing-country family planning programs."[43] One does not have to stretch the imagination too far to speculate on how this technology could be abused.

One of the more controversial developments on the contraceptive scene is RU 486. Invented by Professor Etienne-Emile Baulieu and produced by a French pharmaceutical company, RU 486 is a steroidal derivative that inhibits the action of progesterone, one of the hormones necessary for sustaining pregnancy. It can be used as a once a month oral or injectable contraceptive, a menstrual regulator, or for the termination of early pregnancy. Clinical trials are now underway in at least ten countries. So far failure rates are relatively high and its long-term safety remains in question. Nevertheless, the drug is already receiving good reviews in the press, reminiscent of the early treatment of the pill.[44] Proper use of RU 486 depends on good clinical backup, but there is a very real danger that the drug could be used illicitly for "do it yourself" abortions, where there would be no medical backup in the event of complications.

Because the United States government cannot support research on drugs that can be construed as abortifacients, research on RU 486 and similar drugs is likely to suffer from a shortage of funds. Pharmaceutical companies are also wary of an antiabortion backlash. Such fears led G. D. Searle Co. to withdraw its application for FDA approval of a Japanese prostaglandin drug, Preglandin, which can be used as either a cervical dilator or an abortion inducer in the second trimester of pregnancy.[45]

Meanwhile, male research lags behind, though it is now receiving more attention than in the past. Not surprisingly, concern about safety and side effects appears to be higher in male contraceptive research than in female. "We want to go very slowly," said one researcher at the University of California. The female pill "was applied very rapidly, and later we found a series of very serious complications.[46] The WHO has also found greater reluctance among men than women to volunteer for clinical trials.[47]

Hopes that a male pill, made of Gossypol, a derivative of cotton seed oil, was just around the corner were dashed when clinical trials in China revealed a number of serious side effects, including temporary paralysis and heart ailments caused by a severe drop in blood potassium levels, and a high rate of permanent sterility. The WHO has now withdrawn all funding of Gossypol research in China, but the Chinese government is pressing on. If the potassium side effects can be overcome, Gossypol will be recommended for mass production in China. The fact that it can cause permanent sterility is not viewed as a serious problem, since this fits in with the government's attempts to reduce population growth.[48]

On the more positive side, research is increasing on plants and herbs used for contraception. The WHO has established a network of centers in Hong Kong, South Korea, Sri Lanka, and the United States to select and test plants. They have already identified 400 species of flowering plants grown in 111 countries that have been used by local communities for fertility control. Such a trend is encouraging, for it acknowledges that traditional methods can play a role in modern contraception and that it is not only scientists who have the answers.[49]

At the same time as these developments are occurring, funding for reproductive and contraceptive research has been declining in real terms. 1983 expenditures, for example, were 79 percent of 1979 levels. According to *Family Planning Perspectives*, this decline not only reflects worldwide economic recession, but "the diminution of concern among developed countries about those population issues that helped spur investments in contraceptive research in the mid-1970's."[50]

In response, a number of people within the population establishment are pushing for the formation of a consortium of donors, including WHO, UNFPA, the World Bank, governments, and private foundations, to stimulate and coordinate contraceptive research. Unfortunately, the same old Malthusian motives underlie the proposal. Its proponents argue that the consortium is needed to address "the worldwide health, economic and social consequences of continued rapid population growth rates in the developing world."[51] As long as contraceptive technology is perceived in this way—as a technical fix for the population problem—contraceptive research is likely to be misdirected and misapplied.

There *is* a pressing need for more contraceptive research. The development of new and improved birth control methods of many different varieties, including, not excluding, barrier methods, does have the potential of expanding reproductive choice, but only if the individual's need for safe, reliable, and voluntary contraception figures first. In the end, however, increasing access to and use of contraception is more a social problem than a technical one. It may be a long time—or never—before the "perfect" contraceptive is produced. Meanwhile, the acceptability of the birth control methods already in existence could be greatly enhanced by better health care, counseling, and supervision, and above all by a change in values.

There is no intrinsic reason why women's health and safety have to be sacrificed to contraceptive efficacy or why freedom of choice has to be subordinated to population control. More sensitive and sensible alternatives exist. If there is to be a second contraceptive revolution, let it start with a revolution in values.

PART FOUR

THE WAY FORWARD

The Light at the End of the Demographic Tunnel

The first chapter of this book identified the two basic sets of rights that are critical to an understanding and solution of the population problem. The first is the right of everyone on earth today to enjoy a decent standard of living through access to food, shelter, health care, education, employment, and social security. The second is the fundamental right of women to control their own reproduction.

The two concluding chapters explore how these rights can be translated into concrete social programs and policies, beginning with an examination of the underlying forces behind the demographic transition from high to low birth rates.

THE DEMOGRAPHIC TRANSITION

The value of children as a source of labor and security, son preference, high infant mortality, and the subordination of women all help to explain why people have large families. What motivates them to have fewer children?

Demographers have long searched for clues in the decline in birth rates in Europe over the last few centuries, which could be applied to population trends elsewhere in the world. The European demographic transition used to be thought of in fairly simple and straightforward terms: declining mortality rates as the result of the spread of modern medicine, public health measures, and better food supply, led after a lag to falling birth rates, while economic development reduced the value of children; education and outside employment of women raised the marriage age; industrialization, urbanization, and the spread of communications challenged traditional cultural values, increasing the acceptance of fertility control.

Today, however, demographers have discovered that the wide variation between countries and regions defies simple formulas. Fertility fell more slowly in England than in France, for instance, despite England's faster industrialization and mortality decline. In Hungary and Poland small landowners—usually the most tradition-bound—began to limit their families in the nineteenth century in order that their children could inherit a viable piece of land.

Yet, while country-specific economic, social, and cultural circumstances have certainly determined the shape of fertility decline, by the beginning of the twentieth century the demographic transition was well underway throughout Europe and in North America as well.[1] The Soviet Union and Japan were to follow suit, experiencing even faster fertility declines over a span of forty-five and twenty-five years respectively. Whatever the smaller flourishes, the broad stroke of economic development dominates the picture of demographic transition in these societies. And this transition was achieved *without* any explicit government population control policies.

How relevant is this experience to the Third World today? This question is a subject of much debate. According to demographer John Caldwell, important differences in culture confound attempts to generalize from one to the other. In Europe, for example, well before the onset of the demographic transition, family and social structures made children far more of an economic burden than they are in the typical extended family in the Third World today.[2] For the World Bank, the experience of the now industrialized countries is largely irrelevant: high population growth rates in many Third World countries are "a phenomenon for which economic and demographic history offer no real precedent."[3]

Theories abound as to what key will unlock the door of demographic transition in the Third World. Caldwell maintains that mass education and the penetration of Western values will hasten fertility decline, even in the absence of widespread industrialization. Mead Cain of the Population Council believes that the issue of security is paramount, and that the provision of alternative forms of insurance and improvements in the "environment of risk" could help reduce people's need for children.[4]

Hard-line population control advocates argue that most Third World countries simply do not have the resources to attain the economic level at which the West passed through the demographic transition, and what resources they do have are being eaten away by population growth. Thus population control, not improvement in living standards, they reason, is the only hope for bringing the birth rate down.

But do Third World countries have to come up to the same income levels of the West to achieve a demographic transition? Birth rates in a number of places—China, Korea, Sri Lanka, Taiwan, and the Indian state of Kerala—started to drop when per capita incomes were still only several hundred dollars. What does the experience of these countries reveal?

Let's go back to the initial premise that economic development is the basic force behind the demographic transition. If one measures development simply in terms of GNP per capita, then one finds that countries with higher per capita incomes generally have lower birth rates, though there are important exceptions to this rule. A number of upper-middle-income countries, including Syria, Jordan, Iran, Iraq, and South Africa, have crude birth rates of over forty or more, while two of the world's poorest nations, China and Sri Lanka, have birth rates of 19 and 27 respectively.

Is this simply a statistical anomaly, or is the problem with the concept of development? If one defines development differently, in terms of the number of people who actually benefit from economic growth, then one discovers that more equitable distribution of resources can lead to lower birth rates, even at relatively low levels of GNP per capita.

First of all, this is a matter of income distribution. In Sri Lanka, for example, wealth is more evenly distributed than in many Third World countries: The top 20 percent of households control roughly 43 percent of income, the bottom 20 percent control 7 percent. By contrast, in Kenya, which has a slightly higher per capita GNP of $360, the top 20 percent of households control over 60 percent of income and the poorest 20

INFANT MORTALITY, CRUDE BIRTH RATE, AND GNP PER
CAPITA FOR SELECTED COUNTRIES 1984

	Infant Mortality Rate	Crude Birth Rate	GNP per Capita (U.S. Dollars)
Nigeria	110	50	730
Ivory Coast	106	45	610
Algeria	82	42	2,410
Saudi Arabia	61	43	10,530
Mexico	51	33	2,040
Sri Lanka	37	26	360
China	36	19	310
Costa Rica	19	29	1,190
Cuba	16	17	1,410*
United States	11	16	15,390
Sweden	7	11	11,860

*1981 figure
Source: World Bank, World Development Report 1986.

percent less than 3 percent. Kenya has the highest birth rate in the world.

Brazil has an even worse distribution of income than Kenya, and despite the fact that per capita GNP is over $2,000, its birth rate is 31, 4 points higher than Sri Lanka's. In South Africa, where the black majority has been consistently cut out of the development process, the birth rate of 40 is way out of line with its relatively high per capita income of over $2,500.[5]

The reason for this pattern is not difficult to fathom. A raised standard of living across the population leads to better overall access to health, education, and jobs, all factors that allow people to choose smaller families. Many countries that have more equitable income distribution policies also consciously gear services toward the poor majority, emphasizing mass primary education, for example, rather than expensive higher education for a privileged few. Similarly, countries such as Sri Lanka, China, and Cuba, which have developed extensive public health systems, have managed to bring down infant mortality rates at relatively low levels of GNP per capita, while much richer countries have failed. (See table.)

Also of critical importance is how equitably resources are

distributed between men and women. One of the reasons many relatively rich Middle Eastern countries have such high birth rates may be the restrictions imposed on women's participation outside the home, whereas in Asian countries such as Sri Lanka and Thailand, women's higher status not only gives them greater control over financial resources but over their own reproduction.

The recognition of these factors has led to a recasting of traditional demographic transition theory, in which social and economic justice plays a major role.

RETHINKING THE TRANSITION

Traditional demographic theory identifies three basic stages in fertility decline:

1. *High Mortality and High Fertility*   In preindustrial societies, high death rates, caused by the absence of medical care and poor nutrition, offset high birth rates so that a basic population equilibrium is maintained.

2. *The Lag: Low Mortality and High Fertility*   As societies start to develop, modern technology reduces deaths. At the same time birth rates remain high because of the persistence of traditional attitudes toward childbearing and the lag time between the fall in mortality and people's actual recognition that their children stand a better chance of surviving. The result is rapid population growth. Many Third World countries are stuck in this stage.

3. *Low Mortality and Low Fertility*   Equilibrium is restored when a stage in industrial development is reached in which people choose to have small families because of new values, opportunities for women, and the increasing cost of raising children.

In his "Social Justice Theory of Demographic Transition," Dr. John Ratcliffe challenges this traditional view and recasts the three stages of fertility decline:

1. *High Mortality and High Fertility*   This is not a natural

state of affairs but instead "the demographic pattern typical of highly stratified societies within which social resources are distributed very unequally,"[6] including the vast majority of societies under colonial rule. In these societies, social institutions such as health and education facilities only serve a small ruling elite. Consequently the vast majority of the population suffer from high death rates. The unit for survival is the family, and high fertility is a necessity in the subsistence economy.

2. *Falling Mortality and High Fertility*   This pattern applies to most Third World countries today. It does not result, as traditional demographic theory maintains, from the introduction of modern medical techniques, but instead from the extension of the formal governing system to more—but not all—members of society. This usually occurs with national independence from colonial role. The new nationalist ruling groups come to power promising basic social reforms, but in the end adopt many of the old colonial policies, such as concentrating resources on higher education for the elite rather than mass primary education and emphasizing Western curative medicine for urban areas rather than primary health care for the rural poor.

However, progress is made in terms of building modern communications infrastructure, increasing agricultural production, and providing basic public health measures such as immunization. Since government services reach more people than during colonial times, mortality rates tend to fall, especially in urban enclaves and among the advantaged classes. Those who work in the formal sector also tend to have fewer children.

For the vast majority of the population living in the rural areas, however, life conditions do not change dramatically. Death rates come down somewhat, but fertility levels remain high because the family is still the basic unit of survival.

The lag between low mortality and high fertility is thus really a social gap between the haves and have-nots.

3. *Low Mortality and Low Fertility*   This occurs when governments implement wide-ranging social reforms, including land and income redistribution, educational reforms, the pro-

vision of primary health care, and improvements in women's status. People no longer have to rely on the family as the unit of survival because the government and other institutions provide security and employment.

What are the implications of this view of the demographic transition? Clearly, it is not population control programs that reduce population growth, but the *transformation* of the social and economic institutions that perpetuate poverty and make people dependent on children for survival. The following examples of Cuba, South Korea, Sri Lanka, and Kerala illustrate concretely how this social-justice demographic transition takes place.

CUBA: THE UNSUNG SUCCESS STORY

Most population control literature is strangely silent about Cuba, the country which experienced perhaps the greatest decline in birth rate in the shortest amount of time, and once again at relatively low levels of per capita income. Between 1965 and 1980, Cuba's birth rate fell by nearly half. Shortly after the 1959 revolution, its crude birth rate was 35 births per 1,000 people; today it is only 17, only 1 point higher than the United States, though Cuba's per capita income is roughly one tenth as much. Cuba in fact has the lowest birth rate in all of Latin America.[7]

Before Cuba's revolution, most Cubans had the same poor living standards as the majority of Latin Americans: Life expectancy was low, infant mortality was high, and over half the children were malnourished. Economic and social reforms, combined with a highly effective public health system, led to dramatic improvements in the quality of life.

Today Cuba has the lowest infant mortality rate in Latin America, a life expectancy only two years less than the United States, and high employment and adult literacy. Income differentials are modest, and although sexism is still strong, women are much more emancipated than in most other Latin American countries. Cuban Family Code legislation even specifies that men should share equally in household tasks.

Within Latin America, Cuba stands out as an example of how equality can affect fertility. Venezuela, with a per capita income double that of Cuba, has a birth rate of 33; Mexico with a similar per capita income has a birth rate of 32. In both these countries wealth is concentrated in only a few hands, and in Mexico, the majority are desperately poor.

Cuba achieved its low birth rate without ever once having a population control campaign. Instead family planning services are freely available through the health system to all who want them.

THE KOREAN "MIRACLE"

South Korea also boasts one of the fastest demographic transitions in history, from a crude birth rate of 41 in 1960 to 24 in 1974. (It was 20 in 1984.) In Korea the key appears to be economic and social changes after World War II, which led to advances in equality. These were not the result of a popular revolution, however. As economist Robert Repetto explains:

> The high degree of equality was achieved not through a particularly strong commitment to popular welfare, but through the disruption and devastation of war; through a land reform which was legislated in an atmosphere of fear of Communist intervention and carried through mostly by private land sales or by the U.S. military government; and through an education reform which was also initiated by the U.S. military government.[8]

When Korea was occupied by the Allies at the end of World War II, a feudal system of land tenure prevailed in the countryside, with large landlords controlling much of the land. In 1938, for example, only 19 percent of Korea's farm household heads were full owners of the land. After the United States-sponsored land reform, this figure rose to 72 percent.

At the same time educational reform led to mass access to formal schooling. In 1945, 64 percent of children attended primary school, in 1960, 95.3 percent, and there was steadily increasing attendance in middle school, high school, and college over the period. In 1960 over a quarter of all children could expect to receive a college education, a high figure relative to most societies. These new educational opportunities served as a form of social mobility for poorer families, helping to reduce income disparities.[9]

As the result of the general rise in the standard of living, fertility declined in all regions and across all classes in Korea. Family planning programs had little to do with the initial fall: As late as 1964, well after the decline was underway, only 12 percent of women of reproductive age reported ever using contraceptives, though by 1973 the number had risen to 55 percent. Instead, illegal, though relatively safe, abortion was the most common method of birth control. Education and employment of women also had an impact on fertility, since both raised the marriage age.[10] (Unfortunately, today Korea's family planning program utilizes sterilization incentives, as part of the government's embrace of Western population control philosophy.)

In the 1960s and 1970s, Korea also experienced "miracle" economic growth through the development of export-oriented, manufacturing industries, based on cheap labor. While the conventional view is that this growth also furthered social equality, there is compelling evidence that on the contrary, it has heightened income disparities.[11] Nevertheless, because of the post-World War II reforms, the gap between rich and poor is still less pronounced in Korea than in many other Third World countries.

Taiwan also experienced a similar fertility decline. Its postwar history has much in common with Korea: a United States-sponsored land reform, widening access to education, and rapid industrial growth through export manufacturing.

It is doubtful, however, whether the South Korea-Taiwan model can be readily applied elsewhere. More recent United States-sponsored land reform efforts in countries such as El Salvador and former South Vietnam, for example, have failed dismally because they stopped far short of a genuine distribution of property and power. It is difficult to impose social justice from above, especially in situations where its emergence from below is actively suppressed.

SRI LANKA: ONCE UPON A WELFARE STATE

Sri Lanka is not a rich country. Its 1983 per capita income of only $330 reflects a long history of economic stagnation, stretching back to British colonial rule when the country became dependent on a few cash crops for income. Although Sri Lanka has not been very successful in terms of economic development, it has made great strides in human development. Prior to the election of a conservative government in 1977, Sri Lanka was one of the Third World's few welfare states.

Through sweeping social policies, including free supplementary rice rations, job and old-age security provisions, a progressive tax structure, and free education and health care, Sri Lankans have enjoyed a quality of life far superior to other low-income and even middle-income countries. The infant mortality rate dropped from 150 in 1946 to 37 in 1983, life expectancy is now sixty-nine, and there is virtually universal literacy, except among the exploited Tamil minority on the tea plantations.

Women have also enjoyed real improvements in their lives. By 1977 girls actually outnumbered boys in universities, and many women work outside the home. As a result, late marriage at around twenty-five years is the norm.

The impact of these measures on fertility is predictable. The crude birth rate dropped 20 percent between 1965 and 1983, from 33 to 27, and over half of married women of reproductive age now use contraception. Sri Lanka in fact has one of the lowest birth rates in the Third World.

Under pressure from the International Monetary Fund and the World Bank, the current Sri Lankan government has dramatically cut back welfare measures and is pursuing a strategy of export-oriented economic growth through the establishment of free trade zones for foreign investment. The rationale is that the welfare programs acted as a drain on government resources and a brake on economic development.[12] But would Sri Lanka be where it is today if it had not been a welfare state? Probably not. Instead, infant mortality and birth rates would probably be high, life expectancy low, and the World Bank and IMF would be advising the government to implement harsh population control policies à la India or Bangladesh. Indeed, Sri Lanka's sterilization program already relies on high incentives to achieve results (see Chapter 12).

KERALA: THE EXCEPTION TO THE INDIAN RULE

Anyone who visits India's Kerala state is struck at once by its physical beauty: its lush coconut groves and rice paddies, scenic sea coast and inland waterways. This tropical paradise is also a human paradise in comparison to the rest of India. In Kerala people do not seem as weighed down by poverty as their compatriots. Hunger and disease are much less visible on the streets, most children are in school, and women walk with a pronounced air of self-confidence.

Yet by standard measures, Kerala is poor. Its per capita income and per capita calorie intake are among the lowest in India, while its population density is 550 persons per square kilometer, similar to that of Bangladesh.[13] Other quality-of-life indicators, however, are unusually high. Almost 70 percent of Kerala's people are literate, compared to the all-India average of 36 percent. Kerala's life expectancy is nearly sixty-four years compared to the national average of fifty-two, and its infant mortality rate of 55, compared to India's 125, is the lowest in the country.

In Kerala quality of life has also affected family size. Population growth rates for most other Indian states remain high, yet Kerala is passing through a demographic transition. In 1978 its crude birth rate was 26, in contrast to the Indian average of 33.[14] What has made the difference?

In his work on Kerala, Dr. Ratcliffe describes how mass popular movements brought to power progressive state governments that initiated social reforms. Land reform legislation in the late 1950s and early 1960s, for example, helped to redistribute wealth. On paper these reforms were not much more radical than agrarian legislation in other Indian states, but in Kerala popular pressure ensured their actual implementation. As Indian economist K. N. Raj notes, "Kerala happens to be the only state in India where political pressure based on mass organization and support has been a major factor forcing the pace of land reform and where such reform has constantly received sustained attention."[15]

In addition, strong agricultural labor unions and a relatively high demand for labor have meant that even the landless in Kerala are generally better off than their counterparts elsewhere in India. A 1974 act legislated security of employment for agricultural laborers, as well as welfare and pension funds.

Land reform also brought a nutritional improvement through better food distribution and increased production. Moreover, government ration shops selling food at controlled prices are open to all social groups, unlike in other states where urban and professional classes are the chief beneficiaries of subsidized food.

In the period 1961–1971, in India as a whole the highest income groups increased their proportion of asset holdings by 5 percent. Only in three states did the poorest groups gain on the rich, and it was Kerala that had the largest recorded gain.

Along with redistribution of wealth came improved access to education and health. Primary and secondary schooling receive the lion's share of Kerala's education budget, and today illiteracy among the young has virtually been wiped out. Kerala also has the highest utilization of health facilities in India, even though eight states spend more per capita.

According to Dr. Ratcliffe, better distribution of health services between urban and rural areas is not the only explanation: The politically conscious Kerala populace "uses the power of the press and the vote to force the system to be responsive to their demands." This is unlike most parts of India where "those who lack a clear understanding both of their rights of access to public services and of the political process are easily manipulated and bypassed, and are thus powerless to enter or infuence the system."[16]

Kerala's birth rate decline not only reflects general social development, but the improved status of women. Education has brought more women into the labor force, so they have real alternatives to childbearing. Kerala's average female age at marriage is the highest in India. Unfortunately, there have been instances of excesses in Kerala's family planning program, which relies heavily on sterilization, so that women do not have full reproductive choice.[17]

Of the many lessons Kerala holds for the rest of India, perhaps the most important is that *the foundation of equity rests on the political power of the poor.* Sadly, in most other states politics is largely the prerogative of the rich, and popular movements are routinely repressed. Inequality meanwhile perpetuates the poor's need for children, and they are then held responsible for rapid population growth. The result is mass population control campaigns, instead of the kinds of social and economic developments that would give people more control over their lives.

POLICY PRESCRIPTIONS

What lessons are to be drawn from these case studies?

In neither Cuba, Sri Lanka, Korea, nor Kerala was an intensive population control effort responsible for the demographic transition. Instead, by moving forward on a number of economic and social fronts, these societies, despite their different political systems, created the conditions under which people themselves wanted smaller families. The vital ingredients in their recipe for demographic transition are these:

- income and land redistribution.
- employment opportunities and social security.
- mass education.
- improvements in the position of women, including a later age of marriage.
- accessible health care and family planning services.

Can other countries follow this same recipe?

Certainly, even the most vigorous proponents of population control today recognize that demographic policy must be broadened beyond the simple provision of contraceptives to include social and economic measures to encourage small families. While hard-liners support massive incentive and disincentive schemes, liberals promote the linking of family planning with women's income generation, agricultural aid, Mother and Child Health services, etc. (see Box: The Isolation Exercise).

The trouble with these approaches is that they either lead to coercion or to half-hearted and ineffective social reform measures, since they fail to deal with the unequal power relationships at the root of the problem. Just as people's reasons for having children are complex, so are the solutions to high birth rates. Limited interventions on just one or two policy levels are unlikely to alter people's life conditions to the extent that they want and need fewer children.

In Cuba, Korea, Sri Lanka, and Kerala, as well as in most other societies that have passed through the demographic transition, the goal was not a reduction in the birth rate, but *development in its own right,* of which fertility control was simply one of many aspects and not the most important in terms of improving the quality of people's lives. On paper this distinction may seem subtle, but in practice it is not. By making fertility reduction their main objective, population control advocates *de facto* accept and help to perpetuate inequitable social and economic structures that actually undermine their attempts to reduce birth rates. From a practical and ethical standpoint, the best population policy is to concentrate on improving human welfare in all its many facets.

THE ISOLATION EXERCISE

Today a number of population researchers are trying to isolate those "development indicators"—life expectancy, mortality, literacy, health, per capita GNP growth, access to family planning, etc.—which are the most conducive to fertility decline. All the latest statistical and computer tools are brought to bear on the problem in the hope that, once several are identified, they can form the leading inputs in a neat national population policy. According to Phillips Cutright, author of one of the more recent studies, this is possible because development is not a holistic process, and "fertility is sensitive to certain measures of development and not to others."[1]

Not surprisingly, this approach often indicates that the strength of family planning programs is one of the leading variables in fertility decline. The *World Development Report 1984* confidently asserts that between 1965 and 1975 the availability of family planning accounted for 40 percent of the fertility decline across countries while socioeconomic change accounted for only 27 percent. Furthermore, "for the single goal of reducing fertility, spending on family planning services turns out to be more cost effective . . . than spending on education, health . . . and other programs."[2]

Lately, however, health and education have also been identified as leading causes of fertility decline. This was the conclusion of Cutright's study, as well as demographer Moni Nag in an article on Kerala. Nag maintains that equity in education and health facilities has had a greater impact on fertility decline in Kerala than equity in income distribution. What is the implication? Demographic transition, says Nag, therefore doesn't have to wait for land reforms and other redistributional economic measures; instead, "Equity in educational and health services can perhaps be attained with *less political opposition* [my emphasis] but with more significant demographic consequences. . . ."[3]

It is useful to point out some of the dubious assumptions underlying the exercise. Development *is* a holistic process: One development indicator interacts with another, so that it is difficult, if not impossible, to trace a precise line of causality leading to fertility decline. Family planning efforts can reflect the strength of health services, which in turn reflects more equitable income distribution, which can help determine how many children people want and their receptivity to family planning.

According to demographer John Caldwell, even supposing there were direct relationships between specific development indicators and fertility decline, they would be virtually impossible to prove "because of the tendency for so many economic and social changes to move together." Caldwell in fact criticizes "the use of statisticians and statistically oriented economists" in the analysis of fertility decline, preferring firsthand observation of the individuals and societies in question.[4]

15

Expanding Choices

The kind of social and economic transformation described in the previous chapter is necessary but not sufficient to ensure reproductive choice. Development is an uneven process, and even in the most egalitarian societies in terms of income distribution, or the most "advanced" in terms of industrialization, the gap between the sexes persists. Women's need for safe, voluntary birth control and general reproductive health care is too easily put at the bottom of the public agenda. But for many women it clearly belongs near the top. If one cannot control one's own womb, then what can one control?

Not so long ago the concept of reproductive rights was scarcely known. Now it is gaining currency as women around the globe insist on a new agenda. United in opposition to population control and anti-abortion forces, they are charting a new path.

WOMEN TAKE THE INITIATIVE

In the city of Recife, located in Brazil's impoverished Northeast, a call-in radio show candidly answers questions about contraception in a country where the subject of birth control has long been taboo. Over one hundred people call each month, and letters flow in from the surrounding countryside. The questions and letters are addressed to the reproductive rights organization, SOS Corpo.

SOS Corpo is representative of a number of feminist groups around the globe who are taking bold initiatives to expand women's choices. Established in 1980, SOS Corpo grew out of the feminist movement, which spread among Recife's professional and politically active women in the previous decade. After being introduced to the concept of self-help health care by a Brazilian woman who had lived in France, many women in the movement discovered that despite their relatively privileged positions in society, they knew little about their own bodies and sexuality. As they learned more, they felt a responsibility to share the information. Eight women joined together to form SOS Corpo, receiving their first grant in 1982. Today the group is staffed by an architect, a doctor, a chemical engineer, a journalist, a gymnastics teacher, two social workers, and two sociologists.

SOS Corpo now works with women and young people in the poor neighborhoods of Recife. Its aim is not to impose top-down family planning programs, but to find out what problems women face in regard to sexuality and reproduction as part of the totality of their lives. The group acts as a resource on which the community can draw. In response to women's need for sound birth control information, SOS Corpo, for example, has produced a number of publications and audiovisuals on anatomy and contraception. Their book *How to Avoid Children*, on the pros and cons of birth control methods, is a best-seller in the city. Their radio show reaches people who cannot read, and they are currently working with the Brazilian Health Ministry to develop more educational materials.

Although SOS Corpo does not provide birth control services directly, it engages in vital research on reproductive issues, such as sterilization regret (see Chapter 12). It is currently undertaking research on the diaphragm, based on the premise that if women receive sensitive training and counseling, they can learn to use the diaphragm effectively, regardless of economic class. They have received a grant of diaphragms from the health ministry—on the open market imported diaphragms cost $30 to $40 apiece! Unfortunately, contraceptive jelly too is scarce, since the one company that used to manufacture it has stopped production. SOS Corpo is now investigating ways of producing an inexpensive alternative.

SOS Corpo's basic strategy is to empower people to demand decent health and family planning services from the government. This move comes at an important time in Brazil, since the country's deep pronatalist tradition, backed by the Church, the military, and the traditional left, is under attack from international population control interests. SOS Corpo supports those people within the Health Ministry who are trying to make family planning services freely available, but who oppose their manipulation and misuse in population control programs. In September 1985 the Health Ministry set up a Reproductive Rights Committee with the purpose of surveying and controlling population programs, and as a consequence private population agencies are trying to adopt a more feminist image. The experience of SOS Corpo shows there is great scope in Brazil for a reproductive rights alternative, and that pressure from activists can influence government policy.[1]

In Cuernavaca, Mexico, the women's organization CIDHAL adopts a similar approach. To complement its broader goal of expanding women's economic and political rights through grass-roots organizing, cultural activities, and a resource center, CIDHAL runs a clinic, which provides sensitive contraceptive advice and basic health education. CIDHAL's publication, *Cuerpo de Mujer*, presents the issues of women's sexuality, health, and contraception in accessible language and illustrations.

CIDHAL also works for the legalization of abortion in Mexico, where an estimated 100,000 women die each year from the complications of illegal operations. Because of their courageous activities in this field, CIDHAL's members have suffered harassment from government authorities. In 1984, for example, the police broke into their health clinic on orders from the provincial governor, claiming that CIDHAL was performing illegal abortions. No evidence was found, but the clinic was shut down temporarily. In discussions with the governor and other top officials, the CIDHAL women were accused of encouraging women to undergo abortion simply because they distribute leaflets supporting its legalization. Unfortunately, many reproductive rights organizations face such forms of harassment, for in seeking to increase women's control, they are challenging the control of powerful male-dominated institutions.[2]

In the industrial countries, women's health centers provide an important alternative to conventional medical practices. The New Hampshire Feminist Health Center in the United States, for instance, offers sixteen different types of fertility control and general well-woman care. Health workers explain the risks and benefits of each birth control method, and no woman is prescribed a method until she has read all the manufacturers' precautions. There is a strong emphasis on self-help and support groups, encouraging women of all ages to learn about their bodies. A counseling service also allows women to discuss the broader social and economic problems they face.[3]

These examples show the fundamental difference between the reproductive rights and population control approaches to family planning. In none of these initiatives are women treated as impersonal demographic agents, whose wombs must be controlled in order to reduce population growth. Instead, these organizations take the time to listen, to find out women's real desires and concerns. Staff members use their own privileged positions in society to serve as a resource, not to impose their will on others less powerful than themselves. They are not acting out of a patronizing attitude of "helping" the poor, but in recognition of the common interest women face in controlling their bodies and lives. The task in the years ahead will be to translate such initiatives into broader public programs, so that more women have a choice.

HEALTHIER APPROACHES

Expanding choices in birth control necessarily involves expanding basic health care, in order to guarantee proper medical backup in family planning programs, to reduce infant and maternal mortality, and to improve the general conditions of people's lives. Today, in a number of countries, health activists are challenging conventional medical delivery systems and creating new models of popularly oriented health services.

In Bangladesh, the People's Health Center (Gonoshasthaya Kendra) has effectively integrated family planning into a broader program of basic health care and social change. Started in 1972, the Center has trained a team of over sixty paramedics to deliver low-cost health and family planning services to the surrounding villages. Most of the paramedics are women from village backgrounds, and they try to involve traditional village midwives in their work as much as possible. The project aims to meet women's needs for contraception, including sterilization if they so desire, and has resulted in a birth rate in the project area one third below the national average, despite the fact—or perhaps because of it!—that population control is not a program goal.

The center has also set up its own nonprofit pharmaceutical factory to produce essential drugs at low cost, challenging foreign multinationals' dominance of the Bangladesh market. It has worked to redesign medical education in Bangladesh, so that medical staff are more responsive to the needs of the poor rural population.[4]

In Nicaragua, the government itself has launched an impressive primary health care program. Despite all the problems the nation faces—the economic devastation inherited from the Somoza regime, the aggression of United States-backed Contras, the lack of good infrastructure—it spends over 10 percent of the national budget on health, one of the highest amounts in Latin America. Moreover, health expenditures are now directed toward serving the many, not the few.

According to the *American Journal of Public Health*, "The prerevolutionary situation in Nicaragua was not unlike that which continues to exist in many Latin American countries: fragmented and disorganized services with a major portion of the available pie taken up by a minority of the population . . . those covered by social security care and living in cities."[5] Today, as even a diplomat from a country hostile to the Sandinistas admits: "Health care is something they have every right to be proud of."[6]

As the result of the government's commitment to health care, infant mortality has dropped considerably, the number of rural health posts has quadrupled, breast-feeding and oral rehydration therapy have been widely promoted, and there have been several mass immunization campaigns. As for family planning, the government's attitude is, according to Dr. Orlando Rizzo, director of maternal and child health, "A woman who wants family planning can have it, but we don't think it is a top priority. We don't believe poverty will end by ending the poor."[7]

Nicaragua is also resisting interventions from population control organizations. At the Women's International Tribunal on Reproductive Rights in 1984, the Nicaraguan delegate told the assembly that the country no longer accepted funds from the IPPF because of pressures to institute population control. "At no time do we accept any conditions from foreign powers in our birth control program," she said. Instead, the country is seeking alternative sources of contraceptive supply.[8]

It is a sad commentary on the state of the world today that these types of health programs are precisely the ones most under attack, since they challenge vested interests. In 1976, a senior paramedic at the People's Health Center in Bangladesh was beheaded by agents of wealthy landowners who feared the project's growing strength. And in Nicaragua the constant threat of a United States-supported invasion is the most serious obstacle in the way of expanding health care.[9]

Birth control and health care, which should be basic rights enjoyed by all, are by necessity heated political issues, requiring organized support.

MAKING THE CONNECTION

In the movement for reproductive rights, isolation is one of the greatest enemies, for it prevents the sharing of information and strategies and the provision of solidarity and support. Today through both formal and informal networks, activists are breaking down barriers of race, class, and nationality in the recognition that population control is a global phenomenon and demands a global response. (See Appendix for a list of the major networks.)

One of the most impressive achievements of this network has been the campaign against Depo-Provera abuse. Pressure from consumer, health, and women's groups, in fact, is largely responsible for regulatory agencies in many Western and Third World countries taking a more cautious attitude toward the drug.

As this network grows, so does its ability to collect and transmit information back and forth. Since most new contraceptives and population control strategies originate in the West, activists there have a special opportunity and responsibility to monitor and publicize the latest developments. Furthermore, they are less subject to the political harassment that faces many activists in the Third World. Groups like the Boston Women's Health Book Collective, authors of *Our Bodies, Ourselves*, have played a vital role in disseminating information around the world.

Third World activists, on the other hand, are better placed to observe the impact of population control programs in the field, and they in turn can alert groups back in the countries where these programs originate. This has happened in Bangladesh, where firsthand reports from rural areas have greatly strengthened the campaign against Western agencies' financing of forced sterilization.

In India women's groups are now closely monitoring trials of the injectable contraceptive NET-EN (see Chapter 9), as well as critically evaluating the methodology and results of past WHO studies of the drug in Europe. They are currently petitioning the Indian Supreme Court to halt the drug trials and the further administration of NET-EN. Indian feminists are calling for women's groups in general to adopt a watchdog role vis à vis the country's family planning program in order to compel government and health personnel to follow officially stated safety and ethical guidelines. They are also demanding more representation on government decision-making bodies and more direct involvement in research on women's real birth control needs.[10]

In addition to fighting against population control, many members of this network are also working for the development of safer contraceptive alternatives and for the defense of women's right to legal abortion. The National Women's Health Network in the United States, for example, is currently trying to influence the direction of contraceptive research in government institutions. Pressure from such groups has at least been partially responsible for the increased allocation of funds to male reproductive research and the renewal of interest in barrier methods. In many countries the campaign for abortion rights is one of the strongest elements of the reproductive rights movement.

Although many contacts are informal, formal networks, particularly ISIS, the Women's International Information and Communication Service, and the Women's Global Network on Reproductive Rights (formerly ICASC), have helped to improve and speed communications. Their efforts led to the 1984 Women's International Tribunal and Meeting on Reproductive Rights in Amsterdam, which brought together over 400 women from seventy different countries in a powerful condemnation of both population control and antiabortion forces.

The reproductive rights network currently faces an important challenge in the form of the international antiabortion, antichoice movement. This movement is manipulating women's legitimate grievances against population control programs to build support for a cutoff of all international aid for abortion and family planning, with the exception of natural methods. It is also attacking programs designed to upgrade women's participation in the labor force on the basis that they are "antifamily" and discriminate against "homemakers."

At the 1985 United Nations Decade of Women Conference in Nairobi, Kenya, members of the antiabortion group PLAN (Protect Life in All Nations) held press conferences and disrupted feminist workshops to attract maximum media attention.[11] The fact that they were able to enlist a number of Third World women to their cause exposes one of the great dangers of population control: the way it easily provokes a backlash against all forms of family planning. The reproductive rights network must now clearly differentiate itself from these conservative forces, defending women's right to abortion and family planning, at the same time that it continues to criticize the ways population control too restricts choice.

ON THE INSIDE

Are these pressures from outside having any impact on the inside of the population establishment?

The answer is a small but hopeful yes. The population es-

tablishment is not a monolith, and there are a number of individuals within it who recognize that population control programs have often failed and have exacted a heavy toll on
women's health. They are looking for alternatives.

"We need a new way of thinking," said one Swedish official.
"A new line which separates us from both the right-wing op-
ponents of family planning and the advocates of population
control, a line which presents birth control in feminist terms."
By stopping the distribution of Depo-Provera overseas and
withdrawing from the World Bank's population project in Bangladesh, the Swedish International Development Authority has
shown it is willing to take concrete actions against harmful
population control programs.

Another European population adviser laments the lack of
sensitive research on the kinds of birth control women really
want. He is willing to have a dialogue with reproductive rights
activists, but doesn't know where to start.

In Latin America a senior official reveals how he wants his
country to establish an independent family planning program,
free of population control pressures, but it is difficult when the
funding and technology are largely controlled by the United
States population control community.[12]

Within that community there are also encouraging trends.
Prochoice forces have coalesced around the formation of the
International Women's Health Coalition. This New York-based
group concentrates on providing technical assistance and
training for voluntary, high quality reproductive health care,
including abortion services, in a number of Third World countries. It believes these services should be organized within a
context of "a strong commitment to the overall well-being of
women." In a refreshing departure from the norm, nowhere
in this organization's brochure is there a mention of the need
for population control.[13]

At the Population Council feminists have written women's
needs onto the agenda, through the articulation of the user
perspective, the building of bridges with the women's health
movement, and the opening of new avenues of research such
as studies on breast-feeding. These developments reflect the
fact that in the late 1980s feminists in professional positions

are finally able to wield some power within the population community.

In October 1986 the International Women's Health Coalition and the Population Council, in cooperation with the Boston Women's Health Book Collective and other U.S. women's health advocates, held a meeting in New York on contraceptive research and quality of care in international family planning programs. The meeting, one of the first of its kind, brought together contraceptive researchers, family planners, and reproductive and health rights activists from the United States and several Third World countries in a free and frank exchange of information and views. Third World participants were not hesitant to expose the way quality of care in national family planning programs has suffered from the emphasis on population control. Similar meetings are planned for other regions of the world.

According to Joan Dunlop, director of the International Women's Health Coalition, the time is ripe for such initiatives: "The threat of AIDS, which is renewing interest in barrier methods, and the right-wing attack on family planning, which is encouraging liberal elements in the population establishment to seek allies among the feminist community, make this an historic opening for those of us who want to make reproductive rights the new cornerstone of population policy."[14]

This optimism is tempered by the recognition that theirs is an uphill struggle. Working within the population establishment, these women must not only overcome the entrenched power of population control hard-liners, but the innate conservatism common to most large bureaucracies. They themselves worry that in order to secure resources, they will have to demonstrate that their approach to family planning is just as demographically effective as the population control approach: They will be trapped by the very donor guidelines that have diminished quality of care in the past. And there is always the danger that these individuals' genuine commitment to women's welfare will be twisted and manipulated by others in the population establishment who want to appropriate feminist language and concepts in order to give population control a better image.

Women health activists, on the other hand, worry about how far they can cooperate with even the most feminist members of the population establishment without losing their independence and credibility.

Despite these difficulties, it is certainly a positive development that a few people on the inside are listening to the people on the outside, because it could help set the stage for reform. In the end, however, population control needs more than just reforming. It needs to be fundamentally transformed, for its underlying values are not compatible with either reproductive choice or basic human rights. Stripped of all the economic arguments and political justifications, population control at heart is a philosophy without a heart, in which human beings become objects to be manipulated. It is a philosophy of domination, for its architects must necessarily view people of different sex, race, and class as inferior, less human than themselves, or otherwise they could not justify the double standards they employ.

Such attitudes are not specific to population control, of course, but are a general affliction of this technocratic age. Technology is expected to solve social problems, and leadership is vested in the managers, who substitute top-down social planning for democratic self-determination. Population control is only one part of this ethos, but it is an important part. It profoundly distorts our world view, and negatively affects people in the most intimate areas of their lives. Instead of promoting ethics and empathy, it encourages us to condone coercion. And even on the most practical level, it is no solution to the population problem.

While it would be naive to hope for a quick reversal of population policy, one can at least take the liberty of imagining what would be possible if all the resources presently wasted on population control were redirected toward expanding reproductive choice. The alternatives are already there. There is a way forward.

Notes

Notes to boxed material will be found at the end of the notes to each chapter.

Most of the initial research for this book was done in 1983–1984. However, in the course of writing the book, I have made a concerted effort to stay abreast of current events and have updated research whenever necessary. While much of the material, particularly books and periodicals, is available in major libraries, I acquired a number of less accessible documents through ongoing personal contacts with people in the population field, development agencies, and feminist organizations. Specialized libraries, such as the International Planned Parenthood Federation Library in London, and resource collections, including those of the Boston Women's Health Book Collective and the Institute for Food and Development Policy in San Francisco, were particularly useful. As in any research endeavor in a major field, one has to follow one's instincts in order to tunnel a path through the mountain of available literature. I have tried to be as comprehensive as possible but also sharply focused in order to render a clear picture of population control.

I RETHINKING THE POPULATION PROBLEM

1. See Rafael Salas, *The State of World Population 1981*, New York, UNFPA, 1981; also World Bank, *World Development Report 1984* (Oxford: Oxford University Press, 1984).

2. Mead T. Cain, "The Economic Activities of Children in a Village in Bangladesh," *Population and Development Review*, vol. 3, no. 3, September 1977.

3. John C. Caldwell, *Theory of Fertility Decline* (London: Academic Press, 1982), p. 69.

4. See, for example, Paul Harrison, "Poverty—the Limit?" *Development Forum*, 1979. In a rather macabre vision, Harrison is optimistic about the potential reduction of birth rates through poverty

in Bangladesh. He claims surveys have confirmed that approval and use of contraception increase as amount of land owned declines. But as long as a peasant can live off the proceeds of land sales, the impact on fertility may be delayed. Once this source of money dries up, the peasant will have no other choice but to limit births. Thus Bangladesh "may be hovering on the brink of a sudden and dramatic drop in the birth rate." Increased poverty thus becomes a blessing in disguise, for a destitution-induced decline in population growth will help the country develop and limit births through more positive means!

5. See Mead Cain, "Risk and Insurance: Perspectives on Fertility and Agrarian Change in India and Bangladesh," *Population and Development Review*, vol. 7, no. 3 (September 1981), and by the same author, "Fertility as an Adjustment to Risk," Population Council, Center for Policy Studies Working Papers, No. 100 (New York: October 1983). Also see Caldwell, *Fertility Decline.*

6. See Caldwell, *Fertility Decline*, for more on how education changes the value of children.

Japan provides an interesting example of how the role of children as a source of security changes. In 1950, at the beginning of Japan's industrial boom, a survey showed that over half the population expected to be supported by children in their old age. By 1961, after a decade of rapid growth, this figure had already declined to 27 percent, and the birth rate had also fallen dramatically. Japan example from William W. Murdoch, *The Poverty of Nations: The Political Economy of Hunger and Population* (Baltimore: Johns Hopkins University Press, 1980), p. 29.

The cost of raising one child in the United States from U.S. Department of Agriculture, Agricultural Research Service, *Family Economics Review*, no. 4 (October 1983). In 1982 college education cost an additional $10,000–25,000.

7. Indian example from Frances Moore Lappé and Joseph Collins, *Food First: Beyond the Myth of Scarcity* (New York: Ballantine Books, 1979), p. 32. Sahel example from Caldwell, *Desertification: Demographic Evidence, 1973–1983*, a report to the U.N. Environmental Program Desertification Section (n.p.; n.d.). Also see Nancy E. Williamson, "Boys or Girls? Parents' Preferences and Sex Control," *Population Bulletin*, vol. 33, no. 1 (1978), and Kathleen Newland, "It's an old prejudice—with deep social roots," *Christian Science Monitor*, 11 April 1983.

8. Rafael M. Salas, *The State of the World Population 1983*, New York, UNFPA, 1983, and 1982 World Population Data Sheet of the Population Reference Bureau.

9. Ray E. Brown and Joe D. Wray, "The Starving Roots of Population Growth," *Natural History*, vol. 83, no. 1 (January 1974).

10. James P. Grant, *The State of the World's Children 1982–83*, New York, UNICEF, 1983, p. 7. Not everyone believes there is such a close correlation between mortality and fertility declines; it is a matter of some dispute.

11. José Villar and José M. Belizan, "Women's Poor Health in Developing Countries: A Vicious Circle," in Patricia Blair, ed., *Health Needs of the World's Poor Women* (Washington, D.C.: Equity Policy Center, 1981).

12. Isabel Nieves, "Changing Infant Feeding Practices: A Woman-Centered View," in Blair, ed., *Health Needs*.

13. Richard D. Lamm, "Linking Third World Aid to Population Control," *International Herald Tribune*, 22 April 1985.

14. Thomas R. Malthus, *An Essay on Population*, Vol. 1 (New York: E. P. Dutton and Co., 1914), p. 6.

15. Douglas C. North and Robert P. Thomas, *The Rise of the Western World: A New Economic History* (Cambridge: Cambridge University Press, 1973), p. 8.

16. Environmental Fund, *Statement on the Real Crisis Behind the "Food Crisis"* (Washington, D.C.: 1975).

17. Quoted in John Tierney, "The Population Crisis Revisited," *Wall Street Journal*, 20 January 1986. See also Dennis Meadows and Donnella Meadows, *The Limits to Growth* (New York: Universe Books, 1972).

18. Ann Crittenden, "Poverty, Not Scarcity Called Chief Cause of World Hunger," *New York Times*, 7 December 1982.

19. Computed from Table 19, "Population and Manpower," in *United Nations 1981 Statistical Yearbook* (New York: United Nations Department of International Economic and Social Affairs, 1983), and Table 1, "Land Use," in *FAO Production Yearbook*, vol. 36 (1983).

20. Paul R. Ehrlich, Loy Bilderbach, and Anne H. Ehrlich, *The Golden Door: International Migration, Mexico and the United States* (New York: Ballantine Books, 1979), p. viii.

21. Colin Clark, *Population Growth and Land Use* (London: Macmillan, 1967), pp. 137–38. Also see Ester Boserup, *The Conditions of Agricultural Growth: The Economics of Agrarian Change Under Population Pressure* (London: George Allen and Unwin, Ltd., 1970).

22. See Terry N. Barr, "The World Food Situation and Global Grain Prospects," *Science*, 4 December 1981; *World Development Report 1984*; Murdoch, *The Poverty of Nations*, pp. 98–99.

23. Cited in Susan George, *How the Other Half Dies: The Real*

Reasons for World Hunger (Montclair, N.J.: Allanheld, Osmun and Co., 1977), p. 35.

24. Amartya Sen, *Poverty and Famines: An Essay on Entitlement and Deprivation* (Oxford: Clarendon Press, 1981), p. 118.

25. On the unreliability of statistics, see Lloyd Timberlake, *Africa in Crisis: The Causes, The Cures of Environmental Bankruptcy* (London: International Institute for Environment and Development [Earthscan], 1985).

26. Quoted in Richard Hall, "Debate Begins on Third World Birth Control," *Observer*, 29 July 1984.

27. Michael F. Lofchie, "Political and Economic Origins of African Hunger," *Journal of Modern African Studies*, vol. 13, no. 4 (1975), p. 554; Richard W. Franke and Barbara H. Chasin, *Seeds of Famine: Ecological Destruction and the Development Dilemma in the West African Sahel* (Montclair, N.J.: Allanheld, Osmun and Co., 1980), and Carl F. Eicher, "Facing Up to Africa's Food Crisis," *Foreign Affairs*, Fall 1982.

28. Nigel Twose, "Food Gets Low Priority in Upper Volta's Agriculture," *OXFAM News*, April–May 1984.

29. Timberlake, *Africa in Crisis*, p. 73.

30. Ibid.

31. Ibid., p. 209; and Paula Park and Tony Jackson, *Lands of Plenty, Lands of Scarcity: Agriculture Policy and Peasant Farmers in Zimbabwe and Tanzania* (Oxford: OXFAM, May 1985). Park and Jackson also describe the many problems Zimbabwe still faces in bringing about a genuine agrarian reform.

32. World Bank, *Poverty and Hunger: Issues and Options for Food Security in Developing Countries*, A World Bank Policy Study. (Washington, D.C.: 1986).

33. Lester R. Brown, et al., *State of the World 1984, A Worldwatch Institute Report on Progress Toward a Sustainable Society* (New York: W. W. Norton and Co., 1984), p. 209.

34. E. Wayne Nafziger, *The Economics of Developing Countries* (Belmont, CA.: Wadsworth, 1984), pp. 185, 188.

35. See section on forests in Center for Science and Environment, *The State of India's Environment 1982, A Citizen's Report* (New Delhi: 1982). This excellent report should be required reading for anyone interested in Third World environmental issues. Government view quoted in Ramachandra Guha, "Forestry in British and Post-British India, A Historical Analysis," *Economic and Political Weekly*, 5 November 1983, n. 166.

36. Bharat Dogra, "World Bank vs. The People of Bastar, Re-

forestation or Deforestation?" *Cultural Survival Quarterly*, vol. 10, no. 1 (1986). Also see other articles in this issue for examples of the negative impact of development projects on the environment and indigenous peoples. For general critique of World Bank development policies, see Cheryl Payer, *The World Bank: A Critical Analysis* (New York: Monthly Review Press, 1982), and Teresa Hayter with Catherine Watson, *Aid: Rhetoric and Reality* (London: Pluto Press, 1984).

37.   Center for Science and Environment, *The State of India's Environment 1982* (New Delhi: 1982), p. 152.

38.   Lappé and Collins, *Food First*, pp. 48–52.

39.   Gregg Jones, "Marcos Profited from Smuggling $1b in Timber, Officials Say," *Boston Globe,* 22 May 1986.

40.   United Nations Environment Program, "Population and Desertification in Kenya," Press Release Feature 84/4, Nairobi, February 1984.

41.   Lappé and Collins, *Food First*, p. 43.

42.   Caldwell, *Desertification.*

43.   *World Development Report 1984*, p. 79.

44.   Population Crisis Committee, "Third World Population Growth from a Business Perspective," *Population*, no. 8 (June 1978).

45.   *World Development Report 1984*, p. 81.

46.   Fred Pearce, "In Defense of Population Growth," *New Scientist*, 9 August 1984.

47.   *World Development Report 1984*, p. 86.

48.   Ibid., Table 26, p. 268.

49.   Ibid., Table 25, p. 266.

50.   Ibid., pp. 87–88.

51.   See Teresa Hayter, *The Creation of World Poverty* (London: Pluto Press, in association with Third World First, 1983), for an explanation of these processes. See also Richard J. Barnet and Ronald E. Muller, *Global Reach: The Power of the Multinational Corporation* (New York: Simon and Schuster, 1974).

52.   Peter Roger, "$55 Billion 'Spirited Away Overseas,'" *Guardian*, 19 June 1984.

53.   On Japan, see Pearce, "Population Growth." On France and West Germany see "Low Birth Rate in Western Europe Means Big Social, Economic Changes are Likely," *Wall Street Journal*, 30 December 1985.

54.   See Robert McNamara, "Time Bomb or Myth: The Population Problem," *Foreign Affairs*, Summer 1984, and Maxwell D. Taylor, "U.S. Objectives in Central America," *San Francisco Chronicle*, 7 September 1983.

55.   U.S. Congress. House. *Population and Development in Latin America and the Caribbean.* Hearing before the Subcommittee on Inter-American Affairs of the Committee on Foreign Affairs, 97th Cong., 2d sess., 8 September 1982, p. 45. For another example see Alan L. Otten, "Population Explosion is a Threat to Stability of Central America," *Wall Street Journal,* 17 February 1984.

56.   Malthus, *An Essay,* Vol. II, p. 260.

57.   Julian L. Simon and Herman Kahn, *The Resourceful Earth* (Oxford: Basil Blackwell, 1984), Introduction.

58.   Julian L. Simon, "Myths of Overpopulation," *Wall Street Journal,* 3 August 1984, and his book *The Ultimate Resource* (Princeton: Princeton University Press, 1981).

59.   "U.S. Policy Statement for the International Conference on Population," reproduced as Attachment A in the Ford Foundation, *The Ford Foundation's Work in Population* (New York: August 1985), pp. 45–46.

60.   For an account of the report, see Constance Holden, "A Revisionist Look at Population and Growth," *Science,* vol. 231, no. 4745 (28 March 1986).

61.   Jonathon Lieberson, "Is Population a Problem?" *The New York Review of Books,* vol. 33, no. 11 (26 June 1986).

62.   World Bank, *Population Growth and Policies in Sub-Saharan Africa* (Washington: 1986), pp. vi, 6.

BOX   The Breast-feeding Connection (pages 10–11)

1.   Ann Wigglesworth, "Space to Live," Background Article, The State of World Population 1983 Press File, prepared by the New Internationalist Publications Cooperative for the UNFPA (Oxford: 1983); Lappé and Collins, *Food First,* p. 337.

2.   Robert Lighthouse Jr. and Susheela Singh, "The World Fertility Survey: Charting Global Childbearing," *Population Bulletin,* vol. 37, no. 1 (March 1982), p. 29.

3.   Beverly Winikoff, *The Infant Feeding Study: Summary,* report submitted to AID by the Population Council (New York: The Population Council, n.d.).

4.   See Lightbourne and Singh, "The World Fertility Survey," and Maggie Jones, "The Biggest Contraceptive in the World," *New Internationalist,* no. 110 (April 1982).

5.   See Wigglesworth, "Space to Live"; Grant, *State of the World's Children 1982–83;* and Kathleen Newland, *Infant Mortality and the Health of Societies,* Worldwatch Paper No. 47 (Washington,

D.C.: Worldwatch Institute, December 1981).

BOX   Africa: Overpopulated, Underpopulated, or Both? (pages 17-18)

1. See *Famine: A Man-Made Disaster?* a report to the Independent Commission on International Humanitarian Issues (London: Pan Books, 1985), and Maaza Bekele, "Explosion in a Vacuum," *Ceres,* July–August 1983.

2. *Famine,* p. 11.

3. See Timberlake, *Africa in Crisis,* Chapter 3. Also on African land use, see FAO, *Land, Food and People* (Rome: 1984).

4. OXFAM Public Affairs Unit, *Lessons to be Learned: Drought and Famine in Ethiopia* (Oxford: 1984).

5. Richard W. Franke, "Mode of Production and Population Patterns: Policy Implications for West African Development," *International Journal of Health Services,* vol. 11, no. 3 (1981).

6. See, for example, Timberlake, *Africa in Crisis.*

2   A WOMB OF ONE'S OWN

1. Peruvian quotation from Audrey Bronstein's interview notes for *The Triple Struggle: Latin American Peasant Women* (London: War on Want Campaigns Ltd., 1982); Senegalese quotation from Mariama Kamara, "Bearing the Brunt," *People,* (IPPF), vol. 10, no. 4 (1983), pp. 17–18; Sri Lankan quotation from "Population Control Practices on the Tea Plantations of Sri Lanka," statement delivered at Women's International Tribunal and Meeting on Reproductive Rights, held at Amsterdam, 22–28 July 1984; U.K. letter from Marge Berer, *Who Needs Depo-Provera?* (London: Community Rights Project, July 1981), p. 25.

2. For a discussion of the impact of colonialism on women, especially in Africa, see Barbara Rogers, *The Domestication of Women: Discrimination in Developing Societies* (New York: Tavistock Publishers, 1981), and Ester Boserup, *Woman's Role in Economic Development* (London: George Allen and Unwin Ltd., 1970).

3. Ronald S. Waife, M.S.P.H., *Traditional Methods of Birth Control in Zaire,* Pathpapers No. 4 (the Pathfinder Fund, December 1978), p. 4.

4. See Lars Bondestam and Staffan Bergström, *Poverty and Population Control* (London: Academic Press, 1980), pp. 43–44; Murdoch, *The Poverty of Nations,* p. 28, and Rogers, *The Domestication of Women,* p. 111.

5. Rogers, *The Domestication of Women*, p. 62.

6. See Marilee Karl, "Women and Rural Development," in ISIS Women's International Information and Communication Service, *Women in Development: A Resource Guide for Organization and Action* (Geneva: 1983). This is a crucial source for anyone interested in women and development. Also see *Follow-Up to WCAARD: The Role of Women in Agricultural Production*, Expert Consultation on Women in Food Production (Rome: FAO, 1983), and other papers in this series.

7. See Ester Boserup, "Economic and Demographic Interrelationships in sub-Saharan Africa," *Population and Development Review*, vol. 11, no. 3 (September 1985).

8. *The Need for Improved Agricultural Extension Services for Women Engaged in Agriculture*, Expert Consultation on Women in Food Production (Rome: FAO, December 1983).

9. See Kathleen Newland, *The Sisterhood of Man* (New York: W. W. Norton and Co., 1979), p. 171.

10. On women in the labor force see Rogers, *The Domestication of Women*, and Newland, *The Sisterhood of Man*. For three excellent case studies see Khin Thitsa, *Providence and Prostitution: Image and Reality for Women in Buddhist Thailand*, CHANGE International Reports: Women and Society (London: 1980), Blanca Figueroa and Jeanine Anderson, *Women in Peru*, CHANGE (London: 1981), and Aline K. Wong, *Economic Development and Women's Place: Women in Singapore*, CHANGE (London: 1980).

11. See Barbara Ehrenreich and Annette Fuentes, "Life on the Global Assembly Line," *Ms.*, January 1981.

12. See, for example, Judith Bruce and Daisy Dwyer, eds., "Women and Income in the Third World," publisher to be announced. Many papers in this volume are available from the Population Council.

13. See Helen Ware, *Women, Demography and Development*, Development Studies Center Demography Teaching Notes No. 3 (Canberra: The Australian National University, 1981), p. 61; and Amartya Sen, *Family and Food: Sex-Bias in Poverty* (All Souls College, Oxford: November 1981).

·14. Vina Mazumdar, "Another Development with Women: A View from Asia," *Development Dialogue* (Uppsala), nos. 1–2 (1982).

15. Itziar Lozano Urbieta, *Women, the Key to Liberation* (New York: Women's International Resource Exchange Service, n.d.). Peru saying—personal communication with Judith Condor.

16. Newland, *The Sisterhood of Man*, p. 202.

17. Rashid Faruquee and Ravi Gulhati, *Rapid Population Growth*

in *Sub-Saharan Africa: Issues and Policies*, World Bank Staff Working Papers, No. 559 (Washington, D.C.: World Bank, 1983).

18.   Mead Cain, Syewda Rokeya Khanam, and Shamsun Nahar, "Class, Patriarchy and Women's Work in Bangladesh," *Population and Development Review*, vol. 5, no. 3 (September 1979), p. 432.

19.   Study finding from Debbie Taylor, "Women: An Analysis," in *Women: A World Report* (London: Methuen Ltd., 1985), p. 12. This is an excellent source for up-to-date material on women, and it has lively chapters on women in different countries written by women journalists and novelists. See also Newland, *The Sisterhood of Man*, p. 187.

20.   Personal interview with Paula Park.

21.   See Taylor, "Women: An Analysis," p. 71; Murdoch, *The Poverty of Nations*, p. 41; and *World Development Report 1984*, pp. 109–10.

22.   D. Mandelbaum, *Human Fertility in India* (Berkeley: University of California Press, 1974), quoted in Ware, *Women, Demography and Development*, p. 84.

23.   Female literacy rate from Kristin Helmore, "The Neglected Resource: Women in the Developing World," *Christian Science Monitor*, 20 December 1985. Further education figure from Taylor, "Women: An Analysis," p. 73. Also see Valsa Verghese, Maria Teresa Chadwick, and Ximena Charnes, "Education and Communication," in *Women in Development*, ISIS Resource Guide.

24.   *World Development Report 1984*, p. 110.

25.   Robert Lighthouse Jr. and Susheela Singh, "The World Fertility Survey: Charting Global Childbearing," *Population Bulletin*, vol. 37, no. 1 (March 1982), pp. 42–43. See also ibid., p. 130.

26.   Perdita Huston, *Message from the Village* (New York, Epoch B Foundation, 1978).

27.   Bronstein, *The Triple Struggle*, p. 260.

28.   On Bangladesh, see Betsy Hartmann and James K. Boyce, *A Quiet Violence: View from a Bangladesh Village* (London: Zed Press; San Francisco: Institute for Food and Development Policy; India: Oxford University Press, 1983), and Jenneke Arens and Jos van Beurden, *Jhagrapur: Poor Peasants and Women in a Village in Bangladesh* (Bombay: Orient Longman, 1979), and Loes Keysers, *Does Family Planning Liberate Women?*, Master of Development Studies thesis (The Hague: Institute of Social Studies, May 1982). On Kenya see Gill Shepherd, *Responding to the Contraceptive Needs of Rural People, A Report to OXFAM on Kenya in 1984* (Oxford: OXFAM, 1984). There are serious limitations to Shepherd's interview methods, however, since she fre-

quently began her discussions with women by stating that Kenya had an urgent need for population control. For statements by Third World women's organizations, see *Divided in Culture, United in Struggle,* Report of the International Tribunal and Meeting on Reproductive Rights, Amsterdam, 22–28 July 1984 (Amsterdam: Women's Global Network on Reproductive Rights, 1986).

29.   Bangladesh statistics from Zafrullah Chowdhury, "A Double Oppression in Bangladesh," in Blair, ed., *Health Needs,* p. 5. Anemia statistic from Taylor, "Women: An Analysis," p. 43.

30.   World Health Organization, Division of Family Health, *Health and the Status of Women* (Geneva: 1980), and "Healthier Mothers and Children Through Family Planning," *Population Reports,* Series J, No. 27 (May–June 1984), p. J661.

31.   Newland, *The Sisterhood of Man,* p. 52.

32.   Huston, *Message from the Village,* p. 131.

33.   *World Development Report 1984,* p. 130, and Population Crisis Committee, "World Abortion Trends," *Population,* no. 9 (April 1979).

34.   WHO, "Health and the Status of Women." Bolivian figures from Newland, *The Sisterhood of Man,* p. 61.

35.   Population Crisis Committee, "World Abortion Trends."

36.   Huston, *Message from the Village,* p. 119.

37.   See Christine Oppong and Elina Haavio-Mannila, "Women, Population and Development," in Philip M. Hauser, ed., *World Population and Development* (Syracuse, N.Y.: Syracuse University Press, 1979), p. 480.

38.   Huston, *Message from the Village,* p. 109.

39.   *World Development Report 1984,* p. 135.

40.   On travel time, see Shepherd, *Responding to the Contraceptive Needs,* p. 8. Refusal of birth control, personal communication with Paula Park.

41.   Dr. S. Okun Ayangade, *International Journal of Obstetrics and Gynecology,* vol. 15, no. 6 (1978), p. 499, quoted in Waife, *Traditional Methods of Birth Control.*

42.   Nawal El Saadawi, "On Women's Shoulders," *People,* (IPPF), vol. 6, no. 4 (1979). This article is an excerpt from her book *The Hidden Face of Eve: Women in the Arab World* (London: Zed Press, 1979).

43.   See World Bank, *Population Growth and Policies in Sub-Saharan Africa,* p. 60.

44.   Gavin Jones, "Towards an Optimum Population: The Malaysian Case," *People* (IPPF), vol. 12, no. 4 (1985).

45. Peru information from Rosa Domingo Trapasso of the Peruvian women's group Promoción Cultural "Creatividad y Cambio." A coalition of Peruvian women's groups has now mounted a campaign for public family planning services.

46. See Robin Morgan, ed., *Sisterhood Is Global: The International Women's Movement Anthology* (New York: Anchor Press/Doubleday, 1984), p. 2, and Newland, *The Sisterhood of Man*.

47. See Joe Joyce, "Dublin Scents Victory in Fight to Legalize Condoms," *Guardian*, 18 February 1985.

48. Rosalind P. Petchesky, " 'Reproductive Choice' in the Contemporary United States: A Social Analysis of Female Sterilization," in Karen L. Michaelson, ed., *And the Poor Get Children: Radical Perspectives on Population Dynamics* (New York: Monthly Review Press, 1981), p. 69.

49. Rate from W. J. Weatherby, "The Future New York Offers the World," *Guardian*, 27 March 1985.

50. Tatyana Mamonova, "The USSR: It's Time We Began with Ourselves," in Morgan, ed., *Sisterhood Is Global*, pp. 684–85.

51. *World Development Report 1984*, p. 157.

52. "Romania Orders Baby Boom," *Guardian*, 19 March 1984, and Eve-Ann Prentice, "Romanian Women Subjected to 'Pregnancy Tests' at Work," *Guardian*, 21 June 1986.

53. Thanks to Adele Clark for drafts of articles on this subject. List is also drawn from literature of various reproductive rights organizations. Also see Adele Clark and Alice Wolfson, "Socialist-Feminism and Reproductive Rights: Movement Work and Its Contradictions," *Socialist Review*, vol. 14, no. 6 (November–December 1984).

3 THE PLAN BEHIND FAMILY PLANNING

1. See Donald Warwick, *Bitter Pills: Population Policies and Their Implementation in Eight Developing Countries* (Cambridge: Cambridge University Press, 1982), for a fascinating account of these interventions.

2. Ibid., pp. 114–22.

3. Mahmood Mamdani, *The Myth of Population Control: Family, Caste and Class in an Indian Village* (New York: Monthly Review Press, 1972), p. 19.

4. Bernard Berelson, "National Family Planning Programs: A Guide," *Studies in Family Planning*, No. 5, Supplement, 1964, p. 11, quoted in Warwick, *Bitter Pills*, p. 35.

5.   See *World Development Report 1984*, p. 132. Organizations such as the Program for the Introduction and Adaptation of Contraceptive Technology (PIACT) are starting to utilize smaller, in-depth surveys.

6.   Quoted in Goran Djurfeld and Staffan Lindberg, "Family Planning in a Tamil Village," in Bondestam and Bergström, *Poverty and Population Control*, p. 105.

7.   BKBBN, *Basic Information on Population and Family Planning Program* (Jakarta: 1982), p. 52. Also see Keysers, *Does Family Planning Liberate Women?* for the kinds of messages promulgated in Bangladesh.

8.   Mamdani, *The Myth of Population Control*, p. 40.

9.   Lita Paniagua, "Selling Values Through Social Soap Opera," *People* (IPPF), vol. 10, no. 3 (1983).

10.   Paul Harrison, "King of the Market in Bangladesh," *People*, vol. 6, no. 1 (1979).

11.   Warwick, *Bitter Pills*, p. 40.

12.   Quoted in ibid., p. 131.

13.   Ibid.

14.   Westinghouse Health Systems, "Family Planning Program Effectiveness Study," 29 September 1978, in AID, *Family Planning Program Effectiveness: Report of a Workshop*, AID Program Evaluation Report No. 1 (Washington, D.C.: December 1979), p. 52. According to a former population official, corruption is also rife in the Filipino program. When the Filipino Family Planning Association's warehouse burned down, destroying its contraceptive supplies, members reportedly used the money on luxurious new offices rather than on replacing the lost stocks. This same official comments: "Bribery, nepotism, tax evasion and outright theft are probably as prevalent in family planning programs as anywhere else in the aid world."

15.   Warwick, *Bitter Pills*, pp. 154–55.

16.   Personal communication.

17.   John C. Caldwell and Pat Caldwell, "Family Planning in India: A Worm's Eye View from a Rural Area in South India," *South Asia*, vol. 5, no. 1 (June 1982).

18.   *World Development Report 1984*, p. 176.

19.   Quoted in Warwick, *Bitter Pills*, p. 139.

20.   Quoted in ibid., p. 167.

21.   According to the *World Development Report 1984*, p. 135, follow-up surveys of women who have accepted contraception find that discontinuation is largely due to medical side effects. One survey in the Philippines found this reason cited by 66 percent of women

who stopped taking the pill, 43 percent who discontinued the IUD.

22.   See World Bank, *The Population Sector* (Washington: n.d.); also N. Yinger, R. Osborn, D. Salkever, and I. Sirageldin, "Third World Family Planning Programs: Measuring the Costs," *Population Bulletin,* vol. 138, no. 1 (February 1983).

23.   Warwick, *Bitter Pills,* p. 25.

24.   Personal communication.

25.   UNFPA, Population Council and IPPF, *Family Planning in the 1980's: Challenges and Opportunities,* prepared for Report of the International Conference on Family Planning in the 1980s, Jakarta, Indonesia, 26–30 April 1981 (U.S.: 1981, p. 18).

26.   Personal interview, February 1984.

27.   This description of the classic incentive model is from Marika Vicziany's excellent critique of the Indian family planning program, "Coercion in a Soft State: The Family Planning Program of India, Part I: The Myth of Voluntarism," *Pacific Affairs,* Fall 1982, p. 393.

28.   Ibid., p. 393.

29.   Judith Jacobsen, *Promoting Population Stabilization: Incentives for Small Families,* Worldwide Paper 54 (Washington, D.C.: Worldwatch Institute, June 1983), p. 12.

30.   Personal interview with Alex Marshall, UNFPA, February 1984.

31.   Dr. Zafrullah Chowdhury, "Cash Incentives Degrade Both Parties," *People* (IPPF), vol. 9, no. 4 (1982).

32.   Henry David, "Mechai's Way," *People* (IPPF), vol. 9, no. 4 (1982).

33.   *Family Planning in the 1980's,* p. 18.

34.   Indonesia: World Bank project from Jacobsen, *Promoting Population Stabilization,* p. 20; AID quote from AID Office of Population and Health *Indonesia: Family Planning Program,* Orientation Booklet (Jakarta: June 1984), p. 11; Thailand from David, "Mechai's Way."

35.   Jacobsen, *Promoting Population Stabilization,* p. 20.

36.   Ibid.

37.   Kingsley Davis, "Population Control Cannot Be Painless," *People* (IPPF), vol. 9, no. 4 (1982).

38.   *Family Planning in the 1980's,* pp. 97–98.

BOX   Lee's Designer Genes (pages 69–71)

1.   Quoted in Chee Heng Leng and Chan Chee Khoon, *Designer Genes: I.Q., Ideology and Biology* (Selangor, Malaysia: INSAN, Institute

for Social Analysis, 1984), p. 7. This booklet presents an excellent critique of eugenics.

2. Nicholas Cumming-Bruce, "Lee's Brighter Babies Plan Angers Wives," *Guardian*, 22 February 1984.

3. Nuray Fincancioglu, "Singapore's Controversial Incentives," *People*, vol. 11, no. 3 (1984).

4. Cumming-Bruce, "Lee's Brighter Babies."

5. Quoted in Leng and Khoon, *Designer Genes*, p. 13.

6. See C. K. Chan, "Eugenics on the Rise: A Report from Singapore," *International Journal of Health Services*, vol. 15, no. 4 (1985). Chan reports slightly different sterilization incentives than Fincancioglu.

4   THE INDONESIAN SUCCESS AND THE KENYAN FAILURE

1. See Geoffrey McNicoll and Masri Singarimbun, *Fertility Decline in Indonesia: I. Background and Proximate Determinants*, Center for Policy Studies Working Papers, No. 92 (New York: The Population Council, November 1982). Also see T. H. Hull, "Fertility Decline in Indonesia: A Review of Recent Evidence," *Bulletin of Indonesian Economic Studies*, vol. 16, no. 2 (1980), and by the same author, "Indonesian Population Growth 1971–1980," *Bulletin of Indonesian Economic Studies*, vol. 17, no. 1 (1981).

2. BKBBN statistics from AID Office of Population and Health, *Indonesia: Family Planning Program*, Orientation Booklet (Jakarta: June 1984), p. 26. On their reliability, see Peter Kim Streatfield, *The Reliability of the Contraceptive Prevalence Statistics of the Indonesian Family Planning Program*, Research Note No. 23, International Population Dynamics Program (Canberra: The Australian National University, 1 August 1984). Thanks to Dr. Peter Hagul of the Gadjah Mada University Population Studies Center for making this and other publications available to me.

According to a former IPPF official, "When I was in Indonesia, most of the people I talked to put the 'success' of the program down to one thing—the figures are fiddled. Certainly I have rarely seen such a logistically inefficient program and I find it very difficult to believe the Government's figures on 'contraceptive delivery.' " (Personal communication.)

3. *AID's Role in Indonesian Family Planning: A Case Study with General Lessons for Foreign Assistance*, AID Program Evaluation Report No. 2 (Washington, D.C.: December 1979), p. 1.

4. McNicoll and Singarimbun, *Fertility Decline in Indonesia:*

II. Analysis and Interpretation, Center for Policy Studies Working Papers No. 93 (New York: Population Council, December 1982).

5. For the role of the Ford Foundation and other United States institutions, see David Ransom, "Ford Country: Building an Elite for Indonesia," in Steve Weissman, ed., *The Trojan Horse: A Radical Look at Foreign Aid* (San Francisco: Ramparts Press, 1974). On influence of Western-trained technocrats, see *AID's Role in Indonesian Family Planning,* pp. 33–34.

6. See *Family Planning in the 1980's,* p. 34.

7. Jay S. Parsons, "What Makes the Indonesian Family Planning Program Tick?" *Populi,* vol. 11, no. 3 (1984). See this article for a history of the program.

8. *AID's Role in Indonesian Family Planning,* p. 44.

9. AID Office of Population and Health, *Indonesia: Family Planning Program,* p. 6.

10. BKBBN, *Basic Information on Population,* p. 63.

11. AID Office of Population and Health, *Indonesia: Family Planning Program,* p. 25.

12. On use of traditional methods, see McNicoll and Singarimbun, *Fertility Decline in Indonesia I,* and Jon E. Rohde, "Mother Milk and the Indonesian Economy: A Major National Resource," *Journal of Tropical Pediatrics,* vol. 28 (August 1982).

13. KB, "Antara Fakta dan Hura-Hura," *Tempo,* 14 July 1984, parts of which are translated in "Compulsion Being Used in Indonesia's Family Planning Program," *TAPOL Bulletin,* No. 64 (July 1984)

14. McNicoll and Singarimbun, *Fertility Decline in Indonesia, II,* p. 9, and personal communication with health consultant.

15. Terence H. Hull and Valerie J. Hull, *Health Care and Birth Control in Indonesia: Links through Time,* Research Note No. 53, International Population Dynamics Program (Canberra: The Australian National University, 20 March 1986), p. 5. This article sheds an interesting historical light on the program, and has suggestions on how it could be reformed.

16. Diana Smith, "Indonesia Sets New Targets," *People,* (IPPF), vol. 10, no. 4 (1983). Scale down of program, personal communication with recent visitor to Indonesia.

17. *AID's Role in Indonesian Family Planning,* pp. 33–34.

18. See, for example, Parsons, "What Makes the Indonesian Family Planning Program Tick?"

19. *AID's Role in Indonesian Family Planning,* p. 47.

20. See *Tempo,* 14 July 1984, and *TAPOL Bulletin,* No. 64 (July 1984).

21. Ibid.

22. Parsons, "What Makes the Indonesian Family Planning Program Tick?"

23. Ibid.

24. Ibid.

25. Hull and Hull, p. 10.

26. For this view, see Parsons, "What Makes the Indonesian Family Planning Program Tick?"

27. See ibid. for a description of a typical field visit, and the role foreigners play in legitimizing the program.

28. Quoted in Sujaya Mishra, "Poignant Problems," *People*, (IPPF), vol. 10, no. 4 (1983). Also see Faruquee and Gulhati, *Rapid Population Growth in Sub-Saharan Africa*, on position of women.

29. See Boserup, "Economic and Demographic Interrelationships in sub-Saharan Africa."

30. See Shepherd, *Responding to the Contraceptive Needs of Rural People*. Lack of access to contraception is indicated by the prevalence of illegal abortion. See "Abortion in Kenya Today," *Life and Leisure* (Nairobi), 22 March 1985. Paula Park also reports cases of women aborting with herbs.

31. Quoted in Warwick, *Bitter Pills*, p. 77. For history of Kenyan program, see Warwick, and Lars Bondestam, "The Foreign Control of the Kenyan Population," in Bondestam and Bergström, *Poverty and Population Control*.

32. World Bank, *Kenya, Population and Development*, A World Bank Country Study (Washington: 1980), p. 174.

33. See "Interview: Pierre Pradervand," *People*, vol. 6, no. 1 (1979), for discussion of health services in African countries. Doctor/nurse ratios from Chege Mbitiru, "Kenya: the Great Population Debate," *Africa Now*, October 1985.

34. World Bank, *Kenya, Population and Development*, p. 176.

35. See ibid. Park observation from personal interview.

36. World Bank, *Kenya, Population and Development*, p. 181.

37. "African men are such animals. When he wants to he does," *People*, vol. 10, no. 4 (1983).

38. *World Development Report 1984*, p. 139.

39. Letter to author, dated 5 October 1983.

40. See Djibril Diallo, "Overpopulation and Other Myths About Africa," *Christian Science Monitor*, 22 April 1986.

41. See Shepherd, *Responding to the Contraceptive Needs*, p. 15.

42. World Bank, *Kenya, Growth and Structural Change*, vol. 1

(Washington, D.C.: 1983), p. 54. On incentives see pp. 62–64.

43. Moi's warning reported in Chege Mbitiru, "Kenya: The Great Population Debate," and Joe Nugi, "Pope's Message for Kenya," *People*, vol. 13, no. 1 (1986).

5   BIRTH OF AN IDEOLOGY

1. See Vivien Walsh, "Contraception: The Growth of a Technology," in the Brighton Women and Science Group, *Alice Through the Microscope* (London: Virago Press, 1980); Peter Fryer, *The Birth Controllers* (London: Secker and Warburg, 1965); Norman E. Himes, *Medical History of Contraception* (New York: Gamut Press, 1963); and Clive Wood and Beryl Suitters, *The Fight for Acceptance, A History of Contraception* (Aylesbury, U.K.: Medical and Technical Publishing Co. Ltd., 1970).

2. See Linda Gordon, *Woman's Body, Woman's Right, A Social History of Birth Control in America* (London and New York: Penguin Books, 1977), and Bonnie Mass, *Population Target: The Political Economy of Population Control in Latin America* (Toronto: Women's Press, 1976).

3. See Wood and Suitters, *The Fight for Acceptance.*

4. Speech by Margaret Sanger at Hartford, Connecticut, 11 February 1923, quoted in Bonnie Mass, *Population Target*, p. 26.

5. Quoted in David Kennedy, *Birth Control in America: The Career of Margaret Sanger* (New Haven: Yale University Press, 1970), p. 94.

6. Linda Gordon, "Birth Control: An Historical Study," *Science for the People*. January–February 1977, p. 16.

7. Quoted in Mass, *Population Target*, p. 21.

8. First quote from Mass, *Population Target*, p. 29; second and third from Linda Gordon, "Birth Control and the Eugenists," *Science for the People*, March–April 1977, p. 11

9. Quoted in Mass, *Population Target*, p. 29.

10. Quoted in Gordon, "Birth Control and the Eugenists," p. 14.

11. *The Eugenics Review*, April 1936, quoted in Mass, *Population Target*, p. 21.

12. Gordon, *Woman's Body, Woman's Right*, p. 396.

13. Ibid., p. 332.

14. Ibid., p. 326.

15. Quoted in ibid., p. 345.

16. See ibid., Chapter 12.

17. See *Report of the U.S. President's Materials Policy Commission*, quoted in William Barclay, Joseph Enright, and Reid T. Reynolds, "Population Control in the Third World," *NACLA Newsletter*, vol. 4, no. 8, p. 4.

18. See, for example, Steve Weissman, "Why the Population Bomb Is a Rockefeller Baby," *Ramparts*, May 1970, p. 44.

19. Report of the Population Council, Inc., November 1952–December 1955, pp. 5–6, quoted in Mass, *Population Target*, p. 37.

20. T. O. Greissimer, *The Population Bomb* (New York: The Hugh Moore Fund, 1954), quoted in Mass, *Population Target*, p. 40.

21. Weissman, "Why the Population Bomb is a Rockefeller Baby," p. 44.

22. See Nicholas J. Demerath, *Birth Control and Foreign Policy, The Alternatives to Family Planning* (New York: Harper and Row, 1976), Chapter 2.

23. Charles K. Wilber, "Population and Methodological Problems of Development Theory," in Wilber, ed., *The Political Economy of Development and Underdevelopment* (New York: Random House, 1979), pp. 55–56.

24. Stephen Enke, "Birth Control for Economic Development," *Science*, vol. 164 (16 May 1969), and Stephen Enke and Richard G. Zind, "Effect of Fewer Births on Average Income," *Journal of Biosocial Science*, vol. 1, no. 1 (January 1969), p. 41. For critique of this approach see Amiya Kumar Bagchi, *The Political Economy of Underdevelopment* (Cambridge: Cambridge University Press, 1982), p. 209.

25. Quoted in Mass, *Population Target*, p. 152.

26. Quoted in Phyllis Tilson Piotrow, *World Population Crisis: The United States Response* (New York: Praeger Publishers, 1973), p. 37.

27. Ibid., p. 39.

28. *Report on the U.S. President's Committee to Study the U.S. Military Assistance Program*, vol. 1 (Washington, D.C.: August 1959), pp. 185–87, quoted in Mass, *Population Target*, p. 41.

29. U.S. Congress. House. Committee on Agriculture. *The Food for Freedom Act of 1966*, 89th Congr., 2d sess., 1966. H.R. Rept. 1558, p. 4.

30. Quoted in Barclay, et al., "Population Control in the Third World," pp. 5–10.

31. Paul Wagman, "U.S. Goal: Sterilize Millions of Third World Women," *St. Louis Post-Dispatch*, 22 April 1977.

32. Quoted in Warwick, *Bitter Pills*, p. 49.

33.   Ibid., p. 50.

34.   Marshall Green, U.S. Department of State, "U.S. Responsibilities in World Population Issues," address to Commonwealth Club of California, San Francisco, 10 September 1976.

35.   Quoted in Piotrow, *World Population Crisis*, p. 200.

36.   Quoted in Mass, *Population Target*, p. 66.

37.   Chinese and Indian statements quoted in William F. Ryan and Peter J. Henriot, "Message from Bucharest for Washington and Rome," *America*, 2 November 1974. See also by the same authors, "Opposing Views on Population," *Worldview*, February 1975.

38.   Quoted in Ryan and Henriot, "Message from Bucharest," p. 248.

BOX   Selections from the World Population Plan of Action (pages 109–110)

1.   U.N. Department of Economic and Social Affairs, *The Population Debate: Dimensions and Perspectives*, vol. 1, Papers of the World Population Conference, Bucharest, 1974 (New York: 1975).

6   THE POPULATION ESTABLISHMENT TODAY

1.   "Sources of Population and Family Planning Assistance," *Population Reports*, Series J, No. 26 (January–February 1983), p. J621. See for overview of population and family planning organizations.

2.   The Ford Foundation, *The Ford Foundation's Work in Population* (New York: August 1985), p. 20.

3.   AID, *Congressional Presentation, Fiscal Year 1984*, Main Volume, and Budget of Office of Population Program, FY1981–FY1985.

4.   Personal interview, February 1984.

5.   AID, *Congressional Presentation, Fiscal Year 1985*, Main Volume, p. 42.

6.   Ibid., pp. 40–41.

7.   See *Population Reports*, Series J., No. 26.

8.   See Ibid., *UNFPA 1982 Report, UNFPA 1985 Report*, and recent UNFPA publications. Officials' comments from personal interviews, February 1984.

9.   *World Development Report 1984*, p. 180, and World Bank, *Population Growth and Economic and Social Development*, Addresses by A. W. Clausen, p. 26.

10.   Personal interview, February 1984.

11. World Bank, "The Population Sector."

12. IPPF, *Report to Donors, October 1983* (London: 1983), p. 3.

13. See Planned Parenthood Federation of America, "Current Events Related to IPPF," memorandum, New York, 7 August 1985.

14. Population Council, *1985 Annual Report* (New York: 1985).

15. Warwick, *Bitter Pills,* p. 59.

16. The Ford Foundation, *The Ford Foundation's Work.* On India, see Demerath, *Birth Control and Foreign Policy.*

17. The Ford Foundation, *The Ford Foundation's Work,* p. 16.

18. See Population Crisis Committee, "Private Organizations in the Population Field," *Population,* No. 16 (December 1985).

19. Personal interview, February 1984.

20. Population Crisis Committee, *Highlights of 1983 Activities,* Summary Report (Washington: 1983), p. 3.

21. Population Crisis Committee/Draper Fund, *Report of Activities, 1980–81* (Washington: 1982), p. 7.

22. PCC, *Highlights of 1983 Activities,* pp. 8–9.

23. Ibid., p. 3.

24. The Global Committee of Parliamentarians on Population and Development, "Statement on Population Stabilization by World Leaders," *New York Times,* 20 October 1985.

25. Warwick, *Bitter Pills,* p. 16.

26. Robert S. McNamara, "Time Bomb or Myth."

27. Ibid., p. 1127.

28. *World Development Report 1984,* pp. 156–61.

29. Ibid., p. 155.

30. Ibid., pp. 160–61.

31. Bernard Berelson and Jonathon Lieberson, "Government Efforts to Influence Fertility: The Ethical Issues," *Population and Development Review,* vol. 5 no. 4 (December 1979), p. 609.

32. Ibid., pp. 596, 603.

33. Personal interview, February 1984.

34. Jyoti Shankar Singh, "Ten Years On . . ." *Development Forum,* June 1984.

35. Amy Goodman and Krystyna von Henneberg, "Population Conference Ignored Key Issues," *Boston Globe,* 29 August 1984.

36. "U.S. Policy Statement for the International Conference on Population."

37. Personal communication with Ireen Dubel, who attended the conference as an observer.

7   THE "NEW LOOK" IN FAMILY PLANNING

1.   World Bank, "The Population Sector."
2.   See Barbara Rogers, *The Domestication of Women.*
3.   Quoted in IPPF, *Report of the Meeting of the Working Group on Community Participation in MCH/FP in the Context of PHC* (London: 16–17 July 1983), p. 5.
4.   See for example Marilee Karl, "Income Generation for Women," in ISIS, *Women in Development.* This article provides a good overview and analysis of income generation.
5.   Anita Anand, "Rethinking Women and Development," in ISIS, *Women in Development,* p. 10.
6.   United Nations, *Fertility and the Family: Changing Conditions and Perceptions* (New York: May 1984), p. 3.
7.   Ieda Siqueira Wiarda and Judith F. Helzner, *Women, Population and International Development in Latin America: Persistent Legacies and New Perceptions for the 1980's,* Program in Latin American Studies Occasional Papers Series No. 13 (Amherst: University of Massachusetts International Area Studies Programs, 1981), p. 36.
8.   See Judith Bruce, "Income Generating Schemes: The Bangladeshi Experience," *Populi,* vol. 12, no. 2 (1985), for overview of the issues involved in income generating/family planning schemes.
9.   Personal interview with Alex Marshall, UNFPA.
10.   World Bank, *Recognizing the "Invisible" Woman in Development: The World Bank Experience* (Washington: 1979), p. 15, quoted in Keysers, *Does Family Planning Liberate Women?,* p. 162.
11.   Stan D'Souza, *Sex-biased Stereotypes, Sex Biases and National Data Systems* (New York: United Nations, n.d.), quoted in Naila Kabeer, *Minus Lives: Women of Bangladesh,* CHANGE International Reports: Women and Society (London: n.d.) p. 5.
12.   Kabeer, *Minus Lives,* p. 5.
13.   For analysis of the reasons why, in addition to population control, the Bank and others want rural women integrated into the cash economy, see F. McCarthy and S. Feldman, "Rural Women Discovered: New Sources of Capital and Labor in Bangladesh," *Development and Change,* vol. 14 (1983).
14.   See *World Development Report 1984,* p. 175. For history of the project, see Tahrunnessa Abdullah and Sondra Zeidenstein, *Village Women of Bangladesh: Prospects for Change* (Oxford: Pergamon

Press, 1982); also Bruce, "Income Generating Schemes: The Bangladeshi Experience."

15. Kirsten Westergaard, *Pauperization and Rural Women in Bangladesh*, Project Paper A.82.5 (Copenhagen: Center for Development Research, March 1982), pp. 73-74.

16. Ibid., p. 82.

17. Joke van der Laan and Sultana Krippendorff, *Remember the Words of the Poor: Report of the Mission on Women and Emancipation to Bangladesh*, March 1981, quoted in Kabeer, *Minus Lives*, p. 6.

18. F. McCarthy, S. Sabbah and R. Aktar, *Rural Women Workers in Bangladesh*, working paper (Dhaka: Bangladesh Ministry of Agriculture and Forestry, 1978), quoted in Keysers, *Does Family Planning Liberate Women?*, p. 210.

19. Bruce, "Income Generating Schemes."

20. Personal interview, February 1984.

21. Personal interview with Bruce, February 1984. For description of new research on women's roles, see Daisy Hilse Dwyer, *Women and Income in the Third World*, Population Council, International Programs Working Paper No. 18 (New York: June 1983).

22. See Peggy Antrobus, *Hanover Street: An Experiment to Train Women in Welding and Carpentry*, a pamphlet in the *Seeds* series, a project of the Carnegie Corporation, the Ford Foundation, and the Population Council (New York: 1980), and Marty Chen, *The Working Women's Forum: Organizing for Credit and Change*, a *Seeds* pamphlet (New York: 1983). Also see other pamphlets on women's projects in the *Seeds* series.

23. Personal interview, February 1984.

24. Both quoted in Warwick, *Bitter Pills*, p. 48.

25. Debabar Banerji, "Political Economy of Population Control in India," in Bondestam and Bergström, *Poverty and Population Control*, p. 86.

26. Bronstein, *The Triple Struggle*, p. 31, on El Salvador. Dominican Republic quote from Warwick, *Bitter Pills*, p. 169.

27. Personal interview.

28. First figure from "Condensed Background for Journalists," press release, The State of the World Population 1981 Press File, prepared by the New Internationalist Publications Cooperative for the UNFPA (Oxford: 1981). On health care priorities in general, see Dianna Melrose, *Bitter Pills: Medicines and the Third World Poor* (Oxford: OXFAM, 1982).

29. David Morley, John Rohde, and Glen Williams, eds., *Prac-

ticing Health for All (Oxford: Oxford University Press, 1983), pp. ix–x. This book is an excellent source on issues in primary health care and has a number of interesting case studies.

30.   *World Development Report 1984*, p. 150. See also Ruth Leger Sivard, *World Military and Social Expenditures, 1981* (Leesburg, Virginia: World Priorities, 1981).

31.   See Linda Golley, "Health Policy in ASEAN: Addressing Human Needs or Protecting the Status Quo?" *Southeast Asia Chronicle*, No. 84 (June 1982). This issue, devoted to Health Care in Southeast Asia, is a good source of both facts and analysis.

32.   "Healthier Mothers and Children Through Family Planning," *Population Reports*, Series J, No. 27 (May–June 1984), p. J660.

33.   AID, *AID's Role in Indonesian Family Planning*, p. 65.

34.   BKBBN, *Basic Information on Population*, p. 68.

35.   Letter from Dr. Henry Mosley, 13 August 1984, quoted with his permission.

36.   "Interview with Halfdan Mahler, Director General, WHO," *New Internationalist*, No. 127 (September 1983).

37.   IPPF, *Community Participation in Family Planning: Issues and Examples*, working paper (London: July 1982), p. i.

38.   IPPF, *Report of the Meeting of the Working Group*, p. 12.

39.   IPPF, *Community Participation*, p. 25.

40.   McNicoll and Singarimbum, *Fertility Decline in Indonesia, II*, pp. 13–14. For a refreshingly frank case study on how community participation can be subverted, see Glen Williams and Satoto, "Sociopolitical Constraints on Primary Health Care: A Case Study from Indonesia," in Morley et al., eds., *Practicing Health for All*.

41.   IPPF, *Report of the Meeting of the Working Group*, p. 14.

42.   Emanuel de Kadt, "Community Participation for Health: The Case of Latin America," in Morley et al., eds., *Practicing Health for All*, p. 243.

43.   Judith Bruce, "Implementing the User Perspective," *Studies in Family Planning*, vol. 11, no. 1 (January 1980).

44.   Judith Bruce, *Users' Perspectives on Family Planning: Some Operational and Research Issues* (draft) (New York: Population Council, January 1983).

45.   See Bruce, "Implementing the User Perspective," and George Zeidenstein, "The User Perspective: An Evolutionary Step in Contraceptive Service Programs," *Studies in Family Planning*, vol. 11., no. 1 (January 1980).

46.   Personal communication.

8 CHINA—ONE CHILD, ONE TOO FEW?

1. Murdoch, *The Poverty of Nations*, p. 80.
2. William Vogt, quoted in Lappé and Collins, *Food First*, p. 83.
3. Population Reference Bureau, *1983 World Population Data Sheet*, and *World Development Report 1984*.
4. See Leo A. Orleans, "China's Experience in Population Control: The Elusive Model," *World Development*, vol. 3, nos. 7 and 8 (July–August 1978).
5. On the decline, see "Population and Birth Planning in the People's Republic of China," *Population Reports*, Series J, No. 25 (January–February 1982), p. J597. "Replacement level" fertility is generally when each woman bears an average of 2.1 to 2.5 children in her lifetime. The measure of this average is called the Total Fertility Rate, or TFR. The 1982 Population Reference Bureau's World Population Data Sheet estimates China's TFR at 2.8 at the end of the 1970s.
6. See *Population Reports*, Series J., No. 25, for a description of the various stages of the population program.
7. See Ashwani Saith, "China's New Population Policies," in Keith Griffin, ed., *Institutional Reform and Economic Development in the Chinese Countryside* (London: Macmillan, 1984), for a presentation of the pressure population growth puts on the economy.
8. Keith Griffin, "Introduction," in ibid. On China's agricultural production record, see Elisabeth Croll, *The Family Rice Bowl: Food and the Domestic Economy in China* (Geneva: U.N. Research Institute for Social Development, 1982).
9. Saith, "China's New Population Policies," p. 180. For vivid and informative description of China's new economic policies and their impact on society, see Orville Schell, "A Reporter at Large: The Wind of Wanting to Go it Alone," *New Yorker*, 23 January 1984.
10. Letter to author from Paul Rice, 24 March 1984. Rice has studied China's agrarian reforms.
11. Quote from WGBH Educational Foundation, "China's Only Child," *Nova* No. 1103, 1984.
12. Ibid.
13. See Elisabeth J. Croll, "Production vs. Reproduction: A Threat to China's Development Strategy," *World Development*, vol. 2, no. 6 (June 1983).
14. WGBH Educational Foundation, "China's Only Child."

15.   Qian Xinzhong, "China's Population Policy: Theory and Methods," *Studies in Family Planning*, vol. 14, no. 12, Part I (December 1983).

16.   See Christopher S. Wren, "Chinese Showing Resistance to National Goals for Birth Control," *New York Times*, 16 May 1982.

17.   "Peking Demand for More Sterilization," *Guardian*, 16 June 1983.

18.   *Population Reports*, Series J, No. 25, p. 604.

19.   Saith, "China's New Population Policies," p. 205. Saith points out (p. 207) the use of incentives and quotas leads easily to coercion: "One lesson which the Chinese family planning drive might well learn from the Indian experience is that it is socially dangerous and politically divisive to give local level administrative officials incentives and instructions to meet quotas related to birth control. When this happens the program tends to degenerate rapidly into an authoritarian system of implementation in which the main ingredient for success is coercion."

20.   Rice letter. Also Schell, "A Reporter at Large"; *Population Reports*, Series J, No. 25; Croll, "Production vs. Reproduction"; and Saith, "China's New Population Policies."

21.   Elisabeth Croll, "Women, Marriage and the Family," *China Now* (London), No. 101 (March/April 1982).

22.   See Saith, "China's New Population Policies," for example.

23.   See Jonathon Mirsky, "The Infanticide Tragedy in China," *The Nation*, 2 July 1983. Also E. Croll, "China's First-Born Nightmare Returns," *Guardian*, 28 October 1983.

24.   1982 census material from *World Development Report 1984*, p. 178.

25.   See *Population Reports*, Series J, No. 25, pp. 609–610; also *World Development Report 1984*, p. 104. Also personal communications.

26.   Croll, "Production vs. Reproduction."

27.   Christopher S. Wren, "China Plans a New Drive to Limit Birth Rate," *New York Times*, 7 November 1982. Also see John Bongaarts and Susan Greenhalgh, "An Alternative to the One-Child Policy in China," *Population and Development Review*, vol. 11, no. 4 (December 1985).

28.   Rice letter.

29.   See Bongaarts and Greenhalgh, "An Alternative to the One-Child Policy in China."

30.   Rice letter.

31.   WGBH Educational Foundation, "China's Only Child."

32. Bongarrts and Greenhalgh, "An Alternative to the One-Child Policy in China."

33. The hard-line position is typified by Lester Brown of the Worldwatch Institute. See Hobart Rowen, "Overpopulation Means Famine and War," *Honolulu Advertiser*, 17 February 1985.

34. Van Arendonk—personal interview February 1984. King quote from Timothy King, "Coercion in Family Planning Programs: Issues for International Agencies," 19 August 1983, unpublished manuscript. This article is an interesting examination of the ethics of population control. Although King identifies certain fundamental rights, he concludes that because of the important need to reduce fertility in some countries, the World Bank's concern should be that population control "is done fairly, not necessarily that it be done without coercion."

35. From personal interview.

36. "Paying for Abortions," *Wall Street Journal*, 9 April 1984. Also see Nick Eberstadt, "Peking's Family Policy," *New York Times*, 22 April 1984. "U.N. Population Fund Reacts to U.S. Aid Cut," *Boston Globe*, 29 August 1986.

37. Holzhausen quote from his letter, dated 18 January 1984, to Dr. Nafis Sadik, assistant executive director, UNFPA, New York, which was leaked to the press. It is reproduced in full in Betsy Hartmann and Hilary Standing, *Food, Saris and Sterilization: Population Control in Bangladesh* (London: Bangladesh International Action Group, 1985), pp. 37–39. Van Arendonk—personal interview.

38. Sinding quotes from personal interview, February 1984.

9   SHAPING CONTRACEPTIVE TECHNOLOGY

1. Quoted in Vaughan, P., *The Pill on Trial* (London: Weidenfeld and Nicolson, 1970), in Walsh, "Contraception: The Growth of a Technology," p. 202.

2. Quoted in Barbara Seaman and Gideon Seaman, M.D., *Women and the Crisis in Sex Hormones* (New York: Rawson Associates Publishers, Inc., 1977), p. 62.

3. Frances Gulick, "The Indian Family Planning Program: The Need for New Contraceptives," staff memorandum, USAID/India, April 1968, quoted in Piotrow, *World Population Crisis*, p. 174. Ironically, Indian officials are still employing the same reasoning to justify the poor performance of the country's family planning program. Prime Minister Indira Gandhi told the WHO General Assembly in 1981:

"Family planning programs are awaiting a big breakthrough. Without a safe, preferably oral, drug, which women and men can take, no amount of government commitment and political determination will avail." Quoted in M. F. Fathalla, "A Synthesis of the Various Experiences and Problems Encountered with Available Methods of Fertility Regulation in Developing Countries," background document, International Symposium, Research on the Regulation of Human Fertility, Needs of Developing Countries, and Priorities for the Future, Stockholm, Karolinska Institute and University of Uppsala, 7–9 February 1983.

4.   Linda E. Atkinson, Richard Lincoln and Jacqueline D. Forrest, "Worldwide Trends in Funding for Contraceptive Research and Evaluation," *Family Planning Perspectives,* vol. 17, no. 5 (September/October 1985), Table 7, p. 204.

5.   Ibid. See also Office of Technology Assessment, *World Population and Fertility Planning Technologies, The Next 20 Years* (Washington, D.C.: U.S. Government Printing Office, 1982), pp. 107–11; *Population Reports,* Series J, No. 26 (January–February 1983).

6.   See OTA, *World Population and Fertility Planning Technologies,* Chapter 6; and Forrest C. Greenslade and George F. Brown, "Contraception in the Population/Development Equation," background paper to the Presentation by George Zeidenstein, Population Council, New York, 1983.

7.   See Constance Holden, "Contraceptive Research Lagging," *Science,* vol. 229, no. 4718 (13 September 1985); Matt Clark, "Contraceptives: On Hold," *Newsweek,* 5 May 1986; and Frank E. James, "With Most Contraceptive Tests on Hold, Couples Face Grim Birth-Control Choices," *Wall Street Journal,* 17 April 1986.

8.   No exact figures on size of the market are available. Estimates from Cary LaCheen, "Population Control and the Contraceptive Industry," in Kathleen McDonnell, ed., *Adverse Effects: Women and the Pharmaceutical Industry* (Penang, Malaysia: International Organization of Consumers Unions, 1986). On profitability of oral and injectable contraceptives, see Marjorie Sun, "Depo-Provera Debate Revs up at FDA," *Science,* vol. 217, no. 4558 (30 July 1982), p. 429; and OTA, *World Population and Fertility Planning Technologies,* p. 116.

9.   See OTA, *World Population and Fertility Planning Technologies,* for description of how public and private sectors interact. See LaCheen, "Population Control," for examples of how industry officials lobby for more population research.

10. LaCheen, "Population Control."

11. Informational brochure, SOMARC, The Futures Group (Washington, D.C.: n.d.) quoted in LaCheen, "Population Control," p. 114. LaCheen presents an excellent analysis of CSM projects.

12. LaCheen, "Population Control," p. 116.

13. Ibid.

14. Ibid.

15. Ibid.

16. See Atkinson et al., "Worldwide Trends in Funding."

17. Personal communication, February 1984.

18. Domination of contraceptive field by men from Judy Norsigian, "Redirecting Contraceptive Research," Science for the People, January/February 1979. Quote from Bruce Stokes, Men and Family Planning, Worldwatch Paper 41 (Washington, D.C.: Worldwatch Institute, December 1980), p. 24.

19. Atkinson et al., "Worldwide Trends in Funding."

20. See Table "Percentage Distribution of Public Sector Expenditures for Development of New Contraceptive Methods, 1978," in OTA, World Population and Fertility Planning Technologies, p. 110.

21. Atkinson et al., "Worldwide Trends in Funding," Table 3, p. 198.

22. Ibid., and OTA, World Population and Fertility Planning Technologies, p. 109.

23. Information in this paragraph and previous one from Seaman and Seaman, Women and the Crisis in Sex Hormones, pp. 73–84.

24. Legislative information obtained from Philip Lee. On regulatory relief, see George Bush, "Opening of the Eleventh Assembly," papers presented at the 11th IFPMA Assembly, Washington, D.C., 7–8 June 1982, p. 8.

25. John W. Egan, Harlow N. Higinbotham, and J. Fred Weston, Economics of the Pharmaceutical Industry (New York: Praeger Publishers, 1982), p. 105.

26. Atkinson et al., "Worldwide Trends in Funding."

27. See Vimal Balasubrahmanyan, "Drug Trials: Charade of 'Informed Consent,' " Economic and Political Weekly (Bombay), vol. 18 no. 25 (18 June 1983).

28. The study is described by Anibal Faundes et al., "Acceptability of the Contraceptive Vaginal Ring by Rural and Urban Population in Two Latin American Countries," Contraception, vol. 24, no. 4 (October 1981). On lack of knowledge concerning long-term effects, see "Injectables and Implants: Long-Acting Progestins—Promise and Prospects," Population Reports, Series K, No. 2, May 1983, p. K-42.

29. Barbara Ehrenreich, Mark Dowie, and Stephen Minkin, "The Charge: Gynocide, The Accused: The U.S. Government," *Mother Jones*, November 1979, p. 32.

30. Personal communication, 1984.

31. *Population Reports*, Series J, No. 27 (May–June 1984), p. J658.

32. See Judith Bruce and S. Bruce Schearer, *Contraceptives and Common Sense: Conventional Methods Reconsidered* (New York: Population Council, 1979), p. 51. This earlier work is sadly out of print.

33. Judith Bruce and S. Bruce Schearer, "Contraceptives and Developing Countries: The Role of Barrier Methods," paper read at the International Symposium, Research on the Regulation of Human Fertility, Needs of Developing Countries, and Priorities for the Future, Stockholm, February 1983, p. 416. This paper, available from the Population Council, is an informative examination of the present neglect and future potential of barrier methods. Also see Helen B. Holmes, "Reproductive Technologies: The Birth of a Woman Centered Analysis," in H. B. Holmes, B. B. Haskins, and M. Gross, eds., *Birth Control and Controlling Birth: Women-Centered Perspectives* (Clifton, N.J.: Humana Press, 1980).

34. George Zeidenstein, "The User Perspective: An Evolutionary Step in Contraceptive Service Programs," *Studies in Family Planning*, vol. 11, no. 1 (January 1980), p. 27.

35. Bruce and Schearer, "Contraceptives and Developing Countries," p. 410.

36. Carl Djerassi, "Future Methods of Fertility Regulation in Developing Countries: How to Make the Impossible Possible by December 31, 1999," paper read at the International Symposium, Research on the Regulation of Human Fertility, Needs of Developing Countries, and Priorities for the Future, Stockholm, February, 1983.

BOX   "Informed Consent" in India (pages 171–172)

1. "Round the World," *The Lancet*, 25 May 1985, p. 1209.

2. "NET-EN Trial Disrupted in India," *Women's Global Network on Reproductive Rights Newsletter*, January–March 1986. Article based on account by Sumati Nair and Vimal Balasubrahmanyan, which appeared in *Manushi*, no. 28 (May/June 1985). Also see Balasubrahmanyan, "Finger in the Dyke: The Fight to Keep Injectables out of India," in McDonnell, ed., *Adverse Effects*.

10   HORMONAL CONTRACEPTIVES AND THE IUD

1.   Quoted in Ehrenreich et al., "The Charge: Gynocide,"
p. 34.

2.   Hale H. Cook, Clarence J. Gamble, and Adaline P. Satter-
thwaite, "Oral Contraception by Norethynodrel: A 3-Year Field
Study," *American Journal of Obstetrics and Gynecology*, vol. 82, 1961,
reprinted in Jay Katz, *Experimentation with Human Beings* (New York:
Russell Sage Foundation, 1972), pp. 739, 741. See Katz's book for
excellent material on the introduction of the pill and the controversies
it generated.

3.   Gregory Pincus, John Rock, and Celso R. Garcia, "Field
Trials with Norethynodrel as an Oral Contraceptive," *Report of the
Proceedings of the Sixth International Conference on Planned Parent-
hood* (London: IPPF, 1959), reprinted in Katz, *Experimentation with
Human Beings*, p. 745.

4.   Information on Searle and quote from Seaman and Seaman,
Women and the Crisis in Sex Hormones, pp. 66–69.

5.   FDA Advisory Committee on Obstetrics and Gynecology,
Second Report on the Oral Contraceptives (Washington, D.C.: 1 August
1969), reprinted in Katz, *Experimentation with Human Beings*, pp.
761–765. Hellman quote from "Testimony of Dr. Louis M. Hellman,"
22 Jan. 1970, reprinted in Katz, p. 765.

6.   Personal communication with Norma Swenson of the Boston Women's Health Book Collective. Also see Alice Wolfson, "The
Reselling of the Pill," *CARASA News*, vol. 7, no. 4 (July–August 1983).
The pill in fact engendered vociferous debate among the medical
profession on the individual woman's right to full disclosure of side
effects. At issue was the basic power relationship between doctor and
patient. Dr. Alan Guttmacher, former president of Planned Parenthood, expressed the view of many of his colleagues:

*Unfortunately, the physician has to make the decisions for pa-
tients. . . . Now, I certainly feel the more we can instruct the
American physician about the intricacies of the birth control
pill, the wiser the effort. My feeling is that when you attempt
to instruct the American womanhood in this, which is a pure
medical matter which I am afraid she has not the background
to understand, you are creating in her simply a panic reaction
without much intellectual background. . . . I think that the dis-*

penser of the therapy is the person who must be educated and not the recipient.

> *Quotation from "Testimony of Dr. Alan F. Guttmacher," 25 February 1970, reprinted in Katz, Experimentation with Human Beings, pp. 774–775.*

7. See "Oral Contraceptives in the 1980's," *Population Reports*, Series A, no. 6 (May–June 1982). British statistic from Bruce and Schearer, "Contraceptives and Developing Countries," p. 408.

8. See *Population Reports*, Series A, No. 6.

9. See for example AID, *Indonesia—Oral Contraceptives*, Project Paper (Washington, D.C.: 13 March 1978) for the demographic aims underlying pill promotion. The possibility of side effects are minimized to such an extent in this document that appended in the back is a telegram from headquarters in Washington asking what provisions exist for treatment of pill acceptors who suffer side effects. In virtually every discussion of the pill by population control agencies, the maternal mortality argument is used as the main defense against those who urge greater caution in its distribution.

10. Westinghouse Health Systems, "Family Planning Program Effectiveness Study," in AID, *Family Planning Program Effectiveness: Report of a Workshop*, AID Program Evaluation Report No. 1 (Washington, D.C.: December 1979), p. 27.

11. Stephen F. Minkin, "Abroad the U.S. Pushes Contraceptives like Coca-Cola," *Los Angeles Times*, 23 September 1979.

12. Westinghouse Health Systems, "Family Planning Program," p. 40. Sinding quote from personal interview.

13. Marianne C. Burkhart, "Issues in Community-Based Distribution of Contraceptives," *Pathpapers* No. 8 (Boston: September 1981), p. 30.

14. *Population Reports*, Series J, No. 27, p. J658.

15. See LaCheen, "Population Control."

16. Quoted in S. Minkin, "Bangladesh: where there's a Pill there's a way," *New Internationalist*, No. 79 (September 1979).

17. Manuel Ylanan and Cecilia C. Verzoza, *Commercial Retail Sales of Contraceptives*, PIACT Paper Number 6, Program for the Introduction and Adaptation of Contraceptive Technology (Seattle: n.d.) p. 12, cited in LaCheen, "Population Control," p. 118.

18. Stated by Dr. Stephen Sinding in personal interview.

19. Rheumatic heart disease from *Population Reports*, Series A, No. 6. At least one study has suggested that female circulatory

mortality rates are actually higher in Third World countries such as the Philippines, Mexico, Venezuela, and Chile than in the United States. See Dexter Tiranti, "The Small Miracle," *New Internationalist,* No. 79 (September 1979).

20. See *Population Reports,* Series A, No. 6.

21. See "Breast-feeding and Fertility Regulation: Current Knowledge and Program Policy Implications," *Bulletin of the World Health Organization,* vol. 63, no. 1 (1983).

22. *Population Reports,* Series A, No. 6.

23. Minkin, "Abroad, the U.S. Pushes Contraceptives." One AID-funded evaluation of a household distribution scheme in Bangladesh blamed high dropout rates on "a variety of side effects. The mass distribution strategy unfortunately contributed to this problem. The field staff was given only limited training and even less information was transmitted to the recipients." M. Rahman et al., "Contraception Distribution in Bangladesh: some lessons learned," *Studies in Family Planning,* vol. 2, no. 6 (June 1980), cited in Keysers, *Does Family Planning Liberate Women?,* p. 252.

24. See Minkin, "Abroad, the U.S. Pushes Contraceptives," and Maggie Jones, "The Biggest Contraceptive in the World."

25. S. Bhatia, S. Becker, and Y. J. Kim, "The Effect on Fecundity of Pill Acceptance During Postpartum Amenhorrhea in Rural Bangladesh," *Studies in Family Planning,* vol. 13, no. 6/7 (June–July 1982).

26. *Population Reports,* Series A, No. 6. Also see Wolfson, "The Reselling of the Pill."

27. "Oral Contraceptives and Cancer," *FDA Drug Bulletin,* 1984. For more detail on the cancer debate also see Richard Lincoln, "The Pill, Breast and Cervical Cancer, and the Role of Progestogens in Arterial Disease," *Family Planning Perspectives,* vol. 16, no. 2 (March–April 1984).

28. WHO, *Steroid Contraception and the Risk of Neoplasia,* WHO Technical Report Series No. 619 (Geneva: WHO Scientific Group, 1978).

29. Personal communication with a doctor working in rural Zimbabwe. The reason given for distributing higher dose pills (50 mcg) is that lower dose pills cause more breakthrough bleeding, and that family planning workers are not trained to cope with this. However, in reality 30 mcg. pills do not cause substantially more breakthrough bleeding than 50 mcg. pills, and if women do develop problems, they can change to a higher dose if necessary.

30. See Ehrenreich et al., "The Charge: Gynocide."

31. Pomeroy quote from personal interview, February 1984. "Imperialist arrogance" from discussion with Norma Swenson of the Boston Women's Health Book Collective, who has heard this phrase used by defenders of the pill.

32. See Wolfson, "The Reselling of the Pill." Also *Population Reports*, Series A, No. 6. This issue of *Population Reports* begins with the two subtitles, "Beneficial Effects Noted," and "Risks Limited." See p. A-11 for AID statement to an FDA advisory committee.

33. D. F. Hawkins and M. G. Elder, *Human Fertility Control: Theory and Practice* (London: Butterworths, 1979), p. 109.

34. See "Long-Acting Progestins—Promise and Prospects," *Population Reports*, Series K, No. 2 (May 1983); 11 million figure from Marjorie Sun, "Panel Says Depo-Provera Not Proved Safe," *Science*, vol. 226, no. 4677 (23 November 1984).

35. *Population Reports*, Series K, No. 2.

36. See Ana Blanco, *Norethisterone Oenanthate: The Other Injectable Contraceptive*, briefing paper (London: War on Want and the International Contraception, Abortion and Sterilization Campaign, February 1984). Also Center for Education and Documentation, *Injectables: Immaculate Contraception?* Counterfact No. 3 (Bombay: March 1983). On recent injectables: Marge Berer, "More and More Injectables," Women's Global Network on Reproductive Rights Newsletter (Amsterdam: January–March 1986).

37. Edwin B. McDaniel and Tieng Pardthaisong, "Acceptability of an Injectable Contraceptive in a Rural Population of Thailand," paper presented to the IPPF Southeast Asia and Oceania Congress (n.p., n.d.). It is interesting to note that the disadvantage of having to remember to take the pill each day was not pointed out by the population community until injectables came on the scene. (Personal communication with Norma Swenson of the Boston Women's Health Book Collective.)

38. *Population Reports*, Series K, No. 2.

39. Corea quoted in Quebec Public Interest and Research Group, *Depo-Provera, A Shot in the Dark* (Montreal: 1982), p. 7. For Corea's excellent critique of the drug and drug studies, see "Testimony of Gena Corea," submitted to FDA Public Board of Inquiry on Depo-Provera, Jan. 1983, available from Corea. On Depo as male contraceptive, see S. Minkin, "Nine Thai Women Had Cancer—None of Them Took Depo-Provera: Therefore Depo-Provera is Safe. This is Science?" *Mother Jones*, November 1981.

40. *Population Reports*, Series K, No. 2, p. K-27.

41. There are other possible long-term risks as well. Another

finding from animal studies shows the depression of the immune system following Depo administration. If human immune systems were affected by large doses of progestin, surveillance by epidemiologists would have to be undertaken for another whole set of diseases in addition to specifically reproductive-related ones, for example, higher rates of TB and leukemia. At the present time no studies are underway to test this hypothesis by following women long-term, looking for nonreproductive health effects. See Gena Corea, "Depo Weapon," in Helen B. Holmes, Betty B. Hoskins, and Michael Gross, *Birth Control and Controlling Birth: Women-Centered Perspectives* (Clifton, N.J.: The Humana Press, 1980).

42.   *Population Reports,* Series K, No. 2, p. K-30.

43.   See Seaman and Seaman, *Women and the Crisis in Sex Hormones.* DES, incidentally, is still used as a contraceptive morning-after pill, despite the warnings of its manufacturer.

44.   IPPF, *Statement on Injectable Contraception* (London: October 1982), p. 3.

45.   "Facts about Injectable Contraceptives," *Bulletin of the WHO,* vol. 60, no. 2 (1982), p. 206.

46.   See IPPF, *Statement on Injectable Contraception,* for example. For defense of the animal tests, see Office of Technology Assessment, *World Population and Fertility Planning Technologies,* p. 114.

47.   Quoted in Sun, "Depo-Provera Debate Revs up at FDA."

48.   Judith Weisz, Griff T. Ross, and Paul D. Stolley, "Findings of Fact," *Report of the Public Board of Inquiry on Depo-Provera* (Washington, D.C.: 17 October 1984), pp. 172–80.

49.   Quotes from Marjorie Sun, "Panel Says Depo-Provera Not Proved Safe." This is a good summary article on the board's findings.

50.   "Testimony of Gena Corea," p. 15.

51.   See "Depot-medroxyprogesterone acetate (DMPA) and cancer: Memorandum from a WHO Meeting," *Bulletin of the World Health Organization,* vol. 64, no. 3 (1986).

52.   Letter from Judith Weisz to Frank E. Young, commissioner of food and drugs, FDA, 10 April 1985.

53.   Andrew Veitch, "Women Did Not Know of Drug Injections," *Guardian,* 28 April 1983. For more on Depo use in Britain and the ramifications of the government's decision, see Marge Berer, *Who Needs Depo-Provera?* (London: Community Rights Project, July 1984). Although Britain has approved Depo only for restricted uses, Upjohn is publicizing the decision as a general approval. See Sun, "Panel Says Depo-Provera Not Proved Safe." In France, the Groupe

d'Information et de Soutien des Travailleurs Immigrés in Paris reports that Depo is used especially on immigrants. See their report *Le Depo-Provera: Qui choisit . . . et pour qui* (Paris: April 1983).

54.   On Australia, see "Population Control," *Cultural Survival,* Fall 1981; on New Zealand see *The Politics of Fertility: Depo-Provera at Home and Abroad,* New Zealand Coalition for Trade and Development, Issues Alert No. 2, Wellington, 1983. On New Zealand study, see Phillida Bunkle, "Calling the Shots? The International Politics of Depo-Provera," in Rita Arditti, Renate Duelli Klein, and Shelley Minden, *Test-Tube Women: What Future for Motherhood?* (London: Pandora Press, 1984).

55.   The effects of Depo have been studied on poor black women in Atlanta, Georgia. Journalist Marjorie Sun writes of one such study at Emory University:

> *In 1978, FDA conducted an audit of the Emory University-sponsored study and uncovered serious problems. According to FDA documents, 4,700 black women were tested with Depo Provera over a period of several years, but researchers did not adhere to the protocol approved by FDA. FDA investigators said the study was poorly designed, patient records were inadequate, and researchers did not follow patients who dropped out of the study or provide long-term follow-up to assess potential cancer risk.*

See Sun, "Panel Says Depo Provera Not Proved Safe." According to Sybil Shainwald of the National Women's Health Network, the Indian Health Service routinely gives the drug.

56.   Potts quote from Ehrenreich et al., "The Charge: Gynocide."

57.   Letter from Dr. Griff T. Ross to Dr. Judith Weisz, 23 July 1984, appended p. 181 of the *Report of the Public Board of Inquiry on Depo-Provera.*

58.   Personal correspondence, 29 December 1983. W. Silapa-archa also reports that in Bangkok young prostitutes were brought to a clinic where they received the injection without knowing what it was. Later many developed side effects. In the Philippines, where Depo is ostensibly approved only for research purposes (though it is distributed widely by the voluntary agency World Neighbors), the drug was "tested" in Olangapo and Angeles City, both towns that adjoin United States military bases and have large prostitute populations. See Judy Jacobs, "U.S.A. Drug Companies Promoting Depo-Provera in the Third World," *Plexus,* vol. 8, no. 8 (October 1981).

Also on Philippines, see Lynn Duggan, "From Birth Control to Population Control," *Southeast Asia Chronicle*, no. 96 (January 1985).

59.   *Population Reports*, Series K, No. 2 (May 1983). Also personal interview with Dr. K. Kanagaratnam of the World Bank, February 1984.

60.   *Population Reports*, Series K, No. 2, p. K-22.

61.   Personal communication with Boston Women's Health Book Collective.

62.   "Population Control," *Cultural Survival*, Fall 1981.

63.   Quote from ibid. On Depo in South Africa, also see "Crimes Against Women," *Africa*, no. 170 (October 1985), and Eleanor J. Bador, "Contraception and Control," *Guardian* (New York), Apartheid Supplement, Spring 1986.

64.   Minister quoted in "Curb Black Population Growth or Die of Thirst," *Rand Daily Mail*, 23 May 1984. Government's policy described in Barbara Klugman, "Perspectives on Population in South Africa," unpublished paper presented at Natal Medical School Conference, May 1984.

65.   World Bank, *Population Growth and Policies in Sub-Saharan Africa*, pp. 5, 41–42, 54–55.

66.   "Depo-Provera: Control of Fertility—Two Feminist Views," *Spare Rib* (London), No. 116 (March 1982).

67.   Personal correspondence, 9 February 1984.

68.   Personal communication.

69.   "The Depo-Provera Debate," *Newsweek*, 24 January 1983.

70.   Quoted in Rachel B. Gold and Peters D. Willson, "Depo-Provera: New Developments in a Decade-Old Controversy," *International Family Planning Perspectives*, vol. 6, no. 4 (December 1980).

71.   SIDA quote from the Coordinating Group on Depo-Provera, *Submission to Public Hearing on Depo-Provera* (London: 25 April 1983).

72.   Population Council, *1983 Annual Report*, p. 4.

73.   Greenslade and Brown, "Contraception in the Population/Development Equation," p. 10.

74.   See The Population Council, *Norplant Worldwide*, No. 4 (New York: April 1986).

75.   See Michael Klitsch, "Hormonal Implants: The Next Wave of Contraceptives," *International Family Planning Perspectives*, vol. 9, no. 4 (December 1983), for overview of the method. Some women have developed ovarian cysts while using Norplant, suggesting that further research should be done. Also see *Studies in Family Planning*, vol. 14, no. 6–7 (June–July 1983), a special issue devoted to Norplant.

76. One finds this throughout the literature. For example, the directors of one Chilean study, where the continuation rate was 54 out of 100 after five years, concluded, "Continuation rates in this study show that the method is very acceptable to Chilean women." However, to generalize on the basis of a study of 101 women to the Chilean population as a whole is at best rather hasty. (S. Diaz, et al., "A Five-Year Clinical Trial of Levonorgestrel Silastic Implants (Norplant)," *Contraception,* vol. 25, no. 5 (May 1982).

77. Paola Marangoni et al., "Norplant Implants and the TCu 200 IUD: A Comparative Study in Ecuador," *Studies in Family Planning,* vol. 14, no. 6–7 (June–July 1983), p. 180.

78. The Population Council, "Norplant Contraceptive Implants, Instructions for Clinicians," October 1983, p. 13. Also see Klitsch, "Hormonal Implants."

79. On infection problems see various studies in *Studies in Family Planning,* vol. 14, No. 6–7 (June–July 1983). In the Ecuadorian study a "certain overconfidence" about the ease of the insertion procedures led to "carelessness" (p. 179).

80. Irving Sivin et al., "Norplant: Reversible Implant Contraception," *Studies in Family Planning,* vol. 11, nos. 7–8 (July–August, 1980), on removal advice. Indonesian case from Firman Lubis et al., "One-Year Experience with Norplant Implants in Indonesia," *Studies in Family Planning,* vol. 14, no. 6–7 (June–July 1983). There are also potential problems with screening. Because of the possible risk of birth defects, pregnant women should not be given Norplant. However, even in carefully controlled studies (see above issue of *Studies in Family Planning*) pregnant women have apparently been given the drug by mistake.

81. *Norplant Worldwide,* p. 2.

82. Ibid.

83. Greenslade and Brown, "Contraception in the Population/ Development Equation," p. 14.

84. Draft protocol, "Clinical Study of Norplant—Reversible Hormone Implant Contraception," Bangladesh Fertility Research Program (Dhaka: 1981). Recent reports from Bangladeshi researchers.

85. F. Lubis et al., "One-Year Experience with Norplant Implants," p. 181.

86. Greenslade and Brown, "Contraception in the Population/ Development Equation," pp. 12–13.

87. Christopher Tietze and Sarah Lewitt, eds., *Intrauterine Contraceptive Devices: Proceedings of the First Conference on the IUCD,*

April 30, 1962–May 1, 1962 (Amsterdam, London, New York: Excerpta Medica, 1962).

88. *Population Reports*, Series B, No. 4 (July 1982).

89. Quoted in Jeanie Kasindorf, "The Case Against IUD's: What Your Doctor Never Told You About Infection, Infertility and IUD's," *New West*, 5 May 1980. This is an excellent article for anyone interested in the history of the IUD and its effects.

90. See Jane E. Hutchings, Patti J. Benson, Gordon W. Perkin, and Richard M. Soderstrom, "The IUD After 20 Years: A Review," *Family Planning Perspectives*, vol. 17, no. 6 (November–December 1985). On postpartum use, see for example, "Breast-feeding and Fertility-Regulation," *Bulletin of the World Health Organization*, vol. 63, no. 1, for recommendations against postpartum IUD use. According to Norma Swenson of the Boston Women's Health Book Collective, nursing mothers run an even higher risk of imbedding and perforation, so that contraindication warnings are now being circulated to physicians.

Copper IUDs could have other risks. Jocelyn Knowles, author of a forthcoming book on the IUD, writes (personal communication, 9 March 1984) that copper IUDs were introduced without adequate testing and a real understanding of the effects of copper absorption in the body. At the end of two years, all the copper is gone from the Copper T and Copper 7. According to her, "It is now known that an excess of copper in the body activates Wilson's disease—a relatively rare genetic ailment which was little seen and easy to miss in diagnoses. It affects the brain, liver and kidney, and causes muscular weakness and mental deterioration. With or without Wilson's disease, [copper] affects the functions of the major organs of the body. The copper IUD people claim such minuscule amounts are involved that they can't possibly do any harm, but the fact is that we don't know how minuscule an amount is necessary to cause damages."

91. On estimates of PID risks, see, for example, Ronald T. Burkman, "Intrauterine Device Use and the Risk of Pelvic Inflammatory Disease," *American Journal of Obstetrics and Gynecology*, vol. 138, no. 861 (1980); *Population Reports*, Series L, no. 4 (July 1983); and the results of a recent study in the United States summarized in "New CDC Data Link Contraceptive Method, PID and Infertility," *Contraceptive Technology Update*, vol. 5, no. 11 (November 1984). This study found that users of IUDs had more history of PID than users of the pill. Jocelyn Knowles points out that often PID risk figures "are little better than guesses," helping to explain the variation.

92. For FDA caution, see Kasindorf, "The Case Against IUD's."

93. Quoted in ibid.

94. Ibid.

95. See Sybil Shainwald, "The History of the Dalkon Shield," in National Women's Health Network, *The Dalkon Shield* (Washington, D.C.: 1985), pp. 1–12, for how data was ignored or manipulated. For attorney's testimony, see Barry Siegel, "The 'Yes' that Made Dalkon's Maker Ill," *Boston Globe*, 25 August 1985.

96. Quoted in Ehrenreich et al., "The Charge: Gynocide." Information on AID and the Dalkon Shield from this article.

97. Lord's statement reproduced in the National Women's Health Network, *The Dalkon Shield*, p. 15. Also see Sonja Steptoe, "Women Challenge Right of Robins to Drop Claims," *Wall Street Journal*, 14 February 1986.

98. See, for example, "In Court and 'Out of Control,'" *The Network News* (National Women's Health Network), January–February 1986.

99. See Kaval Guhati, "Compulsory Sterilization: A New Dimension in India's Population Policy," Draper World Population Fund Report No. 3 (Washington, D.C.: Autumn–Winter 1976).

100. Quoted in S. P. Jain, *A Status Study on Population Research in India*, vol. 2 (New Delhi: Family Planning Foundation, 1975), cited in Vimal Balasubrahmanyan, "Women as Targets in India's Family Planning Policy," in Arditti et al., eds., *Test Tube Women*, p. 154.

101. Recounted in Vimal Balasubrahmanyan, "Towards a Women's Perspective on Family Planning," *Economic and Political Weekly*, vol. 21, no. 2 (11 January 1986).

102. Diana Smith, "Chinese Ring Causes Concern," *People*, vol. 12, no. 4 (1985).

103. *Population Reports*, Series A, No. 6, p. A-211.

104. A. Kessler and C. C. Standley, "Fertility Regulating Methods," *WHO Chronicle*, vol. 31, no. 5.

105. See *Population Reports*, Series L, No. 4, and Bruce and Schearer, "Contraceptives and Developing Countries."

106. Hutchings et al., "The IUD After 20 Years: A Review," p. 252. Also see Daniel R. Mishell, Jr., "Current Status of Intrauterine Devices," *The New England Journal of Medicine*, vol. 312, no. 15 (11 April 1985).

107. See Hutchings et al., "The IUD After 20 Years: A Review," James, "Couples Face Grim Birth-Control Choices," and Jacqueline

D. Forrest, "The End of IUD Marketing in the United States: What Does It Mean for American Women?" *Family Planning Perspectives*, vol. 18, no. 2, March/April 1986.

BOX Taking the Pill Is Good for Your Religion (pages 179–180)

1. AID, *AID's Role in Indonesian Family Planning: A Case Study with General Lessons for Foreign Assistance*, AID Program Evaluation Report No. 2 (Washington, D.C.: December 1979), pp. 71–72.

11 BANGLADESH—SURVIVAL OF THE RICHEST

This chapter has greatly benefited from the work of Jane Hughes, with whom I have coauthored articles on the Bangladesh sterilization program in *The Nation, Le Monde Diplomatique, Guardian,* and *Inside Asia.* Also thanks to Hilary Standing, with whom I have worked closely on the issue and coauthored a campaigning document, *Food, Saris and Sterilization: Population Control in Bangladesh* (London: Bangladesh International Action Group, September 1985).

1. See Farida Akhter, "Depopulating Bangladesh: A Brief History of External Intervention into the Reproductive Behavior of a Society," paper delivered to the Women's International Tribunal on Reproductive Rights, Amsterdam, July 1984. Also, see Keysers, *Does Family Planning Liberate Women?*

2. World Bank, *Bangladesh: Staff Appraisal Report, Third Population and Family Health Project* (Washington, D.C.: 21 February 1985), p. 4. The administrative details of the population program's history can be found in this report.

3. See Ibid., p. 3. Also Hartmann and Boyce, *A Quiet Violence.*

4. See Rehman Sobhan, *The Crisis of External Dependence: The Political Economy of Foreign Aid to Bangladesh* (London: Zed Press, 1983); Stefan de Vylder, *Agriculture in Chains: Bangladesh—A Case Study in Contradictions and Constraints* (London: Zed Press, 1982); Francis Rolt and Tom Learmouth, *Underdeveloping Bangladesh* (London: War on Want, 1982); Lawrence Lifschultz, *Bangladesh: The Unfinished Revolution* (London: Zed Press, 1979), on the military; Hartmann and Boyce, *A Quiet Violence;* and North-South Institute, *Rural Poverty in Bangladesh: A Report to the Like-Minded Group* (Ottawa: 1985).

5. Donors' Community in Dhaka, *Position Paper on the Population Control and Family Planning Program in Bangladesh* (draft) (Dhaka, 1 March 1983).

6. Letter dated 30 June 1983.

7. Holzhausen letter, dated 18 January 1984, to Dr. Nafis Sadik, UNFPA, New York.

8. Ershad stated this priority in an interview with Robert Bradnock, "Upazilla Struggle," *Guardian*, 10 May 1985.

9. Information obtained from a field worker for a European voluntary agency.

10. See World Bank, *Bangladesh: Staff Appraisal Report*, p. 22; also Annex 3 of same document.

11. Eighty-five percent figure from ibid., p. 12. AID also supports the activities of the Bangladesh Association for Voluntary Sterilization, which performs 30 percent of all sterilizations in Bangladesh (ibid, p. 10). In FY 1985 AID allocated $27 million in population aid to Bangladesh—see AID, *Congressional Presentation, FY 1985*. Thomas quote obtained by J. Hughes in Dhaka.

12. Clothing handed out after the operation: information obtained from voluntary agency field workers. On the use of the word "incentives," see for example letter from Frank Vogl of the World Bank's Information and Public Affairs Department in *The Nation*, 24 November 1984, and PIACT, *Preliminary Report on a Study of the Motivational and Referral Fee System Under the Population Control Program* (draft) (Dhaka: 24 October 1984), p. 1.

13. For example, in October 1983, after the incentive payments were increased, the number of sterilizations more than doubled from the September figure to 62,399, and rose again to 70,612 in November. In December, when the rice harvest began, they fell to 37,099. These figures were acquired by Jane Hughes from AID in Dhaka.

14. See UBINIG, *Preliminary Report of UBINIG's Study on Incentives and Disincentives System in the Population Control Program of Bangladesh* (Dhaka: February 1986); UBINIG, *Faces of Coercion: Population Control Program of Bangladesh* (Dhaka: Sept. 1986); and Subash Chandra Saha and R. W. Timm, *A Survey of 950 Sterilized Persons in Bangladesh*, (Dhaka: Commission for Justice and Peace of the Catholic Bishops Conference of Bangladesh, 1986).

15. Bangladesh Sterilization Surveillance Team, *"First Four-Partite Review* (September 1983).

16. Ibid.

17. Jane Hughes interview in Dhaka.

18. Saha and Timm, *A Survey of 950 Sterilized Persons*.

19. UBINIG, *Faces of Coercion*, p. 45.

20. PIACT, "Preliminary Report."

21. On the military campaign, see: "A Successful Human Rights

Action Against Compulsory Sterilization," *Asia Link,* vol. 5, no. 1 (January 1984), published by Center for the Progress of Peoples. Thomas quotes from Hughes in Dhaka.

22.   On food aid abuses: communications with field workers from European voluntary agencies: also UBINIG, *Preliminary Report.* The Catholic Commission for Justice and Peace found that thirteen out of their 950 respondents had also been offered food as an inducement.

23.   *Bangladesh Observer,* 14 December 1984.

24.   Letter from David A. Oot, chief of AID's Population, Health and Nutrition Division, Bureau for Asia, to author, dated 28 March 1985; letter from John D. North, director of the World Bank's Population, Health and Nutrition Department, to author, dated 18 April 1985; and Bangladesh Government, Ministry of Health and Population Control, "Office Memorandum: Subject: Grant of Unapproved Inducements for Sterilization Acceptance," 25 March 1985.

25.   Saha and Timm, *A Survey of 950 Sterilized Persons,* and UBINIG, *Preliminary Report.*

26.   *Ittefaq,* 21 January 1986.

27.   For further details of the community incentive scheme, see "New Incentive Measures for Family Planning Program," *Population Bulletin,* vol. 1, no. 9 (October 1983). This is another case where the term "incentives" is freely used by the government in relation to sterilization payments.

28.   SIDA, *Incentives and Disincentives in the Bangladesh Population and Family Health Project,* position and discussion paper (Stockholm–Dhaka: January 1985), p. 1.

29.   See North letter; Kanagaratnam, personal interview, February 1984.

30.   SIDA, *Incentives and Disincentives.*

31.   On the state of infant and maternal health, see Bangladesh Government, Ministry of Health and Population Control, *National Strategy for a Comprehensive Maternal and Child Health Program,* Report of MCH Task Force (Dhaka: February 1985).

32.   World Bank, *Bangladesh: Staff Appraisal Report,* p. 7. Also see North-South Institute, "Rural Poverty in Bangladesh," p. 233.

33.   See Akhter, "Depopulating Bangladesh," and Bangladesh Ministry of Health and Population Control, "Population Control Program in Bangladesh," a status paper prepared for the Bangladesh Aid Group Meeting held in Paris in April 1984 (draft), p. 15.

34.   Budget figures from World Bank, *Bangladesh: Staff Appraisal Report,* p. 11. Aid official quote from Hughes interview, Dhaka. On government priorities, see Ministry of Health and Population Control,

National Strategy for a Comprehensive Maternal and Child Health Program; and World Bank, *Bangladesh; Staff Appraisal Report.*

35.   Quoted in Farida Akhter, *On Population Control Policies and Practices in Bangladesh* (Dhaka: UBINIG, March 1984), p. 10.

36.   Holzhausen letter to Dr. Nafis Sadik.

37.   See World Bank, *Bangladesh Staff Appraisal Report,* pp. 8, 23-24. Findings of ICDDR study reported in James F. Phillips, Ruth Simmons, J. Chakraborty, and A. I. Chowdhury, "Integrating Health Services into an MCH-FP Program: Lessons from Matlab, Bangladesh," *Studies in Family Planning,* vol. 15, no. 4 (July-August 1984).

38.   Phillips et al., "Integrating Health Services into an MCH-FP Program."

39.   UBINIG, *Faces of Coercion,* p. 32.

40.   SIDA, *Incentives and Disincentives.*

41.   On the drug ordinance and the Bangladesh health system in general, see Francis Rolt, *Pills, Policies and Profits* (London: War on Want, 1985).

42.   Letter from C. J. Allison to Gretchen Handwerger, World Bank senior loan officer, 28 March 1985.

43.   Hughes' interview.

44.   Personal communication with James Green of the World Bank, January 1986.

45.   Articles have appeared in the British periodicals *Observer, Guardian, New Scientist, Inside Asia,* and the *Economist Development Report,* as well as in major newspapers in Germany. The Bangladesh International Action Group has launched a campaign against the program.

The program has been discussed on the BBC in England and Cable Network News in the United States. A motion condemning coercive sterilization in Bangladesh has been signed by thirty-eight members of Parliament. In January 1986 the U.S. National Women's Health Network issued a press release about the World Bank Population III Project, criticizing sterilization incentives. The United States representative to the World Bank voted against the project.

12   STERILIZATION AND ABORTION

1.   Quoted in Henry Kamm, "Indian State Is Leader in Forced Sterilization," *New York Times,* 13 August 1976. Dr. Pai is still active in international sterilization circles.

2.   "Band-Aid surgery" and figures on mortality from Pet-

chesky, " 'Reproductive Choice' in the Contemporary United States." Sterilization may have a long-term effect on menstruation, leading to heavier periods in some women, though the evidence is not conclusive one way or the other. See, for example, Coralie Sunanda Ray, "The Long-Term Menstrual Side Effects Associated with Tubal Sterilization, A Literature Review and Case-Control Study with Special Reference to Women in South Asia," unpublished dissertation, London School of Hygiene and Tropical Medicine, September 1983, and "Menstrual Function Following Tubal Sterilization," *AVS Medical Bulletin*, vol. 2, no. 1 (February 1981).

3.   "Vasectomy—Safe and Simple," *Population Reports*, Series D, No. 4 (November–December 1983).

4.   Ibid. Also see Special Issue on Vasectomy, *Studies in Family Planning*, vol. 14, no. 3 (March 1983).

5.   George Zeidenstein, president of the Population Council, expressed this view in a letter to the author. Also see Alaka M. Basu, "Family Planning and the Emergency: An Unanticipated Consequence," *Economic and Political Weekly*, vol. 20, no. 10 (9 March 1985).

6.   Ravenholt quoted in Paul Wagman, "U.S. Goal: Sterilize Millions of World's Women," *St. Louis Post-Dispatch*, 22 April 1977.

7.   Personal interview with Terrrence Jezowski, February 1984, and *Quality of Life, Quality of Service*, Association for Voluntary Sterilization 1982 Annual Report (New York: 1982). I would like to thank Mr. Jezowski for making many materials available to me.

8.   "Reasonable" from personal interview with T. Jezowski; "voluntariness" and quotation from Terrence W. Jezowski and Miguel Trias, M.D., "Programmatic Considerations in Meeting the Demand for Voluntary Surgical Contraception in the 1980's," paper prepared for the Fifth International Conference on Voluntary Surgical Contraception, Santo Domingo, Dominican Republic, 5–8 December 1983, p. 10.

9.   Vijita Fernando, "Heart-Searching in Sri Lanka," *People*, vol. 13, no. 1 (1986).

10.   Jezowski and Trias, "Programmatic Considerations in Meeting the Demand," p. 21.

11.   See James W. Wessman, "Neo-Malthusian Ideology and Colonial Capitalism: Population Dynamics in Southwestern Puerto Rico," in Michaelson, ed., *And the Poor Get Children*. See also chapter on Puerto Rico in Mass, *Population Target*.

12.   Helen Rodriguez-Trias, "The Women's Health Movement: Women Take Power," in Victor W. Sidel and Ruth Sidel, *Reforming*

Medicine: Lessons of the Last Quarter Century (New York: Pantheon Books, 1984).

13. J. M. Stycos, "Female Sterilization in Puerto Rico," *Eugenics Quarterly*, vol. 1, no. 1 (1954), p. 3, quoted in Mass, *Population Target*, p. 95. Also see Petchesky, " 'Reproductive Choice' in the Contemporary United States," for discussion of the context of sterilization choice in Puerto Rico. On contraceptive options today, see Harriet B. Presser, "Puerto Rico: Recent Trends in Fertility and Sterilization," *Family Planning Perspectives*, vol. 12, no. 2 (March–April 1980). The Puerto Rican sterilization program is the subject of a powerful documentary film, *L'Operacion*, directed and produced by Ana Maria Garcia.

14. Dr. Trias' comments from U.S. Congress, House, *Population and Development in Latin America and the Caribbean*. Hearing before the Subcommittee on Inter-American Affairs of the Committee on Foreign Affairs, 97th Cong., 2d sess., 8 September 1982, p. 52.

15. Trias quoted in Alan Riding, "Battleground in Colombia: Birth Control," *New York Times*, 5 September 1984.

16. Ruth Holly, "Population Control in Colombia," paper prepared for the International Contraception, Abortion and Sterilization Campaign, London, 1981.

17. *Ob. Gyn. News*, vol. 15, no. 20 (15 October 1984), cited in ibid.

18. Holly, "Population Control in Colombia."

19. Personal interview, February 1984.

20. "Mental Health and Female Sterilization: A Follow-up: Report of a WHO Collaborative Prospective Study," *Journal of Biosocial Science*, vol. 17, no. 1 (January 1985).

21. This information on Colombia was provided by a reliable source who must remain anonymous.

22. Jezowski and Trias, "Programmatic Considerations in Meeting the Demand," p. 21. I have heard similar reports from British voluntary agency personnel working in Brazil. For status of sterilization in different countries, see John A. Ross and Sawon Hong, "Voluntary Sterilization: A Factbook of International Data from Surveys and Service Statistics," prepared for the Fifth International Conference on Voluntary Surgical Contraception, Santo Domingo, Dominican Republic, 5–8 December 1983.

23. Letter to author from Sonia Corrêa, 4 December 1985.

24. Personal interview with Sonia Corrêa, summer 1985.

25. See Robert del Quiaro, "Where the Best Contraceptive Is Plenty of Money," *Guardian*, 7 August 1984.

26. See Vicziany, "Coercion in a Soft State," for excellent analysis of the program's assumptions and failures.

27. See "Entire Village Sterilized," *India Now*, August 1978.

28. Information on forced sterilization in India from Debabar Banerji, "Political Economy of Population Control in India," in Bondestam and Bergström, *Poverty and Population Control;* Davidson R. Gwatkin, "Political Will and Family Planning: The Implications of India's Emergency Experience," *Population and Development Review*, vol. 5, no. 1 (March 1979); "Delhi to Penalize Couples for Not Limiting Births," *New York Times*, 26 February 1976.

29. McNamara quote from Government of India, Department of Family Planning, *Centre Calling*, Vol. XI (11 November 1976), cited in Banerji, "Political Economy of Population Control in India." Ehrlich quote from 1983 edition of *The Population Bomb*, cited in John Tierney, "Fanisi's Choice," *Science 86* (January–February 1986), p. 42. Van Arendonk quote from personal interview, February 1984. An article published by the Population Crisis Committee, instead of condemning the program, states: "For a coercive program to work, a hugely expanded commitment of administrative and financial resources will be necessary. The world will be watching India's policy closely to see if, and how, state governments follow up their new legislation with bigger budgets and more effective action." See Gulhati, "Compulsory Sterilization."

30. John C. Caldwell, P. H. Reddy, and Pat Caldwell, "Demographic Change in Rural South India," *Population and Development Review*, vol. 8, no. 4 (December 1982), p. 712.

31. "In India, Birth Control Focus Shifts to Women," *New York Times*, 7 March 1982.

32. Basu, "Family Planning and the Emergency."

33. "A Family Planning Story," *Economic and Political Weekly*, vol. 20, no. 40 (5 October 1985), p. 1668.

34. See ibid. and Sunil Sethi, "Reviving the Battle," *India Today*, 31 July 1985.

35. "Birth Control Survey: Sterilization Tops List in U.S.," *Ms.*, January 1984.

36. See Petchesky, " 'Reproductive Choice' in the Contemporary United States."

37. Quoted in Anti-Sexism Committee, National Lawyers Guild, *Reproductive Freedom: Speakers' Handbook on Abortion Rights and Sterilization* reprinted in *Stop Forced Sterilization: A Collection of Reprints about Sterilization and Population Control* (Minneapolis/St. Paul: Twin Cities Reproductive Rights Committee, 1981). Also see ibid.

Possible long-term effects of hysterectomy include early menopause, osteoporosis, and greater susceptibility to coronary disease.

38. Quoted in Rosalind P. Petchesky, "Reproduction, Ethics, and Public Policy: The Federal Sterilization Regulations," *Hastings Center Report*, October 1979.

39. Quoted in ibid.

40. Ibid. These regulations, however, have not been strictly enforced, and groups such as the Committee for Abortion Rights and Against Sterilization Abuse (CARASA) and the National Women's Health Network are now working to ensure that they meet with compliance.

41. *Association for Voluntary Sterilization Annual Report,* 1982, p. 6. See Petchesky, "Reproduction, Ethics and Public Policy," for defense of current moratorium on the sterilization of the mentally handicapped.

42. See OTA, *World Population and Fertility Planning Technologies,* p. 89, and Malcolm Potts, Peter Diggory and John Peel, *Abortion* (Cambridge: Cambridge University Press, 1977), p. 211.

43. On fertility, see Bruce and Schearer, *Contraceptives and Common Sense,* and Lisa Cronin Wohl, "Anti-Abortion Violence on the Rise," *Ms.,* October 1984. On menstrual regulation, see Seaman and Seaman, *Women and the Crisis in Sex Hormones;* Potts et al., *Abortion;* and Boston Women's Health Book Collective, *The New Our Bodies, Ourselves* (New York: Simon and Schuster, 1984).

44. Seaman and Seaman, *Women and the Crisis in Sex Hormones.*

45. K. Kaufmann, "Abortion, a Woman's Matter: an Explanation of Who Controls Abortion and How and Why They Do It," in Rita Arditti et al., eds., *Test-Tube Women.*

46. For a discussion of the basic values underlying the abortion debate, see Kristin Luker, *Abortion and the Politics of Motherhood* (Berkeley: University of California Press, 1984).

47. Potts et al., *Abortion,* p. 2.

48. Although accurate figures are not available, the abortion rate in the Soviet Union may be 115 per 1000 women of reproductive age, compared to 23 in the United States in 1978. See Christopher Tietze, *Induced Abortion: A World Review, 1983* (New York: Population Council, 1983); also OTA, *World Population and Fertility Planning Technologies,* p. 63.

49. Tietze, *Induced Abortion.*

50. Potts et al., *Abortion,* pp. 270–71.

51. Seaman and Seaman, *Women and the Crisis in Sex Hormones,* p. 237.

52.   Rodriguez-Trias, "The Women's Health Movement."

53.   Quoted in Bernard Rosenfeld et al., *A Health Research Study Group on Surgical Sterilization: Present Abuses and Proposed Regulation* (Washington, D.C.: Health Research Group, October 1973), p. 22. Information on England from Marge Berer of the London Women's Reproductive Rights Information Center, and Wendy Savage, "Taking Liberties with Women: Abortion, Sterilization and Contraception," *International Journal of Health Services*, vol. 12, no. 2 (1982).

54.   General IUD cases in Potts et al., *Abortion*. India case from Balasubrahmanyan, "Towards a Women's Perspective on Family Planning."

55.   Zafrullah Chowdhury and Susan Chowdhury, "Abortion in Bangladesh," paper presented at IPPF Expert Panel on Abortion, Bellagio, Italy, 16–18 February 1978, quoted in Keysers, *Does Family Planning Liberate Women?* Information on MR in Bangladesh from Keysers.

56.   See Potts et al., *Abortion*. Also personal experience.

57.   Nancy E. Williamson, "Boys or Girls? Parents' Preferences and Sex Control," *Population Bulletin*, vol. 33, no. 1 (January 1978).

58.   See S. H. Venkatramani, "Born to Die," *India Today*, 15 June 1986.

59.   See Viola Roggencamp, "Abortion of a Special Kind: Male Sex Selection in India," in Arditti et al., eds., *Test-Tube Women*, and Vimal Balasubrahmanyan, "Female Foeticide," *New Internationalist*, no. 127 (September 1983). Also recent communication with Indian doctor.

60.   1984 seminar from Balasubrahmanyan, "Towards a Women's Perspective on Family Planning." Information on Dr. Pai from Staffan Bergström, "Fertility and Subfertility as Health Problems—Population Control Versus Family Planning by the Family," in Bondestam and Bergström, *Poverty and Population Control*, p. 55. Also see articles in the *Economic and Political Weekly*, 23 October 1982, 15 January 1983, 19 February 1983, and 16 April 1983. See for general overview Helen B. Holmes, "Sex Selection: Eugenics for Everyone?" in James Humber and Robert Almeden, eds., *Biomedical Ethics Reviews—1985* (Clifton, N.J.: Humana Press, 1986).

61.   Marsha Saxton, "Born and Unborn: The Implications of Reproductive Technologies for People with Disabilities," in Arditti et al., eds., *Test-Tube Women*, p. 306. See also Anne Finger, "Claiming All of Our Bodies: Reproductive Rights and Disability," in same volume; Gena Corea, *The Mother Machine* (New York: Harper and Row,

1985); and Barbara Katz Rothman, *The Tentative Pregnancy* (New York: Viking Press, 1986).

BOX   Sterilization Side Effects: Unanswered Questions (pages 228–229)

1.   Quoted in Joyce Pettigrew, "Problems Concerning Tubectomy Operations in Rural Areas of the Punjab," *Economic and Political Weekly*, vol. 19, no. 26 (30 June 1984). All Pettigrew quotes from this article.

2.   John C. Caldwell and Pat Caldwell, "Family Planning in India: A Worm's Eye View from a Rural Area in South India," *South Asia*, vol. 5, no. 1 (June 1982).

3.   On Bangladesh, see Chapter 11. On El Salvador, see A. Bronstein, *The Triple Struggle*.

BOX   Is El Salvador Next? (pages 236–237)

1.   Hugh O'Shaugnessy, "El Salvador Poor Given No Choice over Sterilization," *Observer*, 1 April 1984.

2.   In FY 1985 Central America and the Caribbean absorbed two thirds of AID's population budget for all of Latin America, with Guatemala and El Salvador the two biggest recipients. See AID, *Congressional Presentation, FY 1985*, p. 45.

3.   Chris Hedges, "Sterilization of Salvadoreans Promoted by U.S. Agency," *National Catholic Reporter*, 11 November 1983.

4.   O'Shaughnessy, "El Salvador Poor." On IPPF reaction, see O'Shaughnessy, "UK in Birth Control Row," *Observer*, 16 April 1984.

13   BARRIER CONTRACEPTIVES AND NATURAL FAMILY PLANNING

1.   Bruce and Schearer, "Contraceptives and Developing Countries," p. 406.

2.   Balasubrahmanyan, "Women as Targets in India's Family Planning Policy," p. 157. For account of International Tribunal, see Alice Henry, "Population Control: No—Women Decide," *Off Our Backs*, October 1984.

3.   Malcolm Potts, "The Implementation of Family Planning Programs," in R. V. Short and D. T. Baird, *Contraceptives of the Future* (London: The Royal Society, 1976).

4.   Bruce and Schearer, "Contraceptives and Developing Countries," p. 427.

5. Pill and diaphragm use rates from "Studies Show a Dramatic Rise in Sterilization," *New York Times*, 9 December 1984. Recent study results reported in Nadine B. Williams, ed., *Contraceptive Technology 1986–1987* (New York: Irvington Publishers, 1986), p. 103.

6. "New Developments in Vaginal Contraception." *Population Reports*, Series H, no. 7 (January–February 1984), Tables 1 and 2.

7. OTA, *World Population and Fertility Planning Technologies*, p. 89.

8. Bruce and Schearer, "Contraceptives and Developing Countries."

9. See "FDA Advisory Committee Says No to Warning Label on Spermicides," *Medical World News*, 13 February 1984.

10. Allan Parachini, "More Evidence Links Diaphragms, Infection," *San Francisco Chronicle*, 15 July 1985.

11. *Population Reports*, Series H, No. 7, p. H-157.

12. Bruce and Schearer, "Contraceptives and Developing Countries," p. 412. Also see ibid. for details of a number of different studies.

13. Bruce and Schearer, "Contraceptives and Developing Countries," p. 410.

14. Bruce and Schearer, *Contraceptives and Common Sense*, p. 78.

15. *Population Reports*, Series H, No. 7, p. H-181.

16. On Bombay clinic, see Bruce and Schearer, *Contraceptives and Common Sense;* other examples from Bruce and Schearer, "Contraceptives and Developing Countries."

17. *Population Reports*, Series H, No. 7, pp. H182–83.

18. Bruce and Schearer, "Contraceptives and Developing Countries," p. 426.

19. Bruce and Schearer, *Contraceptives and Common Sense*.

20. Quoted in Christine Doyle, "Precautionary Tales," *Observer Magazine* (London), 20 January 1985.

21. See *Population Reports*, Series H, No. 7, and Bruce and Schearer, "Contraceptives and Developing Countries," for specific examples and possibilities.

22. See *Population Reports*, Series H, No. 7; and Bruce and Schearer, "Contraceptives and Developing Countries."

23. Shelton quote from personal interview, February 1984. Indian health writer: Balasubrahmanyan, "Women as Targets in India's Family Planning Policy," p. 157. There are a number of good articles on the sponge. See, for example, Andrea Boroff Eagan, "The Contraceptive Sponge: Easy—But Is It Safe?" *Ms.*, January 1984, and Gwenda

Blair, "Mop 'n Glow: The Absorbing Story of the Contraceptive Sponge," *Village Voice*, 1 May 1984, and "Sponge Survives First Year; Emerges Top Seller," *Contraceptive Technology Update*, vol. 5, no. 7 (July 1984).

24.   Testimony of Barbara Seaman before the U.S. Senate Subcommittee on Health and Scientific Research, 1 August 1979, quoted in National Women's Health Network, *Cervical Cap Information Packet*. (Washington, D.C.: 1983). This packet describes women's efforts to make the cap available in the United States, the battle with the FDA, and the eventual resolution. Also see "FDA Considers Fate of Vimule Cervical Cap in U.S. Trials," *Contraceptive Technology Update*, vol. 5, no. 10 (October 1984).

25.   Personal conversation with Rebecca Chalker. See her *Complete Cervical Cap Guide* (New York: Harper & Row, Publishers, 1987).

26.   Bruce and Schearer, "Contraceptives and Developing Countries," p. 425.

27.   Ibid.

28.   Malcolm Potts and Robert Wheeler, "The Quest for a Magic Bullet," *Family Planning Perspectives*, vol. 13, no. 6 (November–December 1981).

29.   See "Periodic Abstinence: How Well Do New Approaches Work? *Population Reports*, Series I, No. 3 (September 1981); see also "Natural Family Planning: Periodic Abstinence as a Method of Fertility Control," *Population*, no. 11 (June 1981).

30.   See *Population Reports*, Series I, No. 3; for a critique of the Billings method see Katharine Betts, "The Billings Method of Family Planning: An Assessment," *Studies in Family Planning*, vol. 15, no. 6 (November–December 1984).

31.   *Population Reports*, Series I, No. 3.

32.   Audrey Bronstein, "Notes on Family Planning Training Course in El Salvador," background notes to her book *The Triple Struggle*, made available to author.

33.   Quoted in *Population Reports*, Series I, No. 3, p. 154.

34.   Ibid. and Constance Holden, " 'Right to Life' Scores New Victory at AID," *Science*, vol. 229, no. 4718 (13 September 1985).

35.   *Population*, no. 11 (June 1981), p. 7.

36.   Quoted in *Population Reports*, Series I, No. 3, p. I-162. Note this statement by *Population Reports* (I-161): "Teaching and helping couples interested in periodic abstinence to use the method effectively takes time and continued counseling. In fact, in contrast to other family planning methods, which depend on advanced technology and medical

skills, periodic abstinence programs have been described as 'educational delivery systems.' " Other family planning methods could well use such "educational delivery," despite their advanced technical nature.

37. Atkinson et al., "Worldwide Trends in Funding," Table 3, p. 198.

38. See *Population Reports*, Series I, No. 3, and on hand temperature changes, Martin Wainwright, "Scientific Significance in the Cool Feminine Touch," *Guardian*, 10 January 1985.

39. Quoted in *Population Reports*, Series I, No. 3, p. I-63.

40. Holden, " 'Right to Life' Scores New Victory."

41. See Linda E. Atkinson, Richard Lincoln, and Jacqueline D. Forrest, "The Next Contraceptive Revolution," *Family Planning Perspectives*, vol. 18, no. 1 (January–February 1986).

42. Ibid. and Celia Curtis, "Birth Control Vaccine Unveiled," *People*, vol. 13, no. 2 (1986).

43. Atkinson et al., "Worldwide Trends in Funding," p. 206.

44. See Atkinson et al., "The Next Contraceptive Revolution," Rebecca Cook, " 'Contragestion' and the Law," *People*, vol. 13, no. 1 (1986), and Matt Clark, "Contraceptives: On Hold."

45. See Michael L. Millenson, "Publicity Fear Spurs Searle to Sidetrack Drug," *Chicago Tribune*, 13 January 1985.

46. Quoted in Stokes, *Men and Family Planning*, p. 23.

47. A. Kessler and C. C. Standley, "Fertility-regulating Methods: Recent Progress in the WHO Programme of Research in Human Reproduction," *WHO Chronicle*, vol. 31, no. 5.

48. See Mary-Louise O'Callaghan, "Sterility Fear Fails to Halt Chinese Male Pill Tests," *Guardian*, 17 August 1984.

49. See "Herbs for Contraception and Abortion," *ICASC Information*, no. 6 (London: 1981), and Kessler and Standley, "Fertility-regulating Methods." The Ortho Pharmaceutical Corporation is currently investigating the Mexican zoapatle plant—see Seymour D. Levine et al., "The Mexican Plant Zoapatle (*Montanoa tomentosa*) in Reproductive Medicine," *The Journal of Reproductive Medicine*, vol. 26, no. 10 (October 1981). The Voluntary Health Association of India writes (personal communication) that tribal communities in India have long used the oil of the common neem (margosa) tree as a spermicide.

50. Atkinson et al., "Worldwide Trends in Funding," p. 205.

51. Atkinson et al., "The Next Contraceptive Revolution," p. 26.

BOX   AIDS and Barrier Methods (pages 252–253)

1. See Jennifer Dunning, "Woman and AIDS: Discussing Precautions," *New York Times*, 3 Nov. 1986; Richard Saltus, "Heterosexual Contact Suspect in African AIDS," *Boston Globe*, 23 November 1985; Lawrence K. Altman, "More Data Found on AIDS in Africa," *New York Times*, 15 Dec. 1985.

2. See National Institutes of Health, *Request for Proposals No. NICHD-CE-86-9 Primary Prevention Trial of Barrier Contraceptives Against HTLV-III Infection* (Bethesda: 15 April 1986), Section L1.

3. Hugh D. Menzies, "Back to a Basic Contraceptive," *New York Times*, 5 January 1986.

4. See NIH, *Request for Proposals*, and Donald R. Hicks, Linda S. Martin et al., "Inactivation of HTLV-III/LAV-Infected Cultures of Normal Human Lymphocytes by Nonoxynol-9 In Vitro," *Lancet*, 21–28 December 1985.

5. See NIH, *Request for Proposals*.

6. Ibid.

14   THE LIGHT AT THE END OF THE DEMOGRAPHIC TUNNEL

1. See *World Development Report 1984*, Chapter 4. In some European countries, fertility fell while mortality remained high. For a possible explanation, see John Knodel and Etienne van de Walle, "Lessons from the Past: Policy Implications of Historical Fertility Studies," *Population and Development Review*, vol. 5, no. 2 (June 1979).

2. See Caldwell, *Fertility Decline*.

3. *World Development Report 1984*, p. 63.

4. See Cain, "Risk and Insurance," and "Fertility as an Adjustment to Risk." Cain postulates that there may be two stages in fertility decline. In the first, people adjust their fertility to the decline in mortality, but they still need the same number of surviving children to meet their security goals. In the second stage, they start to need fewer surviving children because they have alternative sources of security. The tendency of fertility decline to level off in a number of Third World countries may be because they are caught between the stages. See also Caldwell, *Theory of Fertility Decline*.

5. Figures from *World Development Report 1984*. For more on the relationship between income distribution and fertility decline, see William Rich, *Smaller Families Through Social and Economic Prog-*

ress (Washington, D.C.: Overseas Development Council, January 1973); Murdoch, *The Poverty of Natons;* Robert Repetto, *Economic Equality and Fertility in Developing Countries* (Baltimore: Johns Hopkins University Press, 1979); Michael P. Todaro, *Economic Development in the Third World,* 2d ed. (New York: Longman, 1981), pp. 166–68.

6.   John Ratcliffe, "Toward a Social Justice Theory of Demographic Transition: Lessons from India's Kerala State," *Janasamkhya,* vol. 1 (June 1983).

7.   Salas, *The State of World Population 1982;* and *World Development Report 1984,* Table 20. Analysis in this section from David Werner, "Health Care in Cuba: A Model Service or a Means of Social Control—or Both?," in Morley et al., eds., *Practicing Health for All.*

8.   Repetto, *Economic Equality,* p. 69. Land tenure figures from Repetto.

9.   Dae Hwan Kim, *Rapid Economic Growth and National Integration in Korea, 1963–78* (Oxford: Oxford University Press, 1985), pp. 239–40.

10.   Repetto, *Economic Equality.*

11.   See Kim, *Rapid Economic Growth.*

12.   See Murdoch, *The Poverty of Nations,* pp. 69–75. Recent figures from *World Development Report 1985.*

13.   Ratcliffe, "Toward a Social Justice Theory."

14.   John Ratcliffe, "Social Justice and the Demographic Transition: Lessons from India's Kerala State," in Morley et al., eds., *Practicing Health for All.*

15.   K. N. Raj, "Land Reforms and Their Effects on Distribution of Income," *Poverty, Unemployment and Development Policy: A Case Study of Selected Issues with Reference to Kerala,* ST/ESA/29 (New York: United Nations 1975), quoted in Ratcliffe, "Social Justice and the Demographic Transition," p. 81.

16.   Ratcliffe, "Social Justice and the Demographic Transition," p. 71.

17.   See, for example, Vicziany, "Coercion in a Soft State," and Vimal Balasubrahmanyan, "A Bizarre Medley of Carrots," *Women's Global Network on Reproductive Rights Newsletter,* January–March 1986. This article is a collection of recent newspaper clips on population control excesses in India.

BOX   The Isolation Exercise (pages 284–285)

1. Phillips Cutright, "The Ingredients of Recent Fertility Decline in Developing Countries," *International Family Planning Perspectives*, vol. 9, no. 4 (December 1983).
2. Ibid. and *World Development Report 1984*, pp. 118, 121.
3. Moni Nag, "Fertility Differential in Kerala and W. Bengal, Equity-Fertility Hypothesis as Explanation," *Economic and Political Weekly*, vol. 19, no. 1 (7 January 1984).
4. Caldwell, *Fertility Decline*, pp. 154–55.

15   EXPANDING CHOICES

1. Information based on personal interview with Sonia Corrêa. Also see Robert del Quiaro, "Where the Best Contraceptive."
2. On the harassment of CIDHAL, see Judy Norsigian, "Health Clinic Faces Harassment," Letter to the Editor, *New Women's Times*, July 1984.
3. See Judith Bruce, "Women-Oriented Health Care: New Hampshire Feminist Health Center," *Studies in Family Planning*, vol. 12, no. 10 (October 1981).
4. See Melrose, *Bitter Pills*, for description of the project.
5. Alfred Yankauer, "Venceremos," *American Journal of Public Health*, vol. 74, no. 10 (October 1984).
6. Harry Nelson, "Nicaragua: Putting an Emphasis on Health," *The Nation's Health*, October 1983.
7. Ibid.
8. Testimony of the Nicaraguan delegate to the Women's International Tribunal on Reproductive Rights, Amsterdam, July 1984.
9. Bangladesh: See People's Health Center, *Progress Reports*, no. 7 (Savar, Bangladesh: 1980); Nicaragua: See Nelson, "Nicaragua: Putting an Emphasis on Health." Also ibid.
10. "NET-EN Trial Disrupted in India"; Balasubrahmanyan, "Towards a Women's Perspective on Family Planning"; and personal correspondence with Sumati Nair and other Indian feminist and health activists.
11. See Adrienne Germain, *Reproductive Health Issues at the U.N. Women's Decade Conference in Nairobi and Beyond* (New York: International Women's Health Coalition, 21 August 1985).
12. Statements of these officials from personal interviews.
13. International Women's Health Coalition 1985 publicity brochure.
14. Personal communication, November 1986.

Appendix:
Networks

It is not possible to list here the many groups around the world whose work concerns reproductive rights. The following organizations play a vital role in maintaining contact between these groups and making information accessible on an international level.

WOMEN'S GLOBAL NETWORK ON REPRODUCTIVE RIGHTS

P.O. Box 4098, 1009 AB Amsterdam, Netherlands
Telephone: 020-923900

Formerly the International Contraception, Abortion, and Sterilization Campaign, the Women's Global Network on Reproductive Rights represents women's groups from many different countries who are active in campaigning for reproductive rights and related women's health issues. Its aims are to support women's right to decide if and when to have children and to have access to safe, effective contraception, including legal abortion. The network campaigns against coercive and racist population-control policies, the dumping of dangerous contraceptives in the Third World, insufficient information given to women on the benefits and risks of contraceptives, and restrictive laws and practices. It collects and shares information, publishes a bulletin, and organizes conferences such as the Women's International Tribunal and Meeting on Reproductive Rights in 1984.

ISIS-WICCE (WOMEN'S INTERNATIONAL CROSS-CULTURAL EXCHANGE)

C.P. 2471, 1211 Geneva 2, Switzerland
Telephone: 022-336746

ISIS-WICCE is an international women's resource center. In addition to providing information services, ISIS-WICCE organizes an exchange program, which offers women activists the opportunity to work with women's groups in different cultures. Each year the activities of ISIS-WICCE are focused on a specific theme. The 1985 theme was Women and Health. It publishes the quarterly *Women's World*, which focuses on the link between women in developing and industrialized countries from a feminist perspective.

ISIS INTERNATIONAL

Europe: Via S. Maria dell'Anima 30, 00186 Rome, Italy
Telephone: 06-656-5842
Latin America: Casilla 2067, Correo Central, Santiago, Chile

ISIS International, a sister organization of ISIS-WICCE, is a women's information and communication service. It runs a resource center, and provides background papers, information kits, bibliographics, and research facilities on request. The *ISIS Women's International Journal*, produced jointly with one or more women's groups in the Third World, covers a variety of issues related to women's role in development and serves as a communications channel for feminists in many countries. ISIS International's office in Santiago, Chile, publishes the *ISIS Boletin* (in Spanish) and is establishing a Spanish language documentation center for the region. It recently began coordination of a network of Latin American women's health groups.

The original ISIS group, from which ISIS-WICCE and ISIS International evolved, was set up in 1974. It established a unique network of over 10,000 contacts—both groups and individuals—in 130 countries. The original group published several key resource guides (see References). Both ISIS groups now sponsor the International Feminist Network (IFN), which mobilizes support for women who are being persecuted on the grounds of their sex.

THE BOSTON WOMEN'S HEALTH BOOK COLLECTIVE

47 Nichols Avenue, Watertown, Massachusetts 02172, U.S.A.
Telephone: 617-924-0271

Internationally renowned for its comprehensive guide to women's health and sexuality issues, *Our Bodies, Ourselves*, the Boston Women's Health Book Collective is an important part of the women's health and reproductive rights network. Its Women's Health Information Center, open to the public, has an extensive collection of reference materials. Hundreds of women write, call, and visit the collective each year from countries all over the world. The collective has worked with women's groups in a dozen countries to translate and adapt *Our Bodies, Ourselves* (revised and reissued in the United States in 1984 as *The New Our Bodies, Ourselves*), and in collaboration with ISIS, edited and published the *International Women and Health Resource Guide*. Members of the collective have been instrumental in the campaign against Depo-Provera and population-control abuses.

HEALTH ACTION INTERNATIONAL

Asia: c/o International Organization of Consumers' Unions,
    P.O. Box 1045, Penang, Malaysia
Europe:c/o International Organization of Consumers'
    Unions, 9 Emmastraat, 2595 EG The Hague, Netherlands
    Telephone: 476331, Telex: 33561

Established in Geneva in 1981, Health Action International (HAI) is a broad-based network of consumer and professional groups, which monitors the activities of multinational pharmaceutical companies, including the production and distribution of contraceptives. HAI runs an international clearinghouse for information in the pharmaceutical industry's structure, ownership, and marketing practices, and has set up an international consumer product warning system, the Consumer Interpol. It works for improved drug regulatory procedures and publishes *HAI News*.

Its parent organization, the International Organization of Consumers' Unions (addresses above), is also active in the health and reproductive rights field. IOCU has produced an international anthology on women and pharmaceuticals, *Adverse Effects*, which includes critiques of population-control programs and contraceptive research.

THE NATIONAL WOMEN'S HEALTH NETWORK

224 Seventh St. SE, Washington, D.C. 20003, U.S.A.
Telephone: 202-543-9222

In the United States the National Women's Health Network serves as an umbrella organization for the women's health movement. It closely monitors the activities of the Food and Drug Administration (FDA), produces action alerts and a bimonthly newsletter, and is active in many areas, including reproductive rights, maternal and child health, and occupational and environmental health. Although its major focus is the United States, the network's activities have an international dimension. For example, it has worked for an international recall of the Dalkon Shield and has testified against Depo-Provera approval in the United States. Its knowledge of the FDA, contraceptive research, and the U.S. pharmaceutical industry is an important resource for reproductive rights activists outside the United States.

REFERENCES

More comprehensive lists of organizations, networks, and publications concerned with reproductive, health, and general women's issues can be found in the following: ISIS, *Women in Development: A Resource Guide for Organization and Action* (Geneva, 1983), available in the United States from New Society Publishers, 4722 Baltimore Avenue, Philadephia, Pennsylvania 19143; ISIS and Boston Women's Health Book Collective, *International Women and Health Resource Guide*, 1980 (in Spanish, French, English, German, and Italian); and Boston Women's Health Book Collective, *The New Our Bodies, Ourselves* (New York: Simon and Schuster, 1984).

Index